KINGS AND PROPHETS
OF ISRAEL

ADAM CLEGHORN WELCH

KINGS AND PROPHETS
OF ISRAEL

by
ADAM C. WELCH

edited by
NORMAN W. PORTEOUS

with a
MEMOIR OF HIS LIFE
by
GEORGE S. GUNN

LUTTERWORTH PRESS
LONDON

Printed in Great Britain by The Bristol Typesetting Company
Stokes Croft, Bristol

EDITOR'S PREFACE

I N this volume, the editing of which was undertaken as a
labour of love and as a tribute to the memory of a great
scholar and teacher, there is offered to the public a selection
from the mass of manuscript material which the late Dr.
Welch left behind him. Whether he would himself have
altogether approved of the publication of any of these lectures it is hard to say. The editor has been at pains to include
nothing which might be felt to fall short of the high level of
craftsmanship which the author sought to maintain in all his
published work. He himself took the view that posthumous
publication demanded careful editing. A reasonable liberty
has therefore been taken in occasionally compressing the style
where it seemed redundant and in removing certain colloquial-
isms which were quite in place when the lectures were delivered. Once or twice a brief note has been added where that
seemed necessary, but, though much has been written on the
matters with which these lectures deal since Dr. Welch laid
down his pen, his way of handling a problem or a topic was
so original that it has seemed inadvisable to add learned
comments which the scholar can easily supply for himself
and which might readily detract from the effectiveness of
what the author has to say.

So far as is known, the paper which is printed as the first
section of this book was originally prepared for reading to a
theological club. The remainder consists of lectures on the
history of Israel's religion which were delivered to students at
New College. The course of which they formed part was
prepared to meet the needs of the men who came back from
the First World War, just as *Visions of the End,* one of the
finest of his books, was written with the same generation of
students in view. It is hoped that the lectures which are now

published will enable those who once sat at his feet to recall something of the impression made by his spoken words and of the austere and striking personality which the words revealed. They will be especially glad to have in print the lecture on Saul to which no one ever listened without being deeply moved. In the section on Amos, Hosea and Isaiah the reader will find a maturer and, as Dr. Welch himself believed, more balanced account of those three prophets than is to be found in his early volume of Kerr Lectures, *The Religion of Israel under the Kingdom*.

Dr. Welch's published work—a list of his books is given in an appendix—may be divided into two categories, with the exception of his early volume on Anselm. There is, firstly, that succession of books in which he attacked, and sought a satisfactory substitute for, the Wellhausen theory of the development of Israel's religious institutions and literature. These are perhaps the books with which his name is chiefly associated in the minds of scholars both in this country and abroad. In the second place, there are those other volumes in which he expounded the substance of certain parts of the Scriptures. It was in these writings, and above all in the lecture room, that Dr. Welch revealed himself as one of the greatest Biblical interpreters of his time. What is now published is intended as a supplement to those studies of the prophets and of the prophetic movement, of the Psalms, of Daniel and of the story of Joseph which are already in print.

Not the least welcome feature of this book will be the memoir which has been prepared by Dr. Welch's friend and former pupil, the Rev. Dr. George S. Gunn. There was no other so suitable to whom this task could have been entrusted, no other by whom the subject of the memoir would so willingly have allowed himself to be delineated. Of design no attempt has been made in it to assess Dr. Welch's position as an Old Testament scholar. Those critical theories for which he contended so brilliantly and so gallantly, in particular that concerning the date and origin of Deuteronomy, take their place in the story of Old Testament criticism and the last word about them has not yet been said. The unavoidable delay, however, in the appearance of this volume has made it possible to draw attention to the fact that during the past few years a number of striking tributes have been paid by leading Continental scholars to the value of Dr. Welch's critical work.

Dr. Welch's greatness as a teacher, however, must not be confused with his championship of particular theories about debatable points of criticism. He had an extraordinary gift of entering into the heart of a passage of Scripture and of making it luminous and contemporary in its relevance. In this he was the spiritual successor of A. B. Davidson. In the hands of these two men a study of the history of Israel's religion became theology. They were in a very real sense heralds of the modern revival of Old Testament Theology. His pupils will testify that Dr. Welch was incapable of handling a passage of Scripture without allowing the light of revelation to shine through it. To sit at his feet and listen to his expositions was a profound religious experience and one of the greatest privileges of a man's life. It is unlikely that we shall see his like again. If the publication of these lectures does anything to make more widely felt the influence of a very great teacher, then the long labour of decipherment and transcription will have been amply rewarded.

The editor, who assumes entire responsibility for the final form in which these lectures are presented, desires to express his warmest thanks to another of the professor's former students, the Rev. Dr. R. E. McIntyre, for his kindness in reading through the entire manuscript and making sundry valuable suggestions for improvements in matters of detail, and to the Rev. Dr. G. S. Gunn for help in the correction of the proofs. The General Index has been prepared by the Rev. J. M. Wilkie, B.D., Lecturer in Hebrew in Cambridge University. The Editor's thanks are also due to Mrs. Welch for so freely putting the manuscripts at his disposal and so patiently waiting upon the completion of the work of preparing them for the press.

Edinburgh, 1951. Norman W. Porteous.

CONTENTS

1*

LIST OF PUBLISHED WORKS by ADAM C. WELCH

Anselm and His Work ("The World's Epoch Makers" Series), T. & T. Clark, 1901.

The Religion of Israel under the Kingdom (Kerr Lecture), T. & T. Clark, 1912.

The Story of Joseph ("The Short Course Series"), T. & T. Clark, 1913.

Visions of the End: A Study in Daniel and Revelation ("The Humanism of the Bible" Series), James Clarke, 1922.

The Book of Jeremiah translated into Colloquial English (Series: Books of the Old Testament in Colloquial Speech), National Adult School Union, 1923, 2nd edition, 1928.

Contribution to volume *Immortality* (Edited by Sir James Marchant), entitled "Hebrew and Apocalyptic Conceptions of Immortality", Putnam, 1924.

The Code of Deuteronomy: A New Theory of its Origin, James Clarke, 1924.

Contribution to *The People and the Book*: Edited by A. S. Peake, Essay entitled "The History of Israel", O.U.P., 1925.

The Psalter: in Life Worship and History, O.U.P., 1926.

Genesis Critically Considered (Appendix to the Study Bible: *Genesis*, by E. Griffith-Jones and A. C. Welch), Cassell, 1926.

The Abingdon Bible Commentary: the section on Jeremiah., Epworth Press, 1929.

Jeremiah: His Time and His Work, O.U.P., 1928. Reprint, 1951.

Deuteronomy: The Framework to the Code, O.U.P., 1932.

Post-Exilic Judaism (The Baird Lecture for 1934), Blackwood, 1935.

Prophet and Priest in Old Israel, S.C.M. Press, 1936.

The Work of the Chronicler, its purpose and its date. (Schweich Lectures of 1938), O.U.P., 1939.

The Preparation for Christ in the Old Testament (Vol. 1 of The Four Years' Course for Bible Classes), The Church of Scotland Committee on Youth, *n.d.*

ADAM C. WELCH

A Memoir of his Life

I

"ONE of the most discreditable and discourteous things in life is contempt for what we once loved." So runs one of the many penetrating and memorable sayings which we heard from Professor Welch both in class and in conversation. It was usually in connection with recollections of his own early life that he was speaking. The circumstances in which he passed his boyhood were unusual, and he was inevitably denied much of that affection, understanding and guidance which a child can receive from his parents alone. There was something independent and even stern about the influences which moulded these opening years, and the impression was never effaced. But there was a great deal in that far past that he never ceased to love, and he often recalled with thankfulness what he owed to those who were entrusted with his upbringing. There is some close association also between these early years and the delight which he had in his own happy home and his intense devotion to his own family.

Adam Cleghorn Welch was born on May 14, 1864, at Goshen, Jamaica, where his father, the Rev. John Welch, a native of Johnshaven, was a missionary of the United Presbyterian Church. His mother was Flora Hogg, the daughter of Robert Hogg, farmer at Glendearg in the parish of Melrose. Not only in farming circles was this a well-known Border family—as it still is—but in the life of the Church also. Among the records of the Secession Church at Stow the name often appears, and in the list of the members of a " praying society " which formed the nucleus of that congregation there shines bright the name of Adam Hogg from whom the professor inherited his name and more than his name.

Adam was the sixth of a family of eight children. When he was but an infant he and his brother John were brought home

from Jamaica by their mother who was returning then to
this country for the first furlough in a period of service which
had already extended beyond fifteen years. Two years later
she returned with the children to share her husband's labours
in the field; but their time together was short, for on December
5, 1870, Mr. Welch died of yellow fever, and his wife seven
days later.

Adam remembered little of his parents. The clearest memory
he had was of the family gathered on the veranda of the
Goshen manse, the father reading aloud *The Pickwick Papers*
and the mother sewing. He often used to tell also of the
faithful negro nurse under whose care the children were
brought home to Scotland, and in particular how she gathered
them round with rugged and persistent love to administer
medicine from a large spoon. They were now to be cared for
very devotedly by his mother's sister and brother at the farm
of Haltree near Stow; and there always remained in Adam's
mind a vivid picture of the cold sleety night when they arrived
at Galashiels station, and how he and his brother were packed
into a farm-cart with the luggage, covered with straw for
their greater comfort on the long, slow drive to the farm.

Not yet eight years of age, Adam went with his older
brother to the Academy at Galashiels. For a time the boys
were in lodging together, so that they were early out in the
world on their own. It was an experience by which they were
more closely drawn together in mutual dependence than children normally are in a home. At this period the name of Mr.
Fairley, headmaster at the Academy, deserves recognition, for
Welch always acknowledged that it was to this man that he
owed his pure, chaste sense of good English. When he was
ten, Adam had an accident in the harvest field which involved
several weeks of convalescence in splints, and it was then that
his aunt solved the problem of how to engage an active boy's
time by teaching him to knit—an accomplishment in which
he became proficient, using it to a remarkable extent during
the dark years of the two world wars. Two years later the
whole family came to Edinburgh and were united again. The
oldest brother was now twenty-one and the oldest sister of
seventeen was housekeeper, while the others were at school. It
was a noisy, happy household, and many were the complaints

from the flat below. Adam went to George Watson's College and provided for himself from that time onwards by bursaries and coaching fees. He entered the University at the age of fifteen, graduated in Arts at eighteen, and proceeded to the United Presbyterian Hall. From boyhood he had dedicated himself to the service of the Church, and from that goal he never once took his eye.

A very distinguished course in divinity terminated in 1885 and was followed by a summer with a scholarship at Erlangen. At one stage in his college course he was powerfully attracted to the mission field, to carry on his father's work in Jamaica. It is fascinating to speculate what the effect for good would have been to that mission if Welch had given many years to it; but his subsequent career leaves little room for doubt that he was wisely guided in the decision he made at this time. Nevertheless he was as student, minister and professor, one of the most effective and ardent speakers on the world-wide mission of the Church. When he was " pleading the schemes " as a student, a well-known elder of the time was heard to say, " Adam Welch is the only man who ever made me put the half-crown back into my pocket and take out a pound note instead ".

Welch's pastoral instincts were always strong, and so he welcomed the opportunities which came his way when the Home Mission Committee invited him to undertake work for a new community of miners, some fifteen hundred persons, employed at Straiton, near Loanhead. The conditions were difficult and testing. Rows of small houses had been built, and there was a rule that not more than four lodgers were to be kept; but it was frequently broken by as many as ten youths, working on different shifts, being housed together. There was no place of recreation at all except the public house. The place used first of all for religious meetings was an old farmhouse with some of the partitions knocked out. Adam's own quarters were not luxurious. " If there is anywhere in Scotland colder than this, I don't want to be in it; I can't sleep for cold." His aunt did her best to remedy this by the prompt supply of a shepherd's plaid. It was very uphill work. " I visit them and visit them and they give me a civil reception and promise to come to the meetings—and don't come!" He

sometimes heard interpretations of Holy Writ which would
have surprised the expositors. One old lady said to him, " Ay,
Maister Wailch, thae were wonnerfu' men thae auld prophets.
See thae words o' Jeremiah (sic) whaur he says that ilka mountain and hill shall be brocht low and the crooked roads made
straucht; and see hoo it's a'comin' aboot noo wi' thae rail-
ways. Ay, they were wonnerfu' men thae auld prophets." The
future professor coughed violently. Before he finished his work
at Straiton the meeting place holding about one hundred and
fifty was crowded, and he remembered this short period as one
in which God had granted him true success.

In 1887 he went to Glasgow to be assistant at Dowanhill
Church to Mr. Dickie under whom he had already worked in
Perth. At this period there begins the series of heavy sorrows
which darkened his life for the next seventeen years. In the
summer of this year he went to meet his eldest brother, Robert,
returning from America—to find that he was not on the vessel
and had died before sailing. It was of Robert that he wrote
in later days, " None of us realised how much we owed Bob
without whose influence we might have all gone to the dogs."
The youngest brother, Alex, who had always been the special
joy of the family, was assassinated in Egypt in 1897 when
returning to Alexandria with money to pay workers' wages.
To the memory of this brother he dedicated his book on
Anselm. In the following year the only remaining brother,
John, died in the Straits Settlements. Six years later his own
first-born child died when he was only three months old. All
this, added to the loss of both parents at the same time in
early childhood, amply explains what he wrote in a letter to
Dr. John A Hutton, " I sat astonished to hear you say that
you had had no experience of death. I never knew a time
when I was not pursued by death. It has shot at me as with
arrows from behind trees." Some of his friends who knew him
long have said that the early light-heartedness of Welch disappeared. The explanation is not far to seek, nor is there any
cause for wonder that all through his ministry he was so
amazingly sensitive to the sorrows of men and women.

2

The village of Waterbeck in Dumfriesshire, within a few miles of the birthplace of Thomas Carlyle, is beautiful in its situation and surroundings, and the church there has not only served a widely extended community of farm-workers and shepherds but has in a quite unusual degree won for itself a good name throughout the land. A long succession of remarkable ministers has served this congregation, and the eyes of larger churches in search of a minister have for long been accustomed to turn with enquiring interest towards it. They are a kindly, hospitable, reserved people. Something of their distinctive flavour and humour as well as their precise knowledge of the Bible may be gathered (by those who recognize the reference) from the reply given by a farmer's wife in that parish when her minister, now Principal Hugh Watt, asked, " Well, how are you, Mrs. Z?" " I'm aye keepin' oot Keturah."

Adam Welch was ordained at Waterbeck in November, 1887, and there he spent five happy years, fruitful to his people as to himself. From the beginning the downright ability of the man and the characteristic vigour of all his work were realized by these people with whom he had so much in common; and it is not surprising that they made very definite efforts to retain their minister when the call to Helensburgh came. To this day the hearts of a few older people warm at the mention of his name. He did most of his visiting on foot, an erect, striking figure, clad in the plaid, striding swiftly, with stick in hand, across the moors and hills—and enjoying every moment of it. In later years he often spoke, moved by the memory and moving others by the way he told it, of walking home long distances by moonlight and pondering some of the most profound of the theological issues which were the principal theme of his concentrated study at this period.

He was no recluse. He made it his business and his joy to know people, the conditions in which they lived, and the bearing of these conditions on their personal problems and their faith. Few great scholars have possessed such a wealth of detailed knowledge of the small things that make up the life of ordinary people in the country, and none better than he could cast around these small things the light in which they grow great and vital. There was not a nook of the Border country which he did not know, because he had explored it and searched out its life. Indeed, he was ready to take part in the life of the people in ways which were looked upon as scarcely seemly for a minister half a century ago. When there were wedding festivities to attend, he always went and shared actively in them, so that whispering tongues were known to say that " Waterbeck has got a dancing minister."

One of his best friends in Waterbeck was the precentor who was also the local hairdresser and a man deeply interested in theological discussion. Whenever he was burdened with a problem of this nature, he decided that it was time the minister's hair was cut; and in a leisurely way the question would be unravelled on the floor of the manse kitchen, to the accompaniment of the click of scissors. There was also a fundamental agreement between the two men as to what was seemly in the praise of the Church. When the barber spoke scathingly of certain hymns which were enjoying an undeserved popularity, Welch concurred. "Yes, they are so flimsy," he said, " you can put your fingers through them." This same man regularly attended the minister's Bible Class and detected that quality of incisive seriousness which brought an atmosphere of awe to all his teaching.

During these years in Waterbeck, Welch began to write. " I always had an itch for writing," he says. " It would be more satisfactory to be able to say that this was due to some sense of having a gospel to propagate, but it must be owned that the craving was present before I was conscious of having anything particular to say. It is more in agreement with the facts of the case to set this down to the form taken in my case by what the later generation charitably calls the desire for self-expression, what my generation more bluntly called vanity." There were frequent articles on Biblical themes in the *United Presbyterian Church Monthly,* and in these there was evident a freshness of approach to the Scriptures. Considerable interest in the world of scholarship was aroused by his long review of Cheyne's *Jewish Religious Life after the Exile*. Even these early writings reveal a measure of uneasiness about the Wellhausen theory.

He also wrote a good deal for a short-lived journal called *The Modern Church,* in which Dr. A. B. Bruce was much interested. These articles show how much he was in sympathy with the stirring of the social conscience which was attracting the support of men like D. M. Ross (one of his closest friends) and George Adam Smith. With them he was in fullest agreement that working men will not be satisfied just with mission-halls and tracts. It is in these early days also that Welch first became conscious of what he calls " the chill, unhappy shock of disappointment which accompanies the reading of one's own ' stuff ' in the impersonal medium of print." Nothing he ever wrote could escape this, for what he had to say had to be heard ere its depth and intensity could be appreciated. There was a glow not only in the way he conceived his thought, but still more in the way he delivered it. This is at least a partial explanation of why some of his writings have been calmly ignored and why his main propositions still await an answer.

3

In 1892 the United Presbyterian congregation at Helensburgh was engaged in the selection of a successor to their much loved and honoured minister, Rev. Alex Hislop, D.D., who had been appointed a professor of Practical Training. Welch's name was not on the list of those being considered for the vacancy, but he preached one Sunday in August as a substitute for someone who was unable to come at the last moment, and little doubt remained in any mind that this was to be their minister. From the beginning his dynamic personality made itself felt not only in this church but far beyond its bounds. One of his elders, Mr. William G. Muter, writes, " His preaching was challenging and even daring. He spoke to the conscience and stimulated the imagination. His hearers felt that for him the conduct of public worship and the preaching of the word was a serious and solemn undertaking. Perhaps the most enduring aspect of Mr. Welch's ministry here was his hold upon the young. His grip upon the minds of those whose ideas and philosophy of life were yet in the formative stage was enormous. The Bible Class meetings were filled to overflowing, and were attended by both old and young."

Many letters were received at the time of Professor Welch's death from men and women who were young when he was in Helensburgh, some of them boys and girls; and it is impressive how they agree in testifying to the excellence of his work in the Bible Class. Some of them describe how he used to march to and fro across the platform, chanting with gusto the Hebrew words, defying the enemies of Israel who appeared to be entrenched in the side galleries. He would gladly give a whole evening to any youth who was anxious for fuller light and assurance. The preparation of first communicants and the service of their admission to full membership of the church was so conceived and carried out by him that no one could ever forget these memorable hours. One friend of these days writes to say that, so far as religious instruction goes, she has brought up her family on notes of Welch's sermons and Bible Class addresses. Another says that " Sunday was *the* great day for us; we looked forward to it all the week ", while others declare in their own way that " next to my parents, he was my chief lodestar through life ". If he was adored thus by the young people, he was not neglectful of the old, but very attentive and cheering to them. " What I liked best about him," says one elderly person, " was his sanctified cheek ! "

His work for the congregation at Helensburgh increased with every year, but his energies were not exhausted at the limits of that sphere. Welch would show a real measure of discriminating sympathy with those in the Church to-day who are insisting on the importance of the integration of worship and the common life. He was always moved by a clear recognition of responsibility for a share in the life of the community, and his eagerness to discharge the responsibility was as keen as his recognition was vivid. Every good cause soon learned to turn to him for encouragement and support—and never in vain. He was elected a member of the School Board and served the cause of education for several years. The better housing of the people was a subject he systematically studied even in his Helensburgh days; he made himself master of the relevant facts both for town and country, and he knew how acute the problem was on both sides of it. His transference to Glasgow brought him even more intimately into touch with this problem, as he discharged with diligence the Home Mission part of the work of his congregation.

During the first years of his ministry, Welch's interests were principally in Systematic Theology. The articles which appeared under the pen-name " Rus " revealed that plainly. It was in his Helensburgh period that it began to appear likely that Church History would be the field of his life-work. He felt the necessity of pursuing the history of Christian doctrine down the centuries and of testing it out in the actual life of the Church of the ages. The chief fruit of this line of study is his book on Anselm—a great, vivid book still, worthy to stand beside Dean Church's volume, and more penetrating than it on the purely theological aspects of Anselm's work and time. Welch used to say that his great friend, John Oman, subsequently Principal of Westminster College, Cambridge, compared the style of this book to " the jog-trot of a donkey," adding, " I have never re-read the book to discover exactly the point of the comparison ".

This study in history, with the inevitable judgments it entailed on the Roman legalistic system, had its important bearing on all his later work on the Old Testament. It helped to form in his mind the conviction that (to use his own words) " the Old Testament Church which, during the whole period of its existence, lived in an alien and hostile world, can never have been the merely legalistic institution which it was generally considered to be alike by the critical and the evangelical school. That Church found it necessary to understand more clearly its worth and the work it had to do—a work of such a character that no mere legalism could have fulfilled it." It is a significant fact that it was usually some concrete situation in the life of the contemporary Church which sent Welch back to the examination of one Old Testament problem after another, finding in these problems substantial analogies to the modern conditions. The uneasiness about the Wellhausen position was increased by his Biblical and historical studies, and it is quite certain that from about the year 1901 he saw the

need for recasting the entire critical hypothesis. He was as yet
at the stage only of stating the problem; the lines of his solution had not begun to emerge.

4

As soon as it became known that Claremont Church, Glasgow, had decided to address a call to Welch, the congregation
in Helensburgh made as strenuous efforts to retain their minister as Waterbeck had done. A document signed by every
office-bearer conveyed to him their " earnest desire that you
may see your way to remain with us and to continue a work
more prized and far-reaching than you can measure ". He
had already been invited to two well-known Glasgow
churches, but had declined the invitation. To Claremont,
however, he went in 1902. In the following year he married
Grace, youngest daughter of Thomas Steven, Ardlui House,
Helensburgh, his gifted and devoted companion to the end.
These years in Glasgow have been described by himself as the
busiest and hardest years of his life, and he testified publicly
that he was sure that he would never have come through them
had it not been for the capacity and courage of his wife.

Once again Welch had been chosen to succeed a man called
to the professor's chair. After a most notable ministry of
nearly twelve years in Claremont, Dr. A. R. Macewen had
been elected Professor of Church History at New College,
Edinburgh. Once again also he was to follow a minister who
dwelt in exceptional nearness to the heart of his congregation.

Under Macewen the congregation rapidly rose from a
membership of 400 to more than 1,000. His success as
preacher and pastor was enormous throughout the whole
stretch of his ministry, and he soon became a conspicuous
figure in the life of the city. To succeed such a man was no
easy task. Macewen and Welch resembled each other in
several respects—singular devotion to the Master, the possession of rare gifts, meticulous and sacrificial preparation for
public worship, a capacity for getting near to people of all
sorts, and a nervous intensity which added to the normally
heavy strain of their work. Otherwise they were very different

men. There was more genius in Welch than in Macewen, and more variety of talent in Macewen than in Welch. A layman who knew them both intimately and the congregation they both so honourably served, writes, " Macewen was an organiser to his finger-tips, Welch believed in leaving the details of organisation to his office-bearers. Both in their pulpit ministrations urged the duty of service in the societies of the church, but Macewen pressed home the duty in personal appeal to the individual, whereas Welch left it to the hearers' conscience, believing that those who did not respond were the losers. Macewen was able to suffer fools more gladly than Welch, and Claremont had just the average number of these. Welch's caustic tongue got him into many a scrape which Macewen was able to avoid."

The testimony of one of his assistants in Claremont, Professor William Manson, deserves to be recorded here. " The impressions most deeply wrought upon my mind connect themselves most immediately with the intense devotional atmosphere of his ministry of public worship and with the profound spiritual and ethical quality of his teaching. In particular I recall a series of sermons on Abraham and one on the book of Ruth which for strength and depth of religious insight I have not seen surpassed, not even by anything in his published work. For here the element of human sympathy and inspired imagination had a freer play for their exercise, Welch was a seer to whom Old Testament topics were not merely Old Testament topics but the transparent medium, where men had eyes to see, of God's eternal self-disclosure to our spirit. He saw the Old Testament shot through and through with the light of the Christian revelation; and only so, he would have insisted, has it place and authority for us. The categories of his mind were not either rational or mystical but spiritual—a witness to that which only God's approach to us in revelation creates and maintains in the soul. Life had for him a tragic incompleteness apart from God.

" I look back, therefore, to Claremont Church at that time as to a shrine. He set an immense value on the institutional side of religion. It is possible that there were hearers there, as elsewhere, for whom Welch's profoundly ethical judgment of life signified severity or indifference toward human weak-

nesses and needs. These did not always realise the strictness of
the discipline which the preacher imposed upon himself before
he came with his message to others, nor the intensity of
thought which underlay and expressed itself in the chiselled
purity and restraint of his style. Those who gave their minds
to his teaching recognised the spiritual realism and the devotional beauty of his thought, and would have been prepared
to claim him as the finest preacher of his time."

Alongside of this should be placed the tribute of Dr. A. K.
Walton, one of his successors, delivered at the memorial service in Claremont in February, 1943. " I had not been long
here before I realised that something had gone forward during
the years of his ministry which had left an abiding mark on
the congregation. It was a mark which could only be made
by a man whose life supported and expressed the message
which he uttered. There have been few men with a pro-
founder distaste for saying things which sound well enough
but which do not spring from an overmastering sense of their
truth and reality. Just at that point where most men are
tempted to let themselves go on a tide of emotion and say
what does not have behind it the deep conviction of mind and
heart, he laid on himself an iron restraint. It cannot have been
easy, for he was a man in whom there was deep and even
passionate feeling. He always had to hold in check something
volcanic in himself; and it was the presence of that fire, res-
trained but not hidden, which was part of the secret of his
power.

" His was a great nature, richly human, deeply conscious
of the stresses and strains which are at once the cause of
danger and the way of opportunity for men. He knew where
temptation lurks, and so he could sympathise with his fellows.
But it was never a weak and condoning sympathy. He believed
in men because he believed in God, what He had done for men
and could do in them. And so believing he could speak at
times on the note of severity and demand. It was no easy gospel which came from his lips, and if, because of his fierce
hatred of empty words and insincere amiabilities, he sometimes shocked people and even angered them, those who knew
the deep source of that sternness in his reverence for truth and
his faith that men were too great to be fobbed off with un-

realities, learned to welcome that aspect of his message also.

" A notable and endearing characteristic of his ministry was his profound respect for men and women younger than himself and often immature in their gropings after truth. There was nothing in him of that genial condescension which not infrequently enrages youth. He treated them seriously and so their minds opened ungrudgingly and gratefully to his deeper insights and wider experience. He was a preacher who required more of his hearers than they were always ready to give, but those who had a hunger for what was true and real and who had ears to hear the prophetic note addressed to mind and conscience came by an ever deeper conviction that they were being challenged by the very word of God.

" He was indeed a great preacher; and yet it may well be that those who came to know and love him best of all were troubled folk, who had learned something of life's tragic aspect and were deeply acquainted with grief. It was they chiefly who detected the tenderness and understanding which real human need unfailingly evoked in him."

The cost of such a ministry to such a man was immense. It was not only the preparation for the Sunday services, so astonishingly thorough. The actual conducting of the services exhausted him physically and nervously to such a degree that often at the end of a day he was unable to touch food. It would have been impossible for him to continue the work of this congregation much longer, in conjunction with his other duties and the amount of general Church work which was now steadily growing. The summons to the professor's chair came just in time to secure that his now mature scholarship should be devoted without distraction to its special task for at least twenty-five years.

The name of Adam Welch had become known beyond his own church and country, although as yet the only book he had published was his *Anselm*. It is probable, therefore, that it was mainly on the strength of this volume that the University of Halle conferred upon him in 1909 the Honorary Degree of Doctor of Theology, in connection with the University's celebration of the Calvin Quatercentenary. The magnitude of the honour may be measured by the fact that he was one of three persons in the United Kingdom who received it

at this time. His studies were still mainly in Church History
for, when the Trustees of the Kerr Lectureship invited him to
suggest a subject, his first suggestion was Tertullian, " believing", he says, " that he deserves a more careful and respect-
ful treatment than he has received." The Trustees, however,
insisted on an Old Testament subject, and so in some fashion
Welch's future was determined for him from the outside. The
lectures were published in 1912 under the title *The Religion
of Israel under the Kingdom*. This book, if it never became
in any sense popular, ranked him in the foremost place among
Old Testament scholars. He was deeply gratified to know that
it was being used as a text-book in certain American colleges,
and a little amused to learn that parts of it had been translated
into Kaffir! It was inevitable now that he would be invited to
occupy one of the Old Testament chairs as soon as an opportunity occurred. It came next year; and, as he gave up the
ministry of Claremont Church which his methods of work
and his consecrated purpose had made so heavy for himself,
he published his most valuable little book, *Joseph and his
Brethren*, originally evening addresses to the congregation to
which it is dedicated.

5

The University of Edinburgh conferred upon Welch in
June, 1913, the Honorary Degree of Doctor of Divinity, in
recognition of his eminence as a preacher and scholar and particularly of his work as Kerr Lecturer. The intimation was
made some weeks before his election as Professor, and reached
Mr. and Mrs. Welch in Italy where they were spending a holi-
day as the guests of their congregation, in celebration of his
semi-jubilee as a minister. On May 23, 1913, the General
Assembly of the United Free Church gave itself to a task in
which it always seemed to find some special delight—the election of professors. There were as many as nine candidates
for the Old Testament chairs at Edinburgh and Aberdeen;
but it is significant that seven of the nine were not nominated
as rivals to Welch, and it appeared a certainty that he was
the man for New College. He was supported by 63 out of the

67 Presbyteries, and was very ably commended to the house
by Rev. (later Professor) A. B. Macaulay who, in reference
to the recently-published Kerr Lectures said : " To borrow the
magnanimous hyperbolism of the revered Principal of New
College, Dr. Whyte, ' We have all read it !' "

Welch contributed a very large share to the intellectual and
religious vitality of New College. His finest work was done in
his class-room for twenty-one years, and long before it was
completed he had won recognition as one of the very greatest
Old Testament teachers that the Scottish Church has at any
time produced. As Principal Martin put it—" It is not simply
that during these years he has done inimitably well what
someone else might have done less efficiently, but he has done
for the College and the University and the Church what there
was no one else to do at all."

A specifically theological interest dominated and inspired
all his teaching, and for that reason among others he was
never dull. He had once said of Dr. Oman's *Vision and
Authority* that " it was liable to offend the great body of
people who could not believe that theology was profound
unless it was dull ", and in all his own work he succeeded in
wedding together great depths of thinking with remarkable
movement and liveliness of expression. All that he gave himself to in class was subservient to one commanding purpose—
to make the religious conceptions enshrined in the Old Testament real and relevant for full Christian preaching. This
deserves to be stressed in view of the fact that several of his
books are given almost exclusively to the more technical problems of criticism—although even in them this primary passion
for religious truth shines through, and it was only for the
sake of seeing in better perspective the historical growth of
Israel's religion that he undertook the other task at all. Even
the best students realized that the Old Testament had been
largely a closed book to them until he provided the master key.

Welch was the antithesis of the grammarian type, yet he
believed that normally the theological student ought to be
asked to give himself to the study of the Hebrew language. It
was not that he regarded it in the sacred light of the Scottish
elder who said that he would like to study Hebrew in order
to be able in his prayers to address the Almighty in His own

language! He was convinced, however, that it was a discipline
of a kind all by itself and valuable in itself, that it was a necessary aid to the intelligent use of a good commentary and also,
as he put it in his Inaugural Lecture, that it placed in men's
hands a tool which they might use to prevent themselves being
left at the mercy of what any commentator might say.

It was his custom to open the class every morning with
prayer, and it is likely that what every student remembers about
that class-room with deepest gratitude is the opening prayer,
so carefully prepared, so arrestingly relevant, so profoundly
searching. We had heard from himself and others that, during
his Glasgow ministry, he had been burdened with the necessity
for doing something to help the prayer-life of young men and
women who attended a mission connected with his church,
all of whom lived in over-crowded homes where there was
little opportunity of privacy for prayer. To meet this need
which a man of his strong pastoral instincts could not neglect,
he used to write out sets of short prayers and give them to
these young people to keep beside them and to read, perhaps
on their way to work in the morning. When his work in Glasgow was done and when in many ways people were showing
their appreciation of his ministry, nothing touched him more
than to receive the individual thanks of many of these young
people in the mission for his personal care of them in the most
intimate and sacred region of their life. How often his students
were a little envious of these young folks, and how they have
wished that they had a set of his class prayers beside them!

Welch perhaps did not make upon men the impression of
immense learning, because somehow it sat lightly upon him.
What was most impressive was the distinctive way in which
he said everything, even things that would sound common
enough on other lips. In his lectures he never " got lost in
insignificant detail "; he knew well where he was going and
he kept to his direction. There were also never-to-be-forgotten
days when the lectures, notably one on Saul and another on
Hosea, reached such a height of religious intensity that note-
taking became a sacrilege; every pen was laid aside and men
sat awe-struck and in silence till the teacher swept swiftly out
of the room. It often happened too that students eagerly
sought from him and generously received additional lectures

beyond the requirements of the curriculum. They were only too glad to give some of their free hours each week, especially in the summer term, for this purpose. His normal method was to remain seated during his lectures, and frequently he derived some curious satisfaction, not to say inspiration, from tugging at his shoe laces. On at least one memorable day he delighted the class by kicking the shoe off altogether, and subsequently padding across the room, shoeless in respect of one foot, to point out on a map the course of the Assyrian invasion!

Welch was unrivalled in his understanding of the needs, the eccentricities, and even the subterfuges of students. His relationships with them were friendly and honest, blending inflexible firmness with sympathy and insight. The experience he had gained in earlier years in the work of the College Committee was invaluable to him when he became a teacher. " Men sometimes talk about students", he told the Assembly of 1904, " as if they were an inscrutable species of animal; but in some respects they are very like the ministers I know, and in one respect especially—they are never interested in dead things." When these words were quoted to him years afterwards, he smiled and said that he would modify them only in one respect, in so far as they were too complimentary to the ministers! He rejoiced also that there was at least a proportion of the students always prepared to express, occasionally with a slightly brutal frankness, the things which the more serious thought it wise not to express at all. In his final report as Convener of the College Committee he made a declaration from which he never diverged and in which most students would find themselves in cordial agreement with him—" Our students are almost absurdly over-examined. They are examined at entrance, they are examined throughout the session in their classes, they are examined each year for their exits; and, as though all this were not enough, there are bursary examinations and the Presbyteries have a try at the work too. There is a subtle degradation of mind which is inevitably associated with any system of examinations. But this is greatly increased when, as in our case, the examinations are conducted by different authorities from very different points of view. The necessary outcome is to engender in men's minds the idea that the object of

being examined is to baffle examiners. This matter has grown
steadily clear to me during the years I have served this
Committee." The modifications in detail accomplished in
later years did not change Welch's attitude to this subject, and
that attitude was based broadly on that fundamental respect
for men which was the big thing in his contacts with his
students. It was an enjoyment to him when students did
their work well, apart from any consideration of examination or of the benefit that might be connected with their
place in the results. For the rest, he found a great joy in
mixing freely with young men. His conversation at the dining-
table was rich and human, and sometimes his voice could
be heard high above the general hum of talk, to the accompaniment of dramatic gesture and boisterous laughter.

Welch had the kind of nature which responded in constant, though by no means subservient, loyalty to a leader
and to colleagues. It was wholly fitting, therefore, that when
Principal Martin retired from his chair in 1927, Welch should
be chosen to be the spokesman of the college in the Assembly.
" We are not come here this day to bury Caesar but to praise
him. His roots are wrapped about this heap. There are two
convictions that are fundamental in the Principal's mind—
one that Edinburgh is the centre of Scotland, and the other
that New College is the crown of Edinburgh. These to him
are not arguable propositions; they shine in the luminous self-
evidence which they possess for him. The professors at New
College have their own minds and their own past, and their
own thoughts about things and about one another, which
they have no hesitation in expressing in the unbuttoned hours
around the senate table; but when they come to the world,
they are one in their devotion to the College. They owe that
very largely to the fact that they work together under the lead
of a man who, with a many-sided intellect and very varied
interests, has never forgotten that first and last his duty was
to his chair in the College. The Principal has succeeded in
infecting all his College with his temper—even the Senatus,
two of whom are old United Presbyterians, and these are
tough indiarubber to digest."

Nothing could be more helpful in an estimate of what
Professor Welch was to New College than the judgment of

Principal Martin, and he has written the following tribute :
" In sober truth his influence in the class-room could not.
easily be exaggerated, but his colleagues would speak scarcely
less enthusiastically of the stimulus and enrichment his arrival
in the College meant to themselves and to the common life
generally. The new professor came prepared to find keen
enjoyment in the opportunity opened before him, and he
threw himself into his tasks with an infectious zest and
thoroughness. No academic mustiness, it was quickly felt,
could withstand the impact of this new energising influence.
His sense of the sacredness of the ministerial calling never
left him; his concern that each fresh year's arrivals in College
should profit to the utmost by the fleeting opportunity of an
almost too crowded curriculum was unflagging. Others confessed themselves glad to rekindle their feebler flame at his.

" A term of years in charge of the church's training course
had familiarised him with the problems which fall to be
handled by the governing body of a Divinity College, and
from the first his contributions to discussion in Senate were
as fresh and helpful in substance as their manner of statement might be terse and trenchant. Characteristic of him was
his interposition on the very infrequent occasions when some
point of College discipline fell to be enforced. None realised
more clearly how the policy of the blind eye might be ordin-
arily the only wise one; but in the hundredth case, where
the seemliness and dignity of College life might appear to be
involved, no voice would be raised more decisively for the
firm word being spoken and the just thing done. With individual pupils, specially promising or not, his patience was unwearied. In those dark years, too, when the College benches
were forsaken for the stricken fields of France and the sterner
tasks to be confronted there, no kinsman could have followed
the fighters' fortunes with an intenser anxiety or grieved more
visibly over those who returned no more. The College
memorial to their sacrifice, as often as his eye lit upon it,
never failed to move him.

" In a congenial circle Welch was the most delightful of
companions. His mind belonged perhaps to the variety of the
well-read rather than the specially widely-read, but its contents comprised not a little of what was best in world litera-

ture and were always at command. He could be a most
brilliant talker—when in the humour, which, be it confessed,
was by no means always! There were days, in the later time
especially, when the strain under which the common task
was done and the effect of the buffetings of the world upon a
temperament finely set and keenly sensitive, was only too
apparent. There were days when perhaps he permitted himself too easily to be ' troubled with ill conditions'. But then he
could bear to be told as much—at which the clouds would
break and scatter and, with the irradiating smile which his
intimates love to recall, he would be his irresistible self once
more."

Welch had scarcely begun his work at New College when
the Great War burst upon the world. It was an immense
sorrow to him and the full horror of it broke devastatingly
upon his soul. Through all these dark years—" a horrible
period of moral chaos " he called them—he worked beyond
his strength, undertaking duty in churches whose ministers
had gone on service, and serving as chaplain to the Highland
Light Infantry for a period. When that work was drawing to
a close, he wrote : " Somehow these men and my work with
them have utterly laid hold on me, and the response they
have given and their constant frank kindness are to me ex-
cessively gratifying; they cheer up my heart so that I grudge
that my time is coming to an end." He got on so well with
the men and they so valued his services that they were keen
to persuade him to go with them when they went abroad.
Some of the young officers threatened to kidnap him, if he
would not go peaceably! He was greatly interested in the work
of the Committee on Chaplains, and he spoke to the Assembly of 1916 in terms which made manifest his real grasp of
the many-sided problems of this work. At the same time, to
quote his own words, " he ploughed through much spade
work of a technical kind, partly to deaden thinking during
these dreadful years." When the war ended, he gave himself
enthusiastically to prepare courses of lectures for men who
knew little or no Hebrew. In this way there started a process
of revising and rewriting his lectures which continued all
through the years so that, when he resigned, scarcely a page
of the original survived. One certain effect of these war years

was the undermining of his health, and from 1922 onwards
he had to renounce the pleasures of golf, fishing and cycling
in which he used to share vigorously, and only on rare occasions dare he allow himself to preach, a sore restriction to
himself and a grievous impoverishment to the Church.

A most outstanding day in his career and in the world of
Biblical studies was that day in October, 1921, when he gave
the opening lecture of the session at New College and presented a threefold challenge to the critical theories of the
Pentateuch which had held the field in one form or another
since Wellhausen. This lecture was published in the *Expositor*
of May, 1923, under the title " On the Present Position of
Old Testament Criticism ". Short summaries of this article,
appearing in various journals, suggested to some that he had
broken with all higher criticism and become fundamentalist.
It was an almost amusing error. Although he challenged the
regnant hypotheses, he was equally certain that there could
be no going back to the old view. Its argument had been
foreshadowed in an article by him in the *Expositor* of December, 1913, and he now asserted that " the three cardinal
positions of modern criticism have been seriously shaken ".
Welch often quoted the words of one of his students who
described Old Testament scholars as " a band of cannibals
who refreshed themselves by devouring one another ", and
there is no doubt that he himself set agoing one of the most
controversial ferments of discussion which has agitated this
field for so long. One of the main contentions of his article
is worked out fully in *The Code of Deuteronomy* and
Deuteronomy: The Framework of the Code.

Before that time he had published *Visions of the End*.
The title was not his choice, but Dr. McFadyen's who edited
the series in which it appeared; but it is a really helpful study
of two of the most difficult books of the Bible, Daniel and
Revelation, the cardinal truths of which ought to be published from every pulpit. This book was much prized, especially by men coming back from the war to the University.
Two or three years later there appeared a small, compact
book on the Psalms, in which he makes straight for the religious ideas and uses of this collection of cult hymns. About
the same time he issued a translation of Jeremiah for the

2

Adult Schools, and it is marked by freshness of interpretation
and by a very helpful grouping of the oracles. Jeremiah was
the prophet to whom all along Welch was most attracted.
There is much evidence for this, and of a desire to publish a
book on this prophet years before he actually did so. That
desire was frustrated for various reasons but, when it did
appear in 1928, it was hailed as one of the best studies in
English on the prophet and his period. In some ways the most
successful of his books was the Bible Class Handbook—*The
Preparation for Christ in the Old Testament*. It has been
reprinted often and is used far beyond the Church of Scotland and for larger purposes than that for which it was prepared. There is evidence of vast study of a most detailed
kind behind all these books, and this is particularly true of
his Baird Lectures, " Post-Exilic Judaism ", which he regarded
as the most careful and thorough piece of work he had done.

On attaining the age of seventy, Professor Welch retired
in 1934. His portrait by David Alison was presented to the
College, with a replica for his home, by colleagues, former
students and other friends. On the very same day in February, 1935, when this presentation was made, his book on
Post-Exilic Judaism was published. In the middle of his speech
he hauled a copy from his overcoat pocket and handed it to a
former student who had taken part in the ceremony, adding that
a member of his family had described this volume as " the last
wheeze of the emeritus-professor ". But it was far from that
In the following year one of his most vital books, *Prophet
and Priest in Old Israel,* appeared. During these years of retirement also two of the greatest honours in the realm of Old
Testament scholarship came to him. He was elected President
of the Society for Old Testament Study in 1934, and was
able to travel to London to give his Presidential Address. On
that occasion he first revealed publicly the line of thought
which he developed in his last book, *The Work of the
Chronicler*. It was a particular gratification to him to be invited to deliver the Schweich Lectures, the blue riband in
this field; and he enjoyed his visit to London for this purpose in December, 1938.

During his retirement he developed more extensively an
interest he had pursued for many years—stamp-collecting. As

" Stamp Expert " in *Greatheart* he made the acquaintance of many boys in far-separated places, and his correspondence with them was as real a pleasure to him as it was for them. He devoted a considerable part of the proceeds of his books to do this other fascinating and instructive service for young people in a thorough fashion, and he became a well-known figure haunting the places where rare stamps are on sale.

The outbreak of war in 1939 was a cause of acute distress to Welch. In his book on the Psalms he tells how he wrote prayers of thanksgiving and petition for the services of the Armistice Day of 1918 and destroyed them immediately after the service—" Please God they would never be needed again." The shattering of that hope was bitter almost beyond bearing. So sharply did this renewed world catastrophe make him suffer that he was obliged to give up reading about it in any way, and friends who visited him were aware that it must be kept out of conversation completely. There was only one thing he could do, and so he set himself again to use the art of knitting in which his aunt had trained him during his illness as a boy, and he produced well over one hundred pairs of socks and many pairs of mittens for the soldiers. He had now come back to Helensburgh. There were other old men of his acquaintance there—" we come out like bluebottles in the sunshine ", he said. He enjoyed the sea and the wide views and was able to get quieter walks than would have been possible in the city. To one of his oldest friends, Rev. B. R. H. Mein, he writes, " I am back here where I worked for ten of the happiest years of my life, the years when life is strong in a man and he delights in his job for the sheer satisfaction of putting out all that is in him ". He died on February 19, 1943. In the last conscious moments which terminated several months of weakness he seemed to be repeating the twenty-third Psalm in the Hebrew tongue.

6

At the presentation of Professor Welch's portrait, Principal Martin observed that, if he had not chosen the life of a scholar and instructor, his name would have gone down to future generations as one of the outstanding churchmen of our time. It was inevitable that Welch should devote in some measure his wisdom, candour and incisiveness to the public service of the Church, for his apprehension of truth was essentially of a concrete nature, mediated to his mind through persons and the institutions they formed. While he was a faithful exponent of his firm conviction that a man should first of all do thoroughly what he is paid for, he was impatient of those who so engross themselves in their own congregation's affairs or are so exclusively concerned about the preparation of "their showy little sermons" that they left others to carry the burden of responsibility which is entailed in the fact that we belong to a Presbyterian Church in which our several congregations are but parts of a wider fellowship. He was unwearied in warning his students that, if they neglected this aspect of Christian service, even for the sake of looking well after their own churches, they would be losing something vital without which their very efforts for their own congregations could not be as near the will of God as they might be. There were men, he felt, who evaded their share in this work because they were lazy, and to the indolent he was justly pitiless. Like others whose judgment deserves to be trusted, Welch regarded laziness as the besetting sin of ministers, a temptation inherent in the very conditions in which they are left free to do their work. His view was that laziness always began in a man's thinking, and only after it had won its victory in the things of the mind did it emerge in other noticeable and socially harmful forms.

A man whose roots were so deep in the Secession Church and whose sense of debt to the Church of his fathers remained so keen could hardly be neglectful of the importance of the institution, for the Secession Church attached due significance to it. Welch's gifts in this field of Churchmanship were so apparent to his fellow Churchmen that he was chosen to do two things which he counted as a sacred privilege. The first was early in his minstry when he was asked to be one of the principal speakers at the Jubilee Celebrations of the United Presbyterian Church in 1897. His address on that occasion is an able and characteristic utterance, surveying the inner history of the two sections of that church, its foreign mission interest, the position and influence of that Church in the Scotland of nearly fifty years ago, and its controlling theological tendencies. The following sentences may be quoted : " The two branches of Scottish dissent which united in 1847 had learned to value, as a principle, what they began by accepting as a necessity. The two streams that flowed together were different—so different that some believe the colours are distinguishable after fifty years. Begun as a protest against doctrinal and practical laxity, the Secession had grasped a strong theory of the Church. Finding no adequate outlet for its energies at home, these energies expressed themselves in the foreign mission work which has been our Church's characteristic mark in Scotland. We would judge progress by a low standard were we to think only of the increased numbers who have made up our membership, or of the gifts they have offered, and not also of the purer and higher thoughts of God and His ways with men, which our Church has gladly taught. We have loved our Church and have sacrificed something for her—not simply because she existed, and on her nursing arms were we borne and reared, but because she has long taught and still teaches some truth of Jesus Christ and of His Kingdom which Scotland needs to learn."

The second occasion on which he appeared as the spokesman of the Church of his upbringing was one of which he was even more proud—the two hundredth anniversary of the Secession of 1733. Addressing the General Assembly of the now re-united Church of Scotland, he said, " We of the old United Presbyterian and Secession Churches have given up more for union than anyone else. The Free Church meets in its own hall and the Church of Scotland retains its old name. We of the United Presbyterian Church have lost both place and name; we have let them go without a murmur because we have been allowed to keep our principles. There are things in our Scottish history that are jewels of adventure, like that body of men who came through the Pentlands on a dim morning, having the extraordinary hope that they could make even Edinburgh repent. They proved that the Scot had always believed that the only thing they could do with a conviction, if by God's grace they had got one, was to follow it; and when

they went out riding at its bidding, the next best thing they
could do was not to keep their chin on their shoulder to see
if there was anybody else going to follow them. In that cate-
gory was the act of the four men who, not knowing if they
had anybody with them at all, constituted themselves a presbytery of the Church of Scotland in a wayside cottage on the
road that runs up to Kinross, and made their appeal to the
first free Assembly of the Church of Scotland in vindication
of the thing which they had done."

One of the most responsible tasks which falls to any man
in the Scottish Church is the Convenership of the Assembly's
Committee which supervises the Colleges of the Church and
is responsible for the adequate training of the future ministers. Welch occupied that position for four years, from 1907
to 1911. There is little doubt that the Church called him to
this work because he had already so singularly served this
particular cause as Convener of a special committee which
had been set up to deal with the problems of the training of
the ministry which had of necessity arisen after the Union
of 1900. To read the speeches which Welch gave to the
Assembly during his years of office is to realize how similar the
problems engaging the thought of the Committee were to those
before the Committee at the present time—the retention of
Hebrew language as a compulsory part of the scheme of
study, the necessity for a proper division between language
study and the larger questions of Old Testament history and
theology, the urgency of adequate practical training, the possibility of making one year of compulsory probation after the
close of the college course, and the teaching of sociology and
paedagogy. When at last in 1921 it was agreed to add these
two subjects, Welch said that " the only great difficulty about
these two was that nobody yet knew what they were ". The
question of the theological chairs engaged his thought to a
large extent in his first years as Convener. Even then he had
in a tentative way to turn his mind to the peculiar position
of the theological chairs in the Universities, and he had much
to say on this difficult theme to the Assembly of 1908 and
1909.

With these years of experience behind him and with the
Church's knowledge of how much was owed to him already

in this sphere, it was natural that Welch should be looked to as one of the few men best equipped to devise a satisfying solution of the problem of unifying the resources for theological training possessed and enjoyed by the Church of Scotland and the United Free Church. This was indeed one of the most important of the subordinate questions involved in the Union of 1929.

From the beginning of the wider negotiations for Union, Welch was wholeheartedly committed to the aim which was in view. From stage to stage he saw clearly what was necessary for a true adjustment of difficulties, and he had a deep longing to see the shattered unity of Scotland's Church life restored. In the Assembly debate of 1924, one of the most crucial and heated debates on the subject, Welch spoke with candid fairness and deep emotion. " What we are going to do now will determine not merely the future of the union, but the future of the United Free Church in Scotland. From the very beginning our Established Church brethren have let us know where they stand in connection with this question of teinds. They have said quite definitely that they mean to go on in the expectation, and with the desire, that all the funds should be conserved to the Church of Scotland. They have said that, not merely in the interests of their Church but in the interests of what they believe to be the needs of Scotland and the Kingdom of Christ. The Church of Scotland has put the whole position of their Church into the melting pot. They have submitted their constitution to revision in the interests of union. They have submitted their temporalities to the tender mercy of the Government. The generous and courageous action of a large body of the Church of Scotland in this matter has not quite been recognised in this Assembly. To make the question of the teinds a matter of principle is neither generous nor manly nor honourable conduct on our part. Scotland never allowed a great enthusiasm to die because of the beggarly question of money. We must not slam the door."

Especially in the later stages of the protracted discussions, Welch's sure, unprejudiced judgment was increasingly sought and trusted. Some who were in doubt about the Union were able finally to scatter their hesitations by the reflection that, since Welch was ardently for it, it could not be the wrong

road. Principal Cairns tells that, as they came out together
from the historic service of reunion in St. Giles' Cathedral
on October 2, 1929, there was a look of rapture and thankfulness upon Welch's expressive features, as he said to the
friend at his side, " There's a root of bitterness taken away
now from every parish in Scotland."

7

" We shall never know another Adam Welch. Mind,
character, personality, down to his whimsicalities—dare I
say?—were his own; and all were built on a very unusual
blend of truth and loyalty and love." That is the summing-up
of Principal Martin. Such a man would often express himself
in forceful, incisive and even abrupt ways—it could not be
otherwise—and there are many tales clustering round his
name which show that he could use a liberty of speech which
few are able to risk.

It was when he was preaching in a country church in the
borders at the busy lambing season that he stopped and said,
" I know this is a time of the year when you lose a lot of sleep
and I don't mind you sleeping here; but would someone tell
that man in the second seat from the back not to snore quite
so loudly? I'm afraid that he is disturbing the peaceful slum-
bers of that woman before him." In a very different city
church, when giving out the hymn ' The sands of time are
sinking,' he said, " We shall omit the verse ' I've wrestled
on towards heaven, 'gainst storm and wind and tide '—that
is too strenuous for this congregation!" In the course of his
Presbytery duties in Helensburgh, he was made responsible
for raising a sum of money for a new church and he called
upon a wealthy townsman for a subscription. This man, not
being in his usually generous mood that day, complained
that ministers were always raising funds and wanting dona-
tions, but finally wrote out a considerable cheque. Taking it
and placing it slowly in his pocket-book, Welch replied, " You
know, of course, that the Book says that the Lord loveth a
cheerful giver; but the Presbytery o' Dumbarton canna afford
to be so particular!"

One of Welch's close friends in the Assembly was often troublesome by his frequent and irritating interventions. He was involved, however, in a street accident as the result of which he was laid aside for a time. When Welch heard it, he remarked, " I love the man, but we all have some peculiar way of making a nuisance of ourselves, and it is wholesome to recognise that sometimes Providence in its own rough way takes the matter in hand!" It was in recalling two people whom he had known well in early life that Welch drily observed, " He was a great Liberal; that is to say, in his case, you were perfectly free to think as he did!" and " She was in many ways a noble woman, with one strange characteristic, she would talk at great length on a subject which she said had made her speechless!" As a young minister in the Assembly he declared that " one of the signs of an ecclesiastical mind was to see the wiles of an ecclesiastic where they did not exist." The man must have been a little disconcerted who invited Welch to take some part in his marriage service and got for his answer, " I don't wish to be hauled in by the coat-tails to pronounce the Benediction". On another occasion he referred to someone who reminded him of one of Dostoevsky's characters, "the very embodiment of ambitious mediocrity without enough intelligence to realise how mediocre he really is."

In his sermons, too, dignified as they always were, there were sentences and passages of this kind. A text on which he often preached and recommended students to preach was " Be not ye filled with new wine wherein is excess, but be filled with the Spirit". His opening sentence was " You've got to fill a man with something "—and that indeed was the theme. In the course of another sermon in a church where the thrust might well go home, he said, " We hear much of the dead hand of tradition upon the Church; what I fear more is the living hand of big money". As a professor too he could be cutting, as to the student whose trial sermon he had been hearing. "You will be a New Testament student, Mr. S—", and, when the young man at once disclaimed any such pretentions, he continued, " I thought you might be a New Testament student for you are not an Old Testament student." Welch could say things like these and yet be loved.

There was a wealth of consecrated sagacity in him. Men

2*

brought their troubles and problems to him as much as to any teacher or Church leader. He was prepared to give long stretches of his time to this work of counsel and guidance. After allowing a man to tell his whole story and listening silently to the end, Welch would take up the difficulty and with his wide range of knowledge set it in a larger framework, lay alongside of it analogies from the Bible and his own life's experience, create a sense of other questions which had to be asked, and send the man away feeling always that there was something he could do, some step which he could take with confidence on very solid ground. He was constantly receiving letters from his old students, and not least from some of the Post-Graduate students upon whom his teaching had a most profound influence. It was a sheer delight to him to get these letters, accompanied often by photographs of their wives and children. They had so accurately estimated the kind of man he was that they knew that these friendly, personal contacts and remembrances would bring both happiness and pride to him. These letters reveal also how many men were keeping up the interest in Old Testament studies which he had first stimulated; and they desired his continued guidance as in many parts of the world they encountered some fresh problem, scholastic or practical. He was accustomed to reply with patience and honesty to them all. Occasionally men came to seek his advice concerning articles or treatises which they desired to give to the public. He turned none away; and some of these, when they appeared, were better for having passed the test of his judgment, while for the same reason others never saw the light of the day of publication. One of his deepest concerns in these interviews was to encourage students to carry on their theological studies, for he believed that it was to tell seriously on the quality of the Church's life and faith if this were not done.

Beneath a somewhat austere exterior there lay much warmth of heart and imagination, and upon occasion not a little of a kind of old-world gallantry. Welch could now and then show what has been called " a polysyllabic or even monosyllabic stiffness " which obscured the kindliness of his nature. It is true also that he found it difficult to work with people he did not and could not like, but he had the greatness of character to conceal this when to reveal it would be damaging to some good cause. The essential humanity of Welch was nowhere more apparent than in the happy relationships he was always able to maintain with subordinates, and he used to speak trenchantly of men who were unable to get on with those under them. He gave himself exuberantly to the enjoyment of holidays in this country and on the Continent, and the joy of going back to a place he had visited in earlier years was doubled for him when the time came to see it again through the eyes of his children. The thought of children always brought the warmest glow to his features. In the district in Edinburgh where he lived for nearly thirty years, the children travelling in the same tramcar in the morning got to know him well, and had learned to wait for the broad smile which always came quickly on the back of the brusque command to get up and give him a seat. In his later Claremont days he used to leave very early for Church on Sunday morning, not merely to walk leisurely across the park and to arrive in very good time, but also sometimes to get a chance to play hide-and-seek with his own and other children at an hour when not many Glasgow citizens were abroad, for it would be necessary on the return journey to walk soberly and doucely in the presence of many watchful eyes.

On the very last occasion when the present writer saw Professor Welch, he said something which surely is the central explanation of the strong character which he built up, the ample development of his talents, the unmistakable emphasis in all his teaching and preaching and writing, and his bracing influence on men of diverse sorts. " I am not conscious of any time when I did not know that I was surrounded by stately dependabilities." He was a Christian in the fullest sense, and he knew himself to be used and guarded by a God upon whom he was able utterly to rely. Some of his friends detected in Welch a certain conservative strain. One has heard it said that he was " savagely conservative ". That is a somewhat misleading way of stating a big truth about him. His was a well-anchored life, founded upon a rock, tenaciously holding by the essential and eternal things he had made his own. It would be equally true to say that he was " savagely liberal ". In many respects he was unusually unconventional, even to

the familiar clay pipe and the stentorian " Feed that man!"
when his eye rested upon an empty plate at a students' tea
party in his house. Otherwise his was a progressive and ad-
venturous mind, eager for new truth wherever it lay, not
afraid to search, for he securely held what no new truth could
ever contradict or undermine. He was so sure of what he knew
that he had no fear lest what he did not know might upset it
or rob him of it. It would often be difficult to predict which of
these two attitudes, the conservative or the progressive, would
prevail in a given situation, for there was a splendid unpre-
dictable quality about his manner and his thought; but it is
certain that they were not contradictory, but complementary
in a well-rounded, coherent comprehension of life. Welch
kept his openness of mind to the end. He avoided what he
once described as " the disease common to old age of finding
it difficult to believe that things could be better done than
in the way they had been accustomed to do them ". He was
acidly critical of the closed mind whether in scholars or
ecclesiastics, and he lamented the tendency of some towards
" the distressing practice of running into shunting lines ". Nor
had he any illusions about the past, though he was deeply
sensitive in his perception of the great periods in the life of
the church and the nation. He had no rosy pictures to paint
of the flourishing of religion in the good old days in the parts
of Scotland he knew best. Hence also there seldom, if ever,
appeared on his lips a word of criticism of the younger
generation. He had a strong belief in the rising generation and
he often reflected on how difficult their lot had been made
for them by their predecessors.

In all that he was and in all that he achieved, Adam
Welch was one of the rarest gifts of God to His Church. His
place is sure amid the company of those who are described in
the words of a book which he so skilfully expounded, words
upon which he dwelt with fullness in his lectures on the Old
Testament approaches to faith in immortality, " They that
be wise shall shine as the brightness of the firmament, and
they that turn many to righteousness as the stars forever and
ever."

MOSES IN THE OLD TESTAMENT TRADITION

THE title of this study has been selected in order to define its limitations. No attempt is made to discover the historic Moses. It may be added that the effort to disengage the figure of the founder of the Hebrew faith from the mists of the past must always be conditioned by the fact that our only source of information on the subject is the Hebrew tradition. Now the documents which contain this tradition are all later, some of them much later, than the period with which they deal. It is true that, unless we are to carry scepticism on the subject to an absurd extent and suppose that the nation created its founder out of nothing, we may, even must, credit the authors of the later tradition with having employed earlier sources some of which may have been contemporary. It is also true that the common use of written material has been pushed so far back that no one can deny the possibility that these sources may have been in written form. But to be able to assert that manuscript authorities could have been in existence at the date of the Exodus is no sufficient ground for claiming that in any given case they did exist. Without some positive proof of their actual existence the question must remain in suspense. Further, the writers who embodied the earlier material in the records of Moses which have reached us selected the elements in it which served their purpose and illustrated their own conception of that heroic life. The fragmentary character of what has been recognized as belonging to an earlier tradition is enough to prove that the men to whom we owe its preservation retained what suited their design and fitted it into their picture. The men to whom we owe our earliest conception of Moses were no mean artists. Now, the primary qualification of an artist is his power of selection; he chooses what suits his purpose and ignores what he cannot use. This implies that their account was ill fitted to supply material for a record of Moses in the harder and drier light of history, as we to-day conceive such a figure. They construed his life and his work in the light of what they believed him to have attempted and to have effected, and in doing this they were influenced by their own convictions as to what he had contributed to the life of their nation. There is this subjective element in their picture of the founder of Israel's peculiar life and faith; and it is an element in the situation which we cannot escape in any effort to represent the historic Moses.

We are on surer ground when we attempt to estimate the figure of the leader as the nation, which owed him everything, construed him. When these men described the life of their founder, they told of the purpose which dominated it, how he came to entertain it, and how far he succeeded in fulfilling it. They described the work which he had attempted and the motives which prompted it. Since he had brought Israel into being as a nation, they naturally brought into strong relief the peculiar character he stamped upon it, the ends he set before it and the spirit which was to dominate its communal life. In what he did, however, he was believed to have been the divine agent who was both guided and upheld by God. Hence their conception of his character and work reveals more than their view of him as a man. In all he did, he was the executor of the divine purpose. To discover, therefore, the figure of Moses which any period threw up is to recognize the convictions of that age as to the relation in which Israel stood to its God, and the conditions which were to govern such a relation. In a measure it also brings out the relation in which the nation was believed to stand to its world. To attempt an estimate of this is the purpose of the present study.

The first thing which emerges from a general study of the records is that the Moses who is presented in the Old Testament is not homogeneous. There are two such figures and these are distinct in the date of their composition as they are dissimilar in character. The first of these, which is also the most easily recognized, is that of the law-giver. It would indeed be no exaggeration to say that Moses appears as the law incarnate. In the legal sections of the books of Exodus, Leviticus and Numbers every regulation of the torah was stated to have been issued by him, and when he issued it he did so by the direct authority of God. When his authority was questioned, it, with the authority of his deputies, was guaranteed by the divine intervention. Only those regulations which could claim such august support held final authority in Israel. The generation which produced this figure of the founder of its faith evidently regarded the law as the peculiar possession and glory of Israel. They also counted the relation of Israel to its God to be, at least primarily, that of strict obedience to His commandments. The possession of this law, with the relation to God which it implied, had characterized the national religion from the beginning. This figure, austere and simple, has passed over into the Christian tradition, and, in particular, dominates much of its hymnology and appears in its statuary and church windows. In the last, Moses always appears, either clasping in his arms the tablets of the law or holding these up in a fashion which would be impossible to a Hercules. In the hymns he who brought the law is sharply contrasted with the Lord who revealed Himself as Redeemer. So far as the early artists were concerned, they were doubtless following the directions of the churchmen. The later artists followed their example the more willingly, because the stone tablets, like the harp and crown in the case of David, were unmistakeable. It was unnecessary to put a label round the head of Moses, such as was used in the case of the succession of prophets, for he could be recognized at once by the emblem which was peculiar to him.

There can be no question as to the date of this figure. It came into existence at the time of the Return from Exile and was the outcome of the peculiar needs of that age. On the one side the loss of the national independence made it necessary to find a new bond for Israel, if its peculiar life was to be maintained.

Further, even if the Kingdom had been continued, it could not have supplied what was needed in the conditions in which the people were now living. For Israel had now begun its new life in diaspora, so that a kingdom could no longer supply the needed centre for men who must live under alien authority. The people must look for a different bond, which was capable of making them realize their community of origin and life, and which set clearly out what constituted their distinctive life. They must seek this in something which transcended the limits of Palestine and supplied a bond which united all Jews, wherever exile had cast them. What seemed to supply their need was the cult which was practised at Jerusalem and which had become the only centre for their common worship. Because this cult was the element which remained to them from their past, it continued what was peculiar to their national life, and the practice of it preserved their distinctive character.

But on the other hand, this demanded a more organized form for their religion which adapted it to the new conditions of the time. It also made it necessary to institute a central authority which determined such changes as were necessary and was able to enforce the regulations. Where once, among the diversity of the local sanctuaries, there had been room for a certain diversity in the uses which were practised, there must now be one use which was uniform. The law must go out from Jerusalem and guide all the scattered children of the common faith. Every organized system of religion brings the same necessity in some form. If the system be Presbyterian, the issue is a General Assembly : if it be Episcopal in character, the result is a bench of bishops : if it be Roman Catholic, a pope appears. Judaism lodged its final authority in the Aaronic priesthood, which, it taught, had been instituted at Horeb by Moses at the command of God. When the authorities of Jerusalem took this momentous step, they did not conceive themselves to be putting in force a Priestly Code, which had been invented by a few priests in Babylon and brought into effect by the Persian authority. Like all other church authorities in similar case, they claimed to be the sole possessors of primitive practice. What they enforced was in their view what the founder of the faith had ordered. Moses to that generation became the incarnation of the law which guided and governed Israel, and that law had dominated Israel's relation to its God from the beginning.

This figure forms, accordingly, an epitome of the religious attitude of the men who created it. The founder of Israel had been primarily a lawgiver; the first gift of God to the people He brought into being had been a law; the dominant feature in the relation of the nation to its God was obedience. Now this relation of obedience is a necessary element in every higher religion and is of peculiar significance in Judaism, which must emphasize the moral nature of its God in contrast with the nature-gods of its world. But it was not the only element in such a faith nor had it been the one factor which controlled the religious life of the nation. The sacrifices and offerings of the cult represented the other side, especially after these were construed, as Israel came to construe them, as gifts to their divine head. Every such offering expressed the dependence of the individual or of the nation on Him who gave it all and gave room for gratitude to a heavenly benefactor. It is one of the unfortunate results of setting the sacrifices of old Israel in constant opposition to moral obedience that students have often ignored the way in which these two sides of the religion supplemented each other. Because of its initial resemblance to similar heathen ritual, the early cult in Israel had been a danger to its religion. But, when once the cult came to be construed in the light of a gift to God, and had ceased to be thought of as a means to influence or change Him, it formed a valuable supplement to the obedience to the divine will.

One of the prophets, it is true, enunciated the general principle that obedience was better than sacrifice. But, if we read into the remark that sacrifice was itself opposed to obedience and ought to be done away, we must suppose that he would have nodded in silent agreement with the disciple who made a rapid estimate of a certain box of ointment, and who grumbled because it had been wasted on the impulse of a moment, instead of being spent for the relief of the poor. The Lord, it will be remembered, threw the mantle of His protection over the giver and even blessed the widow who flung her all into the temple-treasury. But He had a different view of the relation of a man to God, and, having this, held a different estimate of the beauty and dignity of sacrifice. What a man brought to God at the lovely compulsion of gratitude, the offering which love brought and which deepened his love, might be unnecessary to Him who owns the cattle on a thousand hills. But its worth to the offerer was incalculable, and was very acceptable to the Master.

The weakness of the generation which followed the Return

was not that the men gave a large place to the sacrifices of
their cult. It was rather that the men brought them into a
system and construed them under the rubric of obedience.
The amount demanded from the individual and the nation
was defined, the seasons when they must be offered were regulated, the constituents for each occasion were prescribed.
Everything there was determined by law. For God from the
beginning had issued His decree on the subject : and Moses
had not only received the tablets of the moral law at Horeb,
but he had also received the regulations of the cult to be
delivered over to the priesthood which controlled it. In the
relation between God and Israel there was room for little else
but a regulated obedience to an original law. And Moses was
the mediator to the people of this law which controlled their
entire religious life.

The initial act by which God entered into relation with Israel
and made it His peculiar people was the covenant He made,
first with Abraham and afterwards with Moses. This became
a dogma which, like many another dogma, was accepted without much thought of what it implied in the character of Him
who initiated it. It came to be construed as the expression of
His sovereign will. He had chosen Israel out of the world and
given it a privileged position, which could not be lost or un-
done. It is true that two later prophets, Deutero-Isaiah and
the author of Jonah, had a larger conception and insisted that
the divine choice of the nation had not merely been intended
to set Israel in a position of privilege. To them Yahweh was
the God of the whole earth, who had a mind to the creations
of His hands. The earliest covenant was made with the whole
world in the days of Noah, and in it was the assurance of His
goodwill toward even the beasts of the earth. When He made
Himself known to Israel, His act was part of this larger purpose, in which even the oppressor-city, Nineveh, with its unconscious children and its cattle, was included. The nation was
chosen to be the sphere of the divine self-revelation and, since
this revelation concerned the world, Israel had a function
which went beyond the preservation and assertion of its peculiar position. It had a mission to the world, because it served
One whose purpose it was that the uttermost ends of the earth
should know the salvation of their God. But these great voices

were at best peripheral, and seem never to have influenced the men who were restoring Judaism at Jerusalem. They even turned Deutero-Isaiah into a propagandist whose chief function was to stir up Zionism among the diaspora and to bring back the dispersed of Israel to the holy land. They construed the covenant with Israel and its election in the light of their belief that the primary possession of the nation was the law which God had made known to Moses. One of them at a later period sought to bring this privileged position of one people into relation to the conviction that Yahweh was the God of the whole earth by means of the theory that the law had been offered to all the nations, but had been accepted by Israel alone.[1] Such a theory proves, more clearly than anything else, the point of view from which the later generation regarded the relation between the covenant and the divine law. The primary task of Israel was to maintain itself as a people apart and to preserve that knowledge of the divine will, which was contained in their law. The divine covenant was essentially an agreement between God and the nation : and their relation to Him was based on and conditioned by their exact obedience to that law. It was apt in the minds of many to appear almost in the terms of a bargain, which assured so much salvation for so much obedience.

There is one constant characteristic of all the church window representations of Moses, which specially reproduces the effect of this late Jewish attitude to him and to the religion which he represented to them. The founder of Israel's religion always gazes blankly out into the void. He never turns his eyes downward to see the nation to which he has brought a revelation. Nor does he, like the prophets in the same windows, look up to receive a revelation from God, for he has received it in its fulness. The man has been transformed into a pedestal which supports on knee or arm the tablets of the Decalogue. To that generation Israel was made for the torah, not the torah for Israel.

Sometimes, in looking at one of those figures, so alike in their desolate and desolating uniformity, there has risen to my

---

[1]This view was taught by the Rabbinic schools of both Ishmael and Akiba in the second century A.D., *vide* G. F. Moore, *Judaism*, Vol. I, pp. 227 ff. [Ed.].

mind the memory of a very different scene. For it is written that, even at the foot of Horeb, Israel forgot its law and demanded another leader than the Moses who had brought to it this revelation of the divine will. It was on the point of being blotted out of existence by the judgment which followed its complete apostasy. Sacrifice could avail nothing, since Aaron, who alone was competent to offer it, had been involved in the national sin. In that hour there was lying prone on his face a man, who had flung down the stone-tablets which he was carrying, and who was pleading with God to remember His covenant with His people, a relation which He Himself had instituted and which was prior to any law. The generation which conceived that figure of the founder of its religion and which set it at the foot of the mountain of the law had a thought of God and of their relation to Him which was richer in content than that of the men of the Return. To them God's purpose had been to redeem a nation and to set it free in order that it might serve Him. He had given that nation a law which was to reveal the character of Him whom they were now free to serve. But a law, which could only be vindicated by the destruction of the people it was meant to guide, undid the purpose of Him who had issued it. The law was threatening to dethrone God.

This illustration may serve to introduce the other figure of Moses which appears in the Old Testament and the source from which it is derived. This emerges, as soon as we turn from the legal sections of the Pentateuch to the stories which have been collected round the name of the great leader in the early chapters of Exodus. It deserves notice that these are the incidents to which every preacher instinctively turns when he attempts to speak about Moses. The reason is not only to be found in the more picturesque and interesting incidents which appear there. He cannot fail to realize that a different spirit, and one which is more closely allied to the Christian standpoint, informs this material. If he has not forgotten all his college lectures on Introduction, he may even recognize that higher criticism has given him a scientific basis for what might otherwise be no more than a personal and subjective judgment on the subject. For the conclusions of modern study have proved that these stories date from a period which is long anterior to the time of the Return, when Moses was construed almost entirely as the giver of the law. At the time when these records reached their present form, the nation had not yet gone into the cloister and attempted to shut itself off from the outside world. It was still living in contact with the wider tides of life. Above all, its religious outlook had not yet become stereotyped round its cult-life, for it was still being fashioned by the most vital influence which was ever brought to bear on any religion, the teaching of its earlier prophets.

The character in which Moses appears throughout these earlier tales is that of the deliverer of Israel, and they describe how he came to undertake the task, how he was equipped for it, and the measure of success which attended his work. He was born into bondage and was said to have escaped the fate of his contemporaries only by the resource and the quick wit of his mother and sister. His rescue by the daughter of the reigning Pharaoh offered the chance of a career altogether beyond the limits of his birth and original upbringing. But, when he became a man, he was unable to deny the claim of his kindred and his sympathy with his own people was not confined to a vague pity or to mere words. The impulsive blow which defended one of his wronged brethren not only showed the man's interest in the condition of his nation : it also revealed the desperate condition into which Israel had fallen. The men were contracting the slave temper which preferred a safe slavery to the dangers which attended the assertion of freedom. They were prepared to deliver the dangerous meddler into the hands of their oppressor, so that the man was forced to take refuge in the land of Midian, not only from the Egyptians, but from his own kindred.

The early tales which have thus been summarized have been collected into a cycle, which has been set alongside similar series of tales which occur in connection with other national heroes. Certain analogies have been pointed out between them and stories which derive from other quarters, especially from Assyria and Babylonia, and occasionally the conclusion has been drawn that the Hebrew account of the founder of the nation is little more than a replica of these alien records. Without entering into any detailed study of the subject, it is legitimate to point out that the comparison in general has only looked for resemblances, has often exaggerated the likeness, and has ignored the no less significant differences. It has thus tended to ignore the peculiar element in the Hebrew record. In all that cycle of stories about the life of Moses till he reached manhood, he does not appear to be endowed with superhuman powers or to be preserved by superhuman protection. He is no demi-god, but remains within the limits of humanity. He is no more than a Jew who loved his own nation, hated to see it oppressed and, though set among conditions which made it natural and easy to deny his kindred, gave up everything in order to attempt their deliverance.

As such, he became capable of receiving and accepting a revelation from God, the burden of which was : I have seen the oppression of my people in Egypt and have heard their cry, and I am come down to deliver them. At once the whole character of the narrative changes. The note of miracle, of the divine intervention in human history, has been struck; and from that time this feature is not only present, but is dominant in the narrative. For now God intervenes and Moses becomes the representative of Him to whom Israel owes its deliverance. Through the somewhat naïve miracles of the hand which became leprous and of the staff which was turned into a serpent, Moses was able to convince the elders of Israel of his divine commission. Through the plagues which culminated in the death of the first-born, he was able to wring from the Pharaoh a reluctant permission that the people should depart. When the Egyptians pursued the fugitives to the shore of the Red Sea, the people needed only to stand still and witness the salvation of their God. By that divine act of intervention in their history, the liberty they had won was made irrevocable. These acts which culminated in the deliverance of Israel were no part of the native endowment of Moses : they resulted from the commission he had received from God and in them all he acted as the agent of Him who had sent him. They were also merely temporary and incidental, since they were conferred upon him in connection with his task of fulfilling the divine purpose with the nation. Their limits were strictly set by the end which they were designed to serve. Thus, when the men who collected those stories multiplied the miraculous features which attended

Moses after his return from Midian, they were not indulging in an orgy of thaumaturgy but were expressing a conviction. In their view the Moses who came back to Egypt after the vision at the bush was the accredited agent of the God who had revealed Himself there. The marvels which from that time attended Moses were the continuation of the initial miracle in which God made Himself known as having seen the affliction of His people and having come down to deliver them. It would be hazardous to pronounce that in this fashion the Jew recognized only one ultimate miracle, *viz.*, that God breaks in on the life of man to make Himself known to the only creature which can receive that knowledge. But it is not hazardous to see that the men to whom we owe this figure of Moses recognized in him primarily the deliverer of his people, who was in all his work the agent and the representative of God. Unless, then, God had had compassion and had Himself come down to deliver them, any leader, however richly endowed by nature and by circumstances, would have been powerless. Israel owed its unique place in the world to the divine election, and God's act had been the outcome of His mere grace. Hence the divine title which recurs in connection with Moses is that of the Lord, merciful and gracious, long-suffering, and abundant in goodness and truth.

This God had intervened both in nature and in history, and his intervention had brought about a new thing. Nor was the new thing a mere forth-putting of His power, for it served the divine purpose. What that purpose was appears in the demand which Moses was said to have made to the Pharaoh : Israel is My son, My firstborn, let My son go that he may serve Me. The divine end was the election of Israel, which did not come about in the outward order of the world or in the ordinary course of human history. God had broken in on both in order to make this redemption a reality. The history of Israel had only confirmed this conviction to the leaders of the people.

The relation, therefore, between Israel and its God was no physical relation, such as was believed to exist between any other nation and its god. It was constituted by an act on His part and, as such, was in the widest sense of the word ethical. The covenant into which He brought Israel embodied this

relation and expressed their redemption and election by Him.
The word used for covenant, *b^erith*, like all theological words
was derived originally from the common life of the people.
It implied an agreement between two, whether individuals or
nations, which defined their mutual relations. It was also
accompanied by an oath, which was sometimes associated
with a sacrifice and by which the contracting parties brought
in the Deity as a third in the agreement and invoked His
vengeance on anyone who might break the covenant. In the
event of one of the contracting parties being the stronger, it
was, accordingly, a distinct favour on his part when he
admitted the weaker to a *b^erith*, since this gave the weaker
party a greater security in all his relations to his more powerful neighbour. Not only could he rely on the other's undertaking, but he could expect the divine support which had
been invoked in the oath. That early Israel construed the
divine covenant along these lines and counted it the supreme
privilege of the nation is clear from the place in which they
set it. It followed the initial act by which God delivered Israel.
It was not something which He demanded from the people
before He stooped to redeem it from Egypt, nor did it condition the act by which He made Israel a nation. It followed
the act of deliverance and formed its completion. The God,
who in His grace had called His son out of Egypt, in the
exercise of the same purpose admitted it into a covenant with
Himself. In both He was fulfilling His own ends with Israel.

Again, the covenant with Israel is not conceived as standing
alone. There were two earlier covenants which preceded that
at Horeb, the covenant with Abraham and the covenant with
Noah.[1] Of these the earlier was made, not merely with the
human survivors of the flood, but with the world, animate
and inanimate, which had suffered from the catastrophe. As
such, it could not have been intended to bind the inanimate
part of creation, and implied merely a pledge on the part of
God Himself that the world would never again be overwhelmed with water. Accordingly, the symbol was something
which the world could neither set up nor undo: it was the
bow which God set in the clouds. Thus the assurance which

---

[1]But the account of the covenant with Noah is generally regarded by
scholars as belonging to the latest source of the Pentateuch. [Ed.].

Israel believed that it had received through the covenant
which God instituted at Horeb was primarily the pledge that
the act by which God had delivered it from Egypt had been
due to no caprice on His part but was the expression of His
immutable purpose toward it. He would never be less to His
people than He had shown Himself to be at the Exodus. In
this great act of deliverance He had revealed His mind toward
Israel and from this, because He had deigned to enter into
covenant with it, He would never depart. The promise
Moses received before he left Midian to return to Egypt,
'Ehyeh 'asher 'ehyeh, has been unfortunately translated
in R.V. as ' I am that I am.' Grammatically it is impossible
Hebrew, because the verb *hayah* is never used in the sense of
absolute existence, but always expresses contingent happening.
Further, the imperfect of a stative verb always implies an
imperfect. *'Eh'yeh* cannot, therefore, mean I have come to
be and so remain what I am; it can only mean I will be. Nor
is it easy to see that a statement of absolute being on the part
of God could have had any sense of suitability in the position
in which the people then were. It must be linked up, on the
one side, with the revelation Moses had received in Midian,
and, on the other side, with the mission with which He had
been charged for the people in Egypt : and thus it must imply
something as to what He will be toward them. God gives His
messenger, who is also His representative, the assurance that
His initial act in coming down to deliver the nation is no
isolated act on His part, but is part of a design which will
unfold itself in their experience and in their history. He will
manifest Himself in the continuous fulfilment of what He has
already done. The covenant, into which He entered with the
nation, was the confirmation of this promise to Moses and
was primarily an act of grace. But, because the relation
between God and Israel was ethical, it implied something on
the part of the nation. This appears at once in the case of the
covenant with Abraham. There God promised to give to the
patriarch and his seed the land of Canaan, so that it also was
fundamentally an evidence of the divine grace. But, because
the relation was now between God and a man, its symbol was
circumcision, which was impressed on the man's flesh. He
accepted the relation, as the world after Noah could not.

Since, now, God had chosen Israel at Horeb and set the nation free to serve Him, He demanded its absolute allegiance. There must be no strange god among them. From the very nature of the relation into which He had brought them they must recognize that the Lord their God was a jealous God. For Israel to depart from its allegiance to Yahweh was no mere failure to implement the conditions which had been laid down in the terms of a covenant relation : it was to lose its identity as a nation. For by that act the people lapsed back into the grey mass of heathenism out of which the divine intervention had brought them.

What then was the relation of the law to the deliverance from Egypt on the one side and to the covenant on the other ? Here again it is unnecessary to enter into the historical question as to whether the decalogue can be carried back so early as the period of Moses. For our business at present is to disentangle the figure of the national leader as that was formulated by a particular generation, and there can be no question that these men incorporated into their account a cycle of stories which associated the origin of the decalogue with the Exodus and with Moses. It may remain an open question whether ten words in the form in which we possess them were really a product of the prophetic movement. But the fact remains that it was an essential part of these men's picture of the founder of their religion to represent him as having received a revelation of their peculiar law.

In connection with this, I quote and expand a very pregnant sentence which appears in *The Theology of the Old Testament* of my honoured predecessor. Dr. Davidson pointed out[1] that the law was given to a nation which was already in covenant with Yahweh, to which I would merely add that it was given to a nation which had already been delivered from Egypt. The law, that is to say, was not a condition of the deliverance, was not even a condition of the new relation which had been instituted between Israel and its God. It followed on both[2] and must be construed in the light of the divine acts of which it formed the sequel and the completion.

[1] A. B. Davidson, *The Theology of the Old Testament*, pp. 280-1.
[2] Yet in the Sinai literary complex, as we have it, the decalogue (Exod. chap. 20) comes before the account of the inauguration of the covenant (chap. 24). [Ed].

As such, it formed part of the revelation of His nature and
His purpose which God had made to the people which He
had elected. Nor are we left to infer this from the course of
events, as they were arranged by the early writers. It is
expressly stated in both the forms in which the decalogue
appears, since the ten words are prefaced by the statement,
"I am the Lord thy God, who brought thee up out of the
land of Egypt, out of the house of slaves". Then follows the
primary law of Israel's being, "thou shalt have none other
gods before me." Yahweh had revealed Himself to this nation.
His first act had been to intervene on their behalf and make
them free to serve Him. His second had been to bring them
into a covenant, so that they might be assured that He would
never be different in His attitude to them from that which
He had thus shown Himself to be. They had been set apart
from their world to be His peculiar people. If they were to be
this, they must know what He required from them. Without
that knowledge, they could not know what made the difference between Him and the other gods, nor yet what made
them different from the rest of the nations. He revealed
this through the ten words. The deliverance from Egypt, the
peculiar relation between Israel and its God, and the decalogue which embodied His mind, were integrally related to
each other as the constituent elements of the life of Israel;
and all these were mediated to them by Moses. But no one
of these could be isolated, as though it in itself were the only
factor in the Mosaic revelation. The primary factor, in the
light of which all the rest must be constituted, was the revelation Moses received in Midian. God had come down to intervene on behalf of Israel. Moses brought this revelation to
Israel and so he appears in all the early cycle of tales
primarily as the deliverer.

All the great prophets who appeared in the course of Israel's
life represented this fundamental conception of the relation
between the nation and its God, but, as was natural with
men of their originality of outlook, they held it with a certain
difference of emphasis. Two of the earliest bring out this
difference very clearly. Thus Amos stated the basis of this
relation in an early passage: "you only has Yahweh chosen
out of all the nations of the earth." The relation of Israel

rested ultimately on an act of God. But Amos developed the meaning of this relation along his own lines. Because God had revealed Himself in the beginning to Israel, and because He had been prompted in this by Himself, Israel had become the sphere of the divine self-revelation. There had never been lacking and there never would be lacking a prophet in Israel. When the people had ignored their messages and stifled the divine voice which spoke to them, God had found a messenger, even in the most unlikely quarter. When He could find no other, said Amos, He took me, who was at first no prophet, but a shepherd on the Tekoa steppes. But the message of these successive prophets had been to their unexpected successor one which dealt with the new relation from the side of what it implied on the part of the people. They have failed here and there and there again to fulfil the duties which their relation to their God involved. They had neglected the voices of their prophets and had ignored their reiterated summons. Therefore God was coming Himself, and His coming to the disobedient nation must imply judgment. Because God had chosen them only out of all the nations of the earth, He must visit upon them all their iniquities. The chief burden of the prophet, because of the side from which he regarded the divine relation to the people, was judgment.

In the same way Hosea saw this relation to be peculiar, but he thought of it primarily, not from the side of what it involved for Israel, but from that of what it involved in God. His very method of stating how the covenant was given revealed his point of view; when Israel was a child, then I loved him and called my son out of Egypt. The original act, without which Israel could not have been, was due to the divine grace, and this, because it was self-moved on God's part, had not been exhausted in the day of the Exodus. The whole life of Israel since that day, during the wandering in the wilderness, in the conquest of Palestine, in the seemly order which followed the conquest, had been a constant proof of the same divine care. God had proved Himself the God of the Exodus, by revealing Himself, not in the appearance of the prophets, but in deeds of history which proved His watchful support. Neither the endurance necessary in the wilderness nor the effort to make themselves masters of their new land would have otherwise been possible for the nation. They had reached their independence through the succour of the God who thus proved the constancy of the love which had been the source of their life. To Hosea, therefore, the root sin of the nation had not been this or that act of disobedience to the voices which had made known to them the divine will. It was their failure to respond to a care which had never failed; it was disloyalty and ingratitude. The judgment which was impending was the declaration of this disloyalty, rather than the punishment due for specific transgressions of the divine commands. Everything which Israel possessed was the outcome of the divine care and it had failed to inspire an answering loyalty. There had been no response on the people's part. In the judgment which was impending, therefore, the nation must be stripped of all the gifts which its God had showered upon it. Especially must it be expelled from Palestine, the home to which Yahweh brought His bride, and must go back, landless and kingless, to the wilderness from which He had led it. It went back to its first beginning, when it possessed nothing, but lived in the open waste, where it knew no leader or protector except its God. Nothing would appear to be left to it; nothing was left to it but the love which prompted Yahweh to come down to its deliverance. But this was left to it, because God could not deny Himself. It is indifferent here whether the story of the prophet's relation to Gomer is interpreted as a page out of Hosea's own life or as an allegory. In either case the point of the story remains the same. The God of Israel was not one who had acted from caprice, so that the love He had for Israel when He brought it out of Egypt could not be defeated, even by the ingratitude of the nation.

That is the conviction which appears in the figure of Moses in the great scene at Horeb to which reference has already been made. At the foot of the Mount, after the deliverance from Egypt, the institution of the covenant and the reception of the law, Israel renounced its relation to Yahweh by setting up the golden calf, of which it said, these are thy gods, O Israel. The sin was the final sin; and not only was the whole nation implicated in the apostasy, but the man who superintended the making of the calf was the high priest. There could be no atonement through any sacrifice, for Aaron was incompetent to offer any such. The wilful rebellion of the nation appeared to have been able to defeat the divine purpose, before it had well begun. Then Moses who had brought the message of the divine intervention on behalf of Israel intervened. He did not plead that the penalty might be averted altogether, for the nation must learn the gravity of the sin into which it had fallen. But, when it appeared as though the result must be the disappearance of Israel, he offered his intercession before God; and that to which he made his appeal was the ultimate thing in the life of the nation, the nature of its God. He who had been the agent of the divine purpose in the redemption of his people appealed to God the redeemer of Israel.

2

SAUL

THE first thing which is apparent about the period of Saul and Samuel is the longer space devoted to it in the Hebrew records, as contrasted, not only with the period which precedes, but with the account of the later kings. One notes even the unnecessarily large space given to the early exploits of David which are not very valuable and a little in the rococo manner.

The records recognize the fact that this was a period of immense significance in the life of Israel, the period, namely, when the nation became a nation through centralization under a king and when the religion became articulate through the appearance of the prophet. The yeasty period of the Judges represented, alongside the success in settling the country, the effort to discover some organization which should represent and confirm its sense of unity. Now, says Israel, we found a king. During the settlement also, in the conscious effort to affirm the national life over against the Canaanites, the nation came to realise that its distinctive life came through its religion and was utterly different from that of the original settlers. What they needed to make clear was what constituted this difference. Now, says Israel, God sent us prophets.

Take first the question of the sources :-

1 Sam. 1-3. This appears to be part of a biography of Samuel. At least it is chiefly interested in him and in the worship of Shiloh. We learn about the sanctuary, its sacrifices, its priesthood, its need for a guiding torah.

1 Sam. 4-6 : A very curious account which is particularly concerned with the ark. Its interest for us here is that it reveals clearly the increasing pressure of the Philistines and so shows the outward cause which led to the rise of the kingdom.

1 Sam. 7-13, are more directly concerned with our aim of understanding how the kingdom originated. And here we have two accounts which have been woven together and which, to speak generally, can be separated into :-

(A) 8 : 1-22, 10 : 17-24. This is closely united on one side to Chapter 7, which relates a great victory won by Samuel over the Philistines, and on the other side to Chapter 12, which tells of Samuel's solemn demission of office.

Now, this story has two broad features which represent its view of the time. Thus we find Samuel judge over all Israel. The people are content with his rule but deeply dissatisfied with his sons and so they demand a king. Samuel objects to the kingdom, which he calls a heathen institution. For Israel to accept this form of rule is to conform in some measure to heathenism. He is forced into the step by the folly of the people to whom Yahweh advises him to give way. The second broad characteristic of this account is that it is definitely hostile to the kingdom on principle. Hence, in both its characteristics, it is closely related to Chapter 7; in the latter of its two characteristics, it is linked with Chapter 12, so that these form in a measure its introduction and its conclusion. Thus Chapter 7 indicates that the kingdom was unnecessary, since Samuel was able to deliver Israel from the Philistines, and makes Samuel judge over a united Israel. Chapter 12 again gives, in the form of Samuel's valedictory address, a grave indictment of the institution of the kingdom in the form of a prophecy of what it will inevitably bring. Here too we see Samuel addressing the entire people.

(B) 9 : 1-27 (omitting v. 9); 10 : 1-16 (omitting v. 8); 11 : 1-11, 15. Thereafter B is continued in Chapter 13.

Here Samuel is not judge, but seer and priest, possessed of very limited authority and confined to the south of Ephraim. So slight is his influence that Saul knows nothing about him. Since Saul is the son of a well-to-do farmer in Benjamin and Samuel is represented as living in the extreme south of Ephraim, this would have been impossible, had Samuel been judge of Israel. Instead of Samuel having defeated the Philistines (*vide* Chapter 7), the situation is of the gravest, the centre of Palestine is overrun and Samuel is represented as seriously troubled about the position of his nation. In the confidence that thereby he is serving Israel's highest interests, and thereby serving the divine will with them and for them, Samuel seeks out Saul, rouses him to action, anoints him in the name of Yahveh and sends him to the prophets.

It is quite clear to me that we must choose between these two accounts. They are incompatible representations of the situation. One can patch up an agreement here and tone down a difference there. But on the broad lines of representing the situation in the nation, they do not agree. The only question that remains is the question as to which we are to select.

Now (B) agrees much better than the other with the conditions of things which prevailed during the period of the settlement. (B) really continues the account of that earlier period. As yet there was no united Israel, consequently there cannot yet be a judge over all Israel. It is also the only account which can be made at all to square with Chapter 11, the story about Nahash and Jabesh-Gilead. The incident not only has a great air of verisimilitude but it stands out as the event to which Samuel sends Saul (10 : 7), the event by which he proves himself to be worthy, the event also by which Israel discovers its needed leader. Now Chapter 11 will not fit in with account (A) on any terms whatever. If Samuel was judge and had just been victorious, why is there no mention of him in the account of Jabesh-Gilead? What is the use of him? Finally (B) agrees best with the later history, which relates the extraordinary difficulty which Saul found in making headway against the Philistines. So far from being broken by Samuel, the Philistines were able to pin Saul to the ground until a considerably later date than his victory over Nahash.

We are bound on purely historical grounds to follow (B). Then we may allow ourselves to note how fresh it is, how touched with the savour of life and vigour, how vividly full of little unconscious sidelights which make one feel its close contact with the ground on which these things happened.

You may perhaps ask how it came about that we have two accounts of the origin of the kingdom, differing in such a remarkable way in their attitude to the institution. It is worth comparing this dual account with the other dual

3

account which we have in the Books of Joshua and Judges.
The chief difference between the early and late accounts of
the conquest and settlement was that the later men overlaid
the idea of a united Israel on a story which still saw the
clans as a loose federation. But here we have two accounts
which imply a radical divergence of judgment on the value of
the kingdom as an institution in Israel. The one sees it as a
gift of God : hence Samuel seeks out Saul and anoints him
beforehand to be king : the people then joyfully accept the
anointed of Yahveh. The other represents Samuel as only
accepting Saul because he cannot resist the pressure of the
nation. But he does it with great reluctance and with a very
pessimistic view of the result.

I think we must see there how Israel came to review its
own history and the course of its development in the light of
later events and especially of the way in which the earlier
institutions evolved. Looking back on the past, the men rewrote the story of their origins from a different angle. Now,
as a matter of fact, the kingdom which cost so much to found
disappointed the high hopes of the men who gave much
sacrifice to found it. The men founded it for high ends and,
in so doing, expected that it would produce nothing but good.
Yet it was a human institution with all the imperfections
which must always attend every human institution. And, as
we shall see, it brought evil as well as good. This is our human
way. We are always imagining that we can save the world by
setting up some better machinery. Enact total prohibition,
give to women a vote, institute a league of nations : in fact,
get a new machinery, and you have men promising that the
millenium will dawn to-morrow. In the day of high enthusiasm, the men who coolly suggest that in the end it is going
to be human beings who run all the machinery and that,
given the old selfish humanity, the men who run the new
machinery will pervert it to the old selfish ends, are called all
sorts of bad names, cynics and drags on the wheels of human
progress. In reality, they may only be Christian men who
insist that the constant need of the world is good men to run
all the machinery, who insist indeed that "Ye must be born
from above."

We older men are often charged with being conservative in

our old age. In reality, as Bernard Shaw says, some of us only become more radical as we grow older. We began by criticizing and desiring to improve every existing institution. We end by criticizing even the new institutions which we should like ourselves to substitute in their place.

Well, Israel found that the kingdom, after it was founded, brought its own dangers. Naturally, when they rewrote the account of its origin, they wrote with these matters in their minds and they found it very difficult to say that the kingdom had been instituted by a prophet who spoke and acted in the name of Yahweh. They said God had a better thing in His mind than that and that He could not have willed the kingdom at all. That is not the way we should put the matter, but that should not hinder us from trying to recognize how other men put it. So the later account sprang up after the kingdom, which had come into existence for the maintenance of Israel's distinctive possession, had proved itself a grave danger even to the distinctive faith.

Views differ as to the date. Dr. A. R. S. Kennedy,[1] e.g., thinks that we must come down as late as the exile. Personally I think we must set it earlier, since I am much impressed by the attitude Hosea took to the kingdom in the period of anarchy which befell the Northern Kingdom. Then, too, one must recognize that the exile did not have the question of the kingdom any more as a burning question. I should set it down to the period which followed Hosea and regard it as a product of Northern Israel. My reason for counting it North Israelite in origin is that Judah never took this attitude to its kingdom. The kingdom there never lost the glamour which David had cast round it.[2]

---

[1]*The New-Century Bible; Samuel,* p. 18.

[2]The outstanding fact about the law of the kingdom in Deuteronomy (17: 14 ff.) is that there the kingdom is regarded as legitimate. Evidently then that law could not have been known in Israel, when Samuel is represented as condemning the desire of the people for a king. If it had been so known, obviously the people would have been able to refer to it and to turn down the prophet's objection to their desire. The account in Samuel cannot precede the law in Deuteronomy. In my judgment we must put the law in Deuteronomy early, before the kingdom had lost the support of the religious men of the nation and while they were still able to believe in and to support it. The account in Samuel dates from a later time of disillusionment.

However that may be, the account which we have elected to follow as more historical brings out the two factors which I have emphasized as having had much to do with the origin of the kingdom—the external factor in the pressure of the Philistines, the internal in the rise of prophecy which represents the uniting factor which bound Israel together.

During Samson's period the Philistines do not seem to have pressed hard on central Palestine: they were content to push back Dan into the hills and prevent Israel from having any foothold in the Shephelah. But not long after, they launched a greater attack by way of the plain of Sharon in the north. Why, one naturally asks, along this road?

There are two possible explanations. Evidently Ephraim under Gideon and Abimelech had been showing signs of finding a certain measure of unity. That in itself was a danger signal to the Philistines. It is even possible that Ephraim was beginning to reach across to the kindred people in Galilee and so was threatening to interfere with the great road by Esdraelon. The locale of the attack may have been due to the Philistines having come north to support the threatened towns of the Plain. Or the attack may have been directed against Ephraim itself. And the locale of the attack may have been due to the fact that it has always been difficult to reach central Palestine from the coast except by the north or by the vale of Aijalon which at this time was held by Israel. The valleys westward to Sharon are narrow and steep and capable of easy defence: the valleys which lead down to Esdraelon are broader and easier. At least the Philistines launched their blow from Aphek at the north end of Sharon. There was a two days' fight. On the second day Ephraim brought up the ark, their palladium, in superstitious confidence, but its priests were slain, the ark captured and Israel routed. The Philistines were then able to force the passes directly east of them, especially the vale of Aijalon and to overrun Benjamin. Probably at this time Shiloh was wrecked and utterly disappeared, and a Philistine garrison was established at Gibeah, south of Shiloh.[1] Now Samuel had been reared at Shiloh and was an

---

[1] Cf. 1 Sam. 13: 3 and 13: 5. See also 1 Sam. 10: 5; Jeremiah 7: 12, 14 and 26: 6, refer to the destruction of Shiloh as well known in his time.

Ephraimite. When the collapse came, he went to live at
Ramah of Ephraim where he continued to act as both prophet
and priest. He had the best reason to recognize the gravity of
the situation. The condition of the people sank into his soul.

To this situation our account (B) links on directly. It is
charmingly full of freshness and the movement of life. Saul
and his servant were out on these hills, seeking his father's
strayed asses. He knows nothing about Samuel but, when
the two are desperate about their search, the servant suggests
making an effort through the seer. Saul's only difficulty is
that the man will naturally expect a fee for his services and
he, with the perennial impecuniousness of youth, is rich in
nothing but hope. The two club their resources and manage
to muster half a shekel. And so they come to the village and
ask the girls who are out with their water cogs the way to the
seer's house. From their answer Saul finds that the day is one
on which the clan sacrifice with its accompanying festival is
held and that Samuel is up to the local *bamah* or high place
acting as celebrant. You note that we are at the period before
it was considered illegitimate to worship at other than a
central shrine : hence Samuel has no hesitation as to such
a rite. On Saul's going to meet Samuel, he is received as not
only expected, but welcome and honoured. Samuel brings him
to the *lishkah,* the banqueting hall where the elders of the
village are met for the sacrificial feast. You are not to think
of this as a mere village jollification : it is part of the sacrificial ritual. After the fat has been taken from the lamb or kid
and burned on the altar, after the blood has been poured
out at the foot of the altar, the greater part of the remaining
flesh is given back to the worshippers that they may use it for
a sacrificial feast before Yahweh. When Samuel has brought
Saul in to the company, he sets the portion of the honoured
guest before him, takes him home to his own house, tells him
not to worry about the asses, because any man with a thought
above himself has graver matters over which to worry, talks
to him till far into the night, and then according to the LXX
sends him to sleep on the flat roof wrapped in his cloak under
the stars. In the morning he calls Saul down, gives him a
convoy on his road, and, when they are parting, suddenly
anoints him with the message that Yahweh needs such men as

he, directs him to go on to a meeting with the prophets and
then bids him do as his hand finds.

It is not possible here to examine more carefully the questions connected with the rise of prophecy in Israel : but it is
necessary to recognize that the prophets to whom Samuel
sent Saul were not men like Isaiah or Jeremiah, but rather
weird creatures who wandered over the country in bands,
fanatics in certain phenomena of their lives, and looked on
dubiously by certain decent elements of the population. So
best can we understand the surprise with which men heard
that the son of a well-to-do sheikh in Benjamin was mixed
up with people of this character. On the other hand the
prophets had a close connection with the cult, as is shown by
the fact that Samuel sends Saul to the place where he will
meet the prophets and that he met them coming down from
the high place.[1]

Only, when you call them fanatics, remember what it was
about which the men were fanatical. They were fanatical
adherents of Yahweh and of all for which, as we have seen,
Yahweh stood at this time—the distinctive element in Israel's
life, the uniting element in its disintegrated life. Because of
this, they stood for national independence as necessary for the
full assertion of the national faith. Hence they supported
Saul, because in him they saw the one means for attaining
that on which they had set their hearts.

Saul goes from Samuel with these new thoughts seething
in his mind, about Israel, about his own responsibility, about
his nation's and his God's claim upon him. And when he
meets the prophets, those representatives of religious and
patriotic enthusiasm, he was swept off his feet, perhaps to
his own amazement, certainly to the amazement of those who
had known him. The thoughts crowding in his mind have
found a channel for expression. The man has been conscious
of powers which found no outlet. Now he goes home with
the recognition that he has also found his life work. But
this does not mean that Saul has any formulated plan given
him by the prophets or conceived by himself. Everything is

[1]Dr. Welch dealt with this important subject in his volume *Prophet
and Priest in Old Israel.* Cf. A. R. Johnson, *The Cultic Prophet in
Ancient Israel.* [Ed.]

still unclear, even to himself. Hence he remains at home, says nothing, hiding from his uncle the whole interview with Samuel, waiting, as the seer bade him, on destiny.

There arrives the news from Jabesh-Gilead with the insult which Nahash has put on all Israel. The Ammonite feels so sure that the spirit of Israel is broken that he does not hesitate to allow the town to send out messengers with an S.O.S. signal. The mission will only serve to publish his victory and his greatness. And indeed, when the news reached Gibeah, its effect was what he had anticipated: the people wept over the sense of their impotence, stung by the sense of how low they had sunk in the eyes of their heathen neighbours.

But Saul, the yeoman with his feet on the land—a man of valour in the Hebrew phrase often means simply a substantial burgher—came home driving his oxen before him. When he heard the news he has no time and no inclination for weeping; he acts and acts at once. He sends out a species of fiery cross, summoning every able-bodied man in Israel, and, with the men who answer his summons, he bursts upon the astonished Nahash and saves his countrymen.

Israel has found its man: and from this time, through all the changing vicissitudes of his unquiet life, Israel supported him to the death. Her allegiance only ended on the fatal hill slopes of Gilboa.

The deed at Jabesh-Gilead has done more than beat back Nahash and avert the ruin of one of the Israelite towns. It has made Israel recognize what it can do, if it will but follow a man who will take his life in his hand and lead.

But the Philistines naturally hear of it and, feeling the new spirit which is stirring among the people they are holding down, they strengthen their garrisons in Ephraim. Israel has rallied round Saul but has hardly measured the issues and the peril of the thing he has undertaken. So the field-army with the fatal weakness of all highlanders, melts away like snow, leaving Saul with a little company of six hundred men to bear the brunt of this great and sudden danger. Saul found himself unable to keep the open field.

How long this lasted it is impossible to say. From the story of the meeting of Saul and Samuel we get the impression that at the time Saul was young. Yet immediately afterwards, according to the narrative, Saul is the father of a grown son, Jonathan. Our account, like all such popular stories, sweeps on from one vivid incident to another and never stops to tell what happened in the interval or how long the interval lasted. Saul may have been a fugitive for quite a number of years. His family found final refuge in the East where Ishbaal set up his little kingdom. Saul may have retreated to the East and held a kingdom together which has been ignored in our present narrative.

But there was a Philistine garrison, keeping the Northern passes to Ephraim, at Michmash (1 Sam. 13 : 23). Evidently it was strong, for there was the danger point. Judah could not support Saul : and, if only the Philistines might hold the Northern passes, they could keep down Ephraim and pin Saul to his native tribe. Below lay a deep rocky ravine which made the position secure. One day Jonathan appeared about the foot of the ravine, when most of its garrison, in their security, had scattered foraging. Lolling over the rocks, one of the Philistines caught sight of the king's son and, saying idly that here at last was one of those Israelites creeping out of his hole into the daylight, bade him come up. Come up he did and he and his armour-bearer overwhelmed the weakened outpost.

The news reached Saul and he was as prompt as in the day of Jabesh-Gilead. Following up the blow, he roused his six hundred, beat the broken detachments of the Philistines and drove the Philistines headlong down the famous pass of Aijalon into their own country.

You will remember the following incident with Saul's vow. Sometimes it is loosely said that this rash vow prevented a complete victory. This is to misinterpret the situation. After all, the victory at Aijalon meant no more than the defeat of a strong garrison. Besides, the strength of the Philistines, then and always, lay in the fact that their strong cities gave them a rallying point so that they could afford to lose such a battle. On the other hand, a couple of days like those at Aphek laid all Israel at the feet of the conquerors.

1 Sam. 14 : 52 represents the real situation : " there was war with the Philistines all the days of Saul." But apparently the first blow was the needed thing to give Israel confidence

that they could hold their own. It vindicated Saul, too, as leader, not only in an effort against a weaker enemy like Ammon, but against the justly dreaded Philistines. And finally it broke open the road to Ephraim. Saul could get no support from Judah, so long as Jerusalem was in possession of the Jebusites. But now he was no longer confined to Benjamin. He had Trans-Jordan through Jabesh-Gilead and he could find a recruiting ground in Ephraim.

Saul, then, gathers up the national consciousness, represents the national spirit, is in sympathy with the national religion, because he not only understands but shares its impulses. Above all, he knows precisely how to use these gifts for the immediate needs of the present hour. So Israel gave him her unquestioning loyalty all his life.

This is the more remarkable in view of two circumstances: First, the quarrel with David. I have no time to enter into detail as to early stories connected with David's attitude toward Saul, and Saul's attitude toward him. They are numerous, rather too numerous: we could well have spared some of them for the sake of authoritative information on other subjects. They are evidently written originally, and collected later, by men who were ardent admirers of the young king, probably at the time when he was in the fair promise of his youth. His romantic exploits in the southern hills, which have been embellished with the familiar, rather rococo Robin Hood melodrama, are of the type which has always been suited to men at a certain stage of culture. They come from different sources, as is manifest from contradictions in them: thus to give only one illustration, you find how, in the account of the battle with Goliath, according to one view of the situation, David was a shepherd lad, utterly unknown to Saul, until he compels attention through his challenge to the giant; according to the other view, he was already the king's armour-bearer, well-known at the little court, before he signalized himself by his courage.

Yet, with all this in their favour, these accounts, which probably would just represent the young captain as more personally popular than his sombre chief, cannot hide the plain fact that David could not maintain himself against Saul. The king was able even to hunt the other out of his own

3*

tribe, Judah, and to compel him finally to seek refuge and
protection beyond the frontier with Achish of Gath. The
Philistines posted him at Ziklag, the site of which is uncertain. But, from the fact that David is represented as able
to make raids on the desert tribes and then to represent these
raids as having been carried on against the southern outliers
of Judah, and from the fact that he sent spoils to these
southern clans in Judah, it is no remote conclusion to suppose
that Ziklag lay south-east of the Philistines and south-west
of Judah. Achish posted him on the dangerous flank, where
the route to Egypt lay exposed to assault from the raiding
Bedawin of the desert.[1]

Second, and more seriously, the quarrel with a number of
the prophets. Unfortunately we are not very well informed
as to the ultimate causes of their quarrel. Still more unfortunately, all the information we have comes from sources
which were definitely unfriendly to Saul. This is true even
of the quarrel with David : there also our informants are
clearly in favour of the man who became the great champion of independent Israel.

The two stories on the subject, which are given in the Book
of Samuel, deserve to be briefly sketched and examined.
According to the one, which appears in 13 : 8 ff., Samuel had
commanded Saul to wait seven days at Gilgal until Samuel
arrived in order to offer sacrifice. The king, after waiting
for the seven days, found his people grow panicky over the
delay and himself sacrificed in order to keep them in heart.
According to the other, Chapter 15, Saul had gone out against
Amalek, had defeated them and was condemned by Samuel
for not carrying out the *herem* (or " ban ") against Agag their
king, a doom which the prophet is said himself to have carried
out.[2]

If one must chose between the two, I should judge that
the latter account is likely to be nearer to the actual course
of events. The law as to a king being judged incompetent and

[1] The Philistines were probably holding the great trunk road in the
interest of Egypt. The desert tribes were able to cut in at the weak
point. The other weak point is in the north-east at Damascus.

[2] It is possible that there we have two different accounts which aim at
giving us the reason why it came to a breach between the young kingdom
and prophecy. We may have to choose as to which of them we are to
follow.

a priest alone being permitted to sacrifice was hardly so much in force as Chapter 13 represents. One remembers the conduct of Solomon and even Ahaz in connection with the temple worship.

But, to leave that question apart, the interesting thing to notice about the two accounts is that in both these cases our modern instincts and our modern religious convictions would make us side with Saul. In the one case, we should be forced to say that Saul did wait the seven days and that he was bearing the heavy responsibility of the condition of Israel. The failure to realize the seriousness of the situation was on the side of the prophet. In the other case, we should be inclined to say that Saul and the people, in refusing to slaughter Agag, were revolting a little from the old brutal desert custom of the *herem,* to which the more conservative prophets still clung as something well-pleasing to Yahweh. We might even see in the incident another illustration of a fact which does not appear here alone in history, viz., that the freer moral instinct of the lay person sometimes judges more surely and goes more certainly to the bottom of a question than that of the professionally religious caste. Religion and religious people have always been strictly conservative. One may add that they will always be : personally I should add that they ought always to be. The reason is that religion is so much wider and richer a spirit than morality. Being that, it is slow to deny : it loves assertion. Goethe was seeing that when he spoke of Mephistopheles as the spirit which continually denies. Well, that spirit is always urging us to break from this and be done with that. Religion is slow to part with anything which human souls have ever asserted and lived by. There was something of truth in what they asserted : and we miss it when we throw out the past as a lie.

Evidently then there is something to be said for Saul even in connection with the quarrel with the prophets; and fortunately we as Protestants are not compelled to believe that prophets were incapable of making mistakes. Don't transfer papal infallibility to the prophets ! Like many other strong religious movements, the movement which produced prophecy was apt to be rigidly conservative and harshly orthodox.

Whatever came from the old desert life must be retained. It
is not difficult to see how and why in an infant community a
conflict arose between the two authorities, secular and religious, one created to meet the needs of the present, the other
holding strictly to the Mosaic past, both recently sprung into
activity, uncertain of their powers, not clear as to their functions in the young community, needing patience and good
temper in order to find some settlement of their respective
claims.

At last there came a clash; and, just because Saul was so
devout a man, the clash was too much for him. This has
always seemed to me the tragedy of the situation, that he was
of the same temper as Samuel, that he was in sympathy
with the prophetic movement. If he had been a hard-mouthed
creature like Jehoiakim who sat with his toes at the brazier
and slit the prophet Jeremiah's roll and tossed it into the
fire, he would merely have hardened his heart and gone his
own way. There are men like that. As it was, he fell a victim
to melancholia and into a morbid condition of soul, of which
a suspicious and haunting jealousy was, as often happens, the
sure symptom. Yet, as a man must, he held on his way. For
Israel's sake the king's government must be carried on.

He united Ephraim and Benjamin : he had enough control
over Judah to be able to hunt David out of his own tribe.
You will note that here Judah begins to find its way quietly
back into its fitting place in the comity of Israel. This is not
proved so much by the appearance of David at the king's
court. For the coming of David might have been an isolated
case; might have meant no more than the natural and
generous response of a high-spirited youth to the appeal of a
gallant leader who was asserting Israel's cause against the
Philistines. It is far more eloquently shown through the presence of David's brothers in Saul's fighting line in the battle
when Goliath appears. David is said to have been sent by
their old father with bread to feed his brothers who are with
Saul as a matter of course. Judah had had greater difficulty
than Ephraim in absorbing its alien elements; but the process
was coming to an end, and the tribe was feeling its way
back to take its place among its kindred. Saul held Benjamin
and Ephraim. He had some authority in Judah and a pretty

firm grasp over East Jordan, for his son found his last rallying point at Mahanaim there. And now I think he was beginning to creep north and to threaten to join up with the
northern tribes beyond Esdraelon with the inevitable threat
this implied to the trade-route. This seems the only satisfactory explanation of how it came about that the decisive battle
of his life was fought at Gilboa.[1]

When it came to battle, Saul's feet were stumbling among
the dark mountains of a difficult world. The fate of Israel
was hanging in the balance, depending on the issues of to-
morrow's fight. He was troubled in mind, because the prophets
had cast him off : and this, in his view of things, really meant
that Yahweh had forgotten him. In his torture he slipped
down in the dark to consult the witch at Endor. To realize
the quality of the man, you must recognize that he really
believed the woman to be no vulgar spae wife, but in touch
with the powers of the other world. He believed that Samuel
did appear in that hour, probably believed that he had heard
the final message : " To-morrow thou and thy two sons shall
be with me."

Yet he went back to his camp and fought the business out.
Whatever else he was, this was a man. Though his life has
been written, if not by his opponents, certainly by dogmatists
possessed by a theory, nothing could quite cancel his largeness.

It is possible to hear in his cry when Samuel intimated his
deposition, " Yet honour me, I pray thee, in the presence of
this people," nothing but the whimper of a beaten man who
asks that he should not be published for what he is. Construe
it along those lines and then, when Samuel complies with the
request, one must see a conspiracy of the spiritual and secular
heads of the state to blind the people and pretend that everything is well, though both know that it is not true. Perhaps
so to judge is merely to betray one's own littleness of spirit.

[1]An explanation was given above (p. 68) of why the battles that are
associated with the ark came to be fought at Aphek. The same
ambiguity is present here ; but it is equally possible that the real concern
of the Philistines was due to the fact that Saul was succeeding too well
in his effort to unite all Israel and hence was threatening the communications along Esdraelon. The reason for so thinking is that all this region
fell easily into David's hands. The process must have begun in Saul's
time.

It is at least possible to read out of the utterance the cry of
a great soul. " I am rejected and doomed; but remember,
there is always this people. There is this people whom we
hoped to serve together, but whom I am not judged worthy
to serve, and who are still the object of God's care. Let us
forget about me and think of this people." Then Samuel's
turning and going with Saul is no effort to hoodwink men,
but the honesty of another great soul who must do his sour
duty and tell Saul that he is not big enough for this work,
but who remembers the first talk far into the night and the
fresh morning and the oil poured on a young man's head
and the common hope that they might deliver Israel. And
it has proved too great a task and they have not been fit to
do it; but there is always this multitude, as sheep not having
a shepherd.

Interpret it along this line, and then we need not see in the
story merely two men who go down to play out a deliberate
farce before the unconscious multitude. We may be able to
see two sincere souls going out to do gravely and simply the
only thing which is sometimes left to us mortal men in this
great and terrible life, which makes havoc of our highest ideals
—make the best we can of a bad business which has broken
in our hands. So it is written, Samuel turned and went unto
his house and saw Saul no more until the day of his death.
Yes, but it is also written " The Lord said unto Samuel : how
long dost thou mourn for Saul, seeing I have rejected him."
This is part of life's tragedy : It is not easy to let go a man
with whom you have worked at some great task, but it is not
possible to go with him.

And Saul went down to meet his end, a great soul face
to face with a ravelled world who refuses to turn his back
on what he has taken upon him, but also a great soul with
a fatal defect in his nature, not quite big enough to do the
thing which his time demanded from its leader, but doing all
which it was left possible for him to do.

So he fell, and surely there are few more sombre and touching pictures, even in the Old Testament, which contains a
whole gallery of such things, than the little company of men
to whom in Jabesh-Gilead the news came of the fall of their
leader on Mount Gilboa. They left their town and slipt in the

sheltering and pitiful night along the trough of Jordan till
they reached Bethshan. And from its walls they took down
at peril of their own lives the marred and dishonoured carcase and bore it reverently back for decent burial in the
town he had saved. " He did not leave us to be the mock of
Ammon : God do so to us and more also if we leave him to
be the mock of the uncircumcised."

And Saul surely had his reward. There is a justice at the
heart of this world. For he made David and the after kingdom possible. Without him they could not have been. Again,
if you would rightly estimate the situation of Saul and the
reward and honour which are due to him, you must see it all
in its Old Testament setting. We are biased in this matter
of reward by our over-developed individualism in its dangerous weakness. We expect all reward to come to us personally
in our own life-time, and we are apt to complain unduly if it
does not come, so that we can savour it to the full. The Old
Testament with its strong sense of the individual as but the
creature of a day, who yet contributes his own act to the
corporate body out of which he has come, who passes himself but who leaves his world richer by what he has sought to
do for it, has a juster sense of what constitutes a due reward.

I find myself wondering at times whether the man who
wrote for us the story of Saul in the Old Testament quite
knew all he did, when he set up this as the figure of the first
king over his people. It remains so much richer, because so
much more suggestive a figure than that of Solomon, who is
a kind of lay figure at best, padded, successful, crackling in
robes which make it difficult to reach the man behind them.

But here is a man, all a man, wrestling with fate and with
the dark powers which hem in every man's destiny, which
limit him at every point in his effort to reach the thing he has
set before him. He fails as the world counts failure, but he
leaves a new temper to the nation and a great example of how
worthy a thing it is to die attempting what may prove, when
all is done, to be beyond one's power.

So great a thing it is to be king over Israel, so great a thing
to be the anointed of Yahweh.

DAVID

I DO not propose to enter into the question of the sources here, partly because the question is a very complicated one and its details would scarcely reward us for the time spent on its discussion, but still more because all our historical material comes from a period comparatively near to the time about which it treats. In the case of the period of the Settlement it would be necessary to separate out the later account, because this represents a much later view of the way in which the Settlement proceeded; and, before we could make up our minds as to the actual history, we would have to face up to a decision as to which representation of it we meant to follow. But, while the accounts of David's reign come from different sources, these do not show a radically divergent view of the reign itself, and the question of the sources accordingly is not of such fundamental importance.

It may, however, be of interest, as showing how such matters as history were dealt with in old Israel, to note one thing which is manifest from the most cursory reading of the book. One cannot but be struck with the full details given us as to two periods of David's life, his relations with Saul at the beginning and his stormy end. The last, which opens with his adultery and comes to a somewhat abrupt conclusion with the account of Absalom's rebellion and its defeat, is, I venture to say, one of the great pieces of the world's literature.

Yet, between these two periods lay the most fruitful period of David's life and the period most significant for the future history of Israel, both externally in the building up of the realm, and internally in consolidating and uniting the tribes and absorbing the Canaanites. How meagrely the period is treated! For the process of building up the kingdom and for the proof of the capacity of the king in war we have chiefly

to depend on hints like those connected with the deeds of the
mighty men, 2 Sam. 21 : 15 ff.; 23 : 8 ff. These show a long
struggle with the Philistines and wars with Syria and Ammon.
And even these we owe to an appendix like the closing
chapters of the book of Judges, no integral part of the book
of Samuel.

Inside the kingdom, as to what David did to centralize and
consolidate the nation, to provide for its economic life, to give
expression to its new judicial authority, to build it into a unity,
we have practically nothing at all. Yet one fact is enough to
show how large a change passed over the whole life in Israel
in this respect. At the beginning of the period so weak is the
central authority and so chaotic are the conditions that Abner
and Joab do very much what they please in the young kingdom. At the end, in spite of two rebellions, one of which led
to the temporary flight of the king, the kingdom was so
powerfully rooted in men's minds that it was able to maintain
itself. This implies long and laborious and valuable work at
internal organization, a work on which Solomon based in
connection with his new developments.

Now on all this our accounts are practically silent. The
writers of history in Israel are still at the stage of loving the
picturesque. David has had the advantage of having his story
written by an ardent admirer, conscious of the weaknesses in
his hero, but very conscious always of the benefits which he
brought to his nation. Further, we must recognize in David a
far abler man in many respects, more conscious of the situation and of its needs and more adequate to meet the latter
than his predecessor. Yet somehow one feels conscious of a
different atmosphere and, I confess, an atmosphere which is
closer and a little more sultry. Saul's effort has the dew of
youth upon it and its charm : it is like the effort of a pure
enthusiasm. Even where he plays the fool and quarrels with
David he does it openly. David can hold his hand and play
a much more secret game, can use Joab for his own ends and
watch an opportunity to get rid of him, can utilize a popular
emotion for his own purposes. I confess to a certain bias
against David and warn you accordingly.

By the fortunate accident of the other Philistine princes
refusing to trust him and to allow him into their ranks, he

began with a clean record before his countrymen. So he can take up the role of being the champion of Israel's cause, and, at the same time, through his alliance with Saul by his marriage with Michal, can lay a certain claim to being the natural successor to the throne. The incident of the slave who brought Saul's wristlet from Gilboa gave him the opportunity to show himself the defender of the memory of the heroic king (2 Sam. 4 : 10); and his lament over Saul and Jonathan struck the right note in proving him able to appreciate the quality of these fine figures. At the same time he is *persona non ingrata* to the Philistines who allow him to set up a petty kingdom in Hebron, possibly tributary, certainly subordinate to them. He has moved further into the heart of the country than Ziklag and may still be of use to them. In setting up the petty kingdom there was no disloyalty to Saul's house on David's part, for, as matters stood, with the Philistines overrunning the hills and Jerusalem still in the hands of the Jebusites, it was sheerly impossible that Ishbaal could ever have hoped to hold the south of Judah. If not to David, it must have fallen to someone else. Only, one could have wished that in his message (2 Sam. 2 : 7), to the men of Jabesh-Gilead, so seemly and worthy in itself, he had omitted the hint at the end as to how Judah had anointed him king. That smells a little of the art of the politician.

Ephraim was again overrun by the Philistines : so Ishbaal must withdraw beyond Jordan and set up his little court at Mahanaim, a court which from the beginning was dependent on the character and quality of the king's uncle Abner. The two petty chiefs—they are nothing more—were tolerated as negligible in the eyes of the Philistines, the more so, because they are jealous of each other. The two might have continued without coming into contact, but each tries to extend his influence over Benjamin : Ishbaal, because he naturally wished to win back his father's tribe and so gain a footing west of Jordan : David, because a man of natural force of character and of ambition, could hardly be content to be penned among the barren hills of South Judah.

Hence you have border warfare between the two, of the type which is admirably brought before us in the story of the fight at the pool of Gibeon (2 Sam. 2 : 12 ff.) Note the small number of the respective contingents engaged. Probably this was not the only incident of the kind. It has been preserved for us because it was the occasion of the death of Asahel at the hands of Abner. This embittered the whole business, by introducing the blood feud between the two generals, and led ultimately to Abner's death.

In this border war the superior quality of David and Joab was gradually wearing down their opponents. Many in the north saw what must be its ultimate issue and even Abner was forced to recognize that his nephew's cause was doomed. But the little kingdom could not pass decently out of life : it fell in rather squalid fashion. Poor Ishbaal grew suspicious of his uncle, the more so because Abner resolved to marry Rizpah, a concubine of Saul. This step was not so innocuous as it may seem to us, for in the East the marriage of a man with a king's widow generally implies a desire to succeed to his dignity. Remembering how Absalom set up the *huppah* on the roof of the palace and publicly took over his father's harem as the sign of a complete break with David.[1] Abner may have been looking for an excuse, for he takes prompt offence and goes off to David to make terms.. David always maintaining his role of being Saul's legitimate successor, makes his *conditio sine qua non* the restoration of Michal, daughter of the first king. When Abner returned to implement this first condition, David carefully sent Joab out of the way. Perhaps he had it in mind to get rid of the too powerful Joab by setting Abner in his place and making the plea for his act, reason of state. If so, it must have been a disappointment to find Joab getting rid of his rival by his favourite left-hand stroke. David was careful to get clear of the accusation of treachery in connection with the deed by his public lamentation over Abner. The feckless Ishbaal, left naked by the loss of his uncle, is butchered by a couple of assassins : but the men, who, like the slave with Saul's wristlet, had hoped for a reward, have their hands and feet hung up before the kites beside the pool at Gibeon.

Things, you notice, have a singular faculty of falling out

---

[1] The step was taken at the advice of his astute privy-councillor, not as an insult to David, but as the definite breach between him and his father—David was thus regarded as practically dead.

happily and conveniently for David. He needs only to wait for circumstances to turn to his advantage. But what this generally means in history is that, in the circumstances of the time, such a man was bound to come out on the top. David was bound to win. He was the competent man, and the only competent man. The nation needed such a man, and every year seems only to have proved the utter incompetence of Ishbaal. David was the man for the position, and, in the circumstances in which he was placed, one cannot deny him the great and rare virtue of moderation. He certainly knew ambition, possibly too he recognized that he must win in the end. He was conscious of great powers and of the real needs of Israel. But he never seems to have forced the pace; and he certainly refused to sully his hands with the commoner, baser crimes of the ambitious man. The result was that, when he came to the throne, he came with tolerably clean hands and a tolerably clean record. Men who had been honourably attached to the house of Saul could fall in behind him and retain their self-respect.

The disappearance of Ishbaal won David Benjamin, E. Jordan, part of Ephraim in addition to his own native tribe. It was patent that sooner or later there must come a breach with the Philistines, patent to both sides. The Philistines saw it so clearly that they seem to have moved first and to have struck with all their available force. This time there is and can be no question of going round by the north and approaching from the Vale of Esdraelon. The danger was vital and was situated at their very door. So they struck at the heart as directly as they did promptly. Besides they may have aimed at separating David from North Israel and may have had the support of Jerusalem and its Jebusite garrison. They overran Bethlehem and Hebron, taking David by surprise so that he was unable to summon his scattered men. I am piecing together the story from the broken accounts left us. Unfortunately the accounts we have make no pretence at indicating the period in the king's reign to which they belong. And naturally this period in the king's life did not receive very much attention in the Israelite narrative. But we should read 2 Sam. 5 : 17 directly after v. 3, and where at present we read of David going down into the hold, we should understand this as meaning the familiar cave of Adullam. Then, between v. 17 and vv. 18-21 of Chapter 5, insert 23 : 13 ff., the story of how David longed for water from the well of Bethlehem and how several of his men broke through to meet even this desire of their beloved leader. My reason for setting the incident there is that we know of no other period in his life when David was so pent in by the Philistines. Probably it is because the story gives an illustration of the devotion the king in his youth could inspire that it has been suffered to survive, though it recalls one of the most desperate periods of his career. For a time David seems to have been reduced to the old fugitive life. Yet that life exactly fitted the Judean Highlanders. They were often most dangerous when defeated, since they took to their hills and guerilla war. So they seem now to have worn out the Philistines, to have defeated them at Gibeon and chased them as far as Gezer in the Shephelah.

No sooner was his tribe cleared of the Philistines than David proved himself abler and more far-seeing than Saul. He saw what Israel needed and he could pursue his ends more resolutely than his predecessor, because he had Israel behind him. He had learned too from his stay in Philistia the value of a central fortress and from Saul's defeat at Gilboa the danger of having none. He seized Jerusalem.

Jerusalem stands on two hills, eastern and western. The citadel of the Jebusites was on the eastern hill. Its situation was in certain respects not unlike that of our Castle rock. The strength of both places lay in the fact that both were approachable from only one narrow quarter, Jerusalem from the north, Edinburgh from the East. The weakness of both lay in the fact that neither side was possessed of water within the walls. Hence the Romans never held Edinburgh in strength, in spite of its obvious advantages for watching the tribes across the Forth. If you go to the north side of the Castle between the rock and the railway you will find an old forgotten building. This was the water supply. The castle garrison approached it by a covered way from what is now the esplanade, and they had the advantage that it was pro- tected from a besieging force by the Nor Loch which filled the valley. Jerusalem's water-supply came from a spring on the east side at the bottom of the hill, what is now known as Sidi Mariam. To reach it the Jebusites had dug a tunnel through the limestone rock. This, I think, was the channel by which David's men made their entry, though the text is too uncertain to make us quite sure.

The advantage of this great success was obvious. To hold Jerusalem meant joining up Judah finally with Israel—a thing which could only remain tentative and dubious so long as the strong fortress divided the tribes. To hold Jerusalem meant also to have a rallying point for Israel directly over against the power of the Philistines.

So soon as he had captured the town and had beaten back the Philistines, the king set himself to make Jerusalem, not merely the military, but the spiritual, centre of the kingdom. To compare small things with great, in precisely the same fashion Bismarck, when he had consolidated the German Empire under the leadership of Prussia, set himself to make Berlin the intellectual, as well as the military centre of Germany.

David, in the same spirit and with the same insight, brought up the ark to his new capital and made preparations for building a temple.

The man had an eye for a situation and the practical mind which can make its insight effective. Notice how eminently fitted Jerusalem was for such a position as David designed for it. I do not mean merely through its being a strong natural fortress, commanding the ford at Jericho, giving quicker access to Ephraim than the Philistines could control. But, besides, it had no associations with the separate tribes, such as might make the northern Israelites unwilling to come to Hebron or the men of Judah resentful at being required to resort to Shechem. Jerusalem did not, like Hebron or Bethel, bring memories of their separate existence or their individual prowess to the tribes who met in her narrow streets. Instead it marked precisely what the tribes had been able to do, when they were happily united, what they had found themselves unable to do, till they were thus united. It stood for united Israel. It was the Israelite capital.

Even in its situation, it stood for the same thing. It had never been reckoned to Judah, but had stood on the margin with the boundary between Benjamin and Judah running through it.

The ark, which David brought into it and for which he planned to erect a temple, was not merely a religious, but a political, emblem. It had always been in the custody of Ephraim, had been associated with Joshua, the hero of Ephraimite blood, and with the worship at Shiloh in Ephraimite country. As such, the bringing of the ark into the new capital was a sign of the great desire of David's life to unite Israel into a single unity. David declared himself, through accompanying the Ark, no mere Judaean but an Israelite.

One may add that the Ark stood for the distinct character of the Yahweh worship among the northern tribes. Its associations were with the conquering tribes, i.e. with the men who had been least time settled in Palestine. We know how inevitably the religion of the tribes became tainted with the Canaanite worship. The influence was strongest where the tribes had been longest settled among the Canaanites and had had least opportunity to share in the new impulse which had come through Moses. It was least in those places where the tribes came fresh from the desert and from the religious quickening connected with the desert that is, it was least in Judah and in the body of opinion which centred round the Ark. It was true that Judah had had grave difficulty in assimilating the foreign elements in its body politic: but, in doing this, it had the advantage that its new country, being little agricultural and almost wholly delivered over to the rearing of sheep, had enabled the tribesmen to preserve their old traditions and maintain their customs. David, a true son of Judah, stood for this element in Judah's life: so did the Ark. They both stood for purer Yahwism.

Winckler says[1] that Yahwism practically dates from David; holds, that is to say, that he came from the desert of Judah with the doctrine of Yahweh's unique character and introduced it in Israel for the first time. The persistent tradition of his adopting the Ark and the large part it played in his life and the fact that the early history of the Ark centred

[1] In *Geschichte Israel's in Einzeldarstellungen*, Teil I, pp. 27 ff.

round Benjamin and Shiloh and Samuel are sufficient to my mind to make this impossible.

The truth which lies in Winckler's remark is what I have been trying to insist on to you. From this time, through the rise of the kingdom, we find a clearer assertion of the distinct life of Israel. And, as the distinct life of Israel centred round and sprang from its faith, you find its Yahwism growing more pronounced. This shows itself even in such a smaller matter as the increase of proper names compounded of Yahweh. These, as Buchanan Gray shows in his *Hebrew Proper Names,* increased greatly from the time of the kingdom.

Nor was this the work merely of a clever statesman. David was able to do all this so powerfully and so naturally because he was a strong adherent of his people's faith. This reveals itself in the story which has been preserved about his dancing before the Ark. As Saul could share the prophetic enthusiasm without shame, David could take his own share in the outward forms of his people's religion. The scoffing of Michal, when she saw him do it, is on the same level as the surprise certain men showed at finding Saul among the prophets. The worldly wise could not quite fathom this naïve power to be moved even by the cruder elements in their common faith. David could represent and gain support for the native faith of the time so thoroughly because he shared it. I do not mean to suggest that he was a great leader of its higher life. This was for other men. But, as is said, his heart was perfect with Yahweh, his God; that is, he was whole-hearted in his allegiance. And this was the religious virtue his time needed and could understand.

In many respects David's capture of Jerusalem with all it implied was the master stroke of his life. It was a sincere effort to discover Israel, united Israel, to itself and to discover for it a common centre of which both north and south might be equally proud. It was also an honest effort to unite it round, not merely a great physical citadel, but the profoundest force which made it, its religion.

Yet this was not all his people's debt to David. To estimate this we must try to piece together our information as to the political situation outside, so far as this is within our power.

Trouble broke out early with Ammon, the growing strength

of which had already become evident in the incident in connection with Nahash, which discovered Saul to himself and to
Israel. In 2 Sam. 10 we have a story which is very difficult
to date, but which probably belongs to the early period of
the new reign. The king of Ammon had died and David sent
messengers to congratulate the son on his accession. The
young king deliberately insulted the messengers. One wants at
once to know the reason. It seems possible that Ishbaal had
been their tributary, as David had been at Hebron the tributary of the Philistines. If this were so, then of course the
situation ceased under David. Even if Ishbaal was not tributary to Ammon, the situation became very different when a
strong power which dominated West Jordan was substituted
for the tottering kingdom at Mahanaim. The situation on the
east of Jordan was materially altered for the worse for all the
little kingdoms there. All the more was it disturbing for
Ammon, because David was evidently on good terms, or
even allied, with Moab. The Book of Ruth goes so far as to
derive his ancestry from a Moabite woman. And, while the
late date of the book and its evident character of propaganda
make its evidence not very reliable, we find it casually mentioned that, when David was in serious danger from Saul, he
sent his father and mother into safe keeping with the king of
Moab.

Evidently it was not only Ammon that felt how gravely
the situation all along east Jordan had been altered, for,
when Ammon flung down the gage of battle, and appealed
for help to the tribes in the north, it received promptly the
aid it required. Ammon, being nearest to this new, strong
rival, was the first to take alarm. But its king was able to
form a coalition with the Syrians of Tsoba, Bethrehob and
Maacab, little states belonging to Aram along the north of
Gilead (2 Sam. 10 : 1-6). Joab was sent against them and was
able to defeat the coalition (vv. 7-14). But the Ammonites
retreated to Rabbath Ammon, while the Syrians retired home.
In their strong fortress Ammon was able to hold out during
the winter. Next spring the Syrians returned, led by
Hadadezer, King of Tsoba, but David defeated them so
utterly that, though Rabbath Ammon still held out, they
became subject (vv. 15-19). Finally Rabbath Ammon was

taken and with it the crown of the god Milkom (11 : 1-17, 12 : 26-30). Through this war the kingdom, you will note, reached out to the desert on the east and was made secure on the flank.

On the north David is able to do what Saul failed in, cross Esdraelon and make Galilee an integral part of Israel, as he had made Judah a permanent part of Israel. The power of the Philistines is gone and, accordingly, the Canaanite towns in Esdraelon, which had always been absorbing Israelite elements, became themselves absorbed. His kingdom stretches to Lebanon and Hermon and David forms a league with Phoenicia. This was obviously to their mutual advantage, for by this time Tyre and Sidon had definitely turned to trade in the Mediterranean, for which their possession of the only decent harbours on the coast peculiarly fitted them. As, however, their towns were penned in by Lebanon behind and their coast territory was only about two to five miles deep and could not feed them, and as their interest, like that of every trading community, was peace, they obtained through David's friendship supply of food and a market for their wares, and they secured decent order in their hinterland. They kept open also their trade-route across Galilee to the Euphrates.

Southward Amalek disappears from history. Edom is conquered and through its conquest Israel reaches the Red Sea, being masters of Elath and Ezion Geber, ports on the sea. There Israel began to trade on her own, particularly under Solomon. One notes also how Solomon, for the protection of this trade and its furtherance, built Tamar. This is not, as it used to be understood, Tadmor or Palmyra, but a fortress in the Negeb, covering the caravan route to Elath by way of Hebron.

All this continues and is confirmed under Solomon. Evidently he was specially interested in all that concerned his country's trade. He was driven to this by his rather foolish love for building with its inevitable expenditure, by the need for maintaining an army which brought its incidental expenses, and by his desire to make his kingdom take its place among those of his neighbours. The one point in which Solomon did not exactly succeed was his relation to Damascus. This kingdom had been, if not tributary, at least subordinate to David. But in Solomon's time a general from the army of Tsoba made his way into Damascus and founded a kingdom. For the present it was negligible, but, like some of the internal conditions in Solomon's time, it was of evil omen for the future, because Damascus became a terror to Israel in later years, especially under Ahab.

All this development, which made David's and Solomon's kingdom for a period the most powerful realm in Syria, was possible because its great neighbours Egypt and Assyria were at the time unable to interfere. Assyria was busy with troubles from what answers to our modern Armenia and from Babylon. Egypt was weakened by its old enemy, internal troubles: the long strip of land along the banks of the Nile has always been difficult to hold together.

One cannot help bringing this impotence of Egypt into relation to the equally sudden collapse of Philistia at the same period. It is just possible that the two are related as cause and effect, that is, that Philistia was subordinate to Egypt, was even in some measure its advance guard along the great Asiatic road. When Egypt grew weak, Philistia of course collapsed before David and enabled the king to capture Jerusalem.

But one can only speculate there. Unfortunately our information is still incomplete as to the precise relations between Philistia and Egypt.

But that this development of Israel might have its check at any time, when one of these strong kingdoms recovered, is shown in Solomon's relation to Egypt. He married a daughter of the Pharaoh, a thing which in itself meant very little. One notes how a Pharaoh, probably the same, receives the fugitive rebel from Edom and gives him in marriage to one of his daughters. In Pharaoh's crowded harem there were daughters enough and, so long as the girl was not a daughter by the chief wife, the gift of her really meant very little. What seems to me more significant is that Pharaoh took Gezer and presented it as his daughter's dowry to Solomon. Why did he need to take the town? Why did Solomon not take it himself? The only possible answer seems to be that Gezer was recognized, as we should say, as lying within Egypt's sphere of influence and that, for Solomon to take it himself, would have meant his ignoring Egypt's claims in Syria. Egypt has not surrendered its old claims and is now coming into a position in which it can venture to make these good. It makes these good in the direction of thereby entering into closer relations to the strongest kingdom south of Lebanon and one which controls most of the trade routes out of Egypt. You see Solomon holds Elath and Ezion Geber, he has Esdraelon and the coast road, has the Negeb and the route into Arabia. It suits Egypt at this time to make peaceful settlement with Israel : but the interest it holds in all this may at any time demand that it take more independent and vigorous action.

Now one sees the nation, strong, independent, self-confident, under a united and uniting authority. There are ugly symptoms that the old cleavage between north and south is only soldered up. Already under David this has shown itself; under Solomon it has only shown itself more clearly. But both kings have been able to keep it down. Israel too is open to the world in a new way. The Canaanites have been absorbed and Israel is seeing more widely into the world of their time. Trade is enlarging their outlook and bringing into the country not only new products and new wants, but new men with their differing ideals and widely differing faith. The old simplicity of life has gone, never to return.

Let me try to put before you what all the change in the condition of the nation brought with it, and how the change also implied a change in the religious attitude and outlook.

To begin with the most obvious change, all this demanded and obtained a different type of army. We saw Saul sending the fiery cross to raise the levy, sitting under a tree at Gibeah with the chiefs of his clan about him. We saw the Israelites scatter from him before the Philistines, so that he was left with the voluntary detachment. We saw David taken by surprise and driven to Adullam again by the Philistines' sudden attack. We saw too how, when they were summoned, certain tribes shirked the summons and sent no volunteers. Such a state of affairs could not meet the new situation. A centralized kingdom with a capital and relations with the world must have means of defence. Hence we find under David a new type

of army. There are the six hundred who had been with him
in the old heroic days against Saul. Gaps in the ranks were
filled by professional soldiers, taken from all quarters. As
generally happens with a Praetorian Guard foreigners were
welcome, especially Philistines. Their leader was Benaiah from
the Negeb, a man from David's own clan, but so largely were
the men recruited from abroad that they even came to be
known as the K^{e}rethim and P^{e}lethim. Besides there were thirty
picked men in peculiarly close relations to David, a kind of
household infantry. These seem to have been gradually
increased, and it is significant to find them under command
of Ittai of Gath, another Philistine. Of course it was necessary
at times to summon the whole nation, and in connection with
this, to prevent any tribe shirking its duty, you have the first
census taken by Joab, the army commander-in-chief, evidently
an effort after better organization.

Now, note how these men, the core of Israel's strength,
stood in a wholly new relation to nation and king as compared with any which old Israel can offer. The old levy
rose for a definite occasion, melted back in the civil population
when the occasion had passed, served the nation's immediate
need, were Israelites, full of Israel's peculiar opinions, more
subject to its ideals, because they risked everything to defend
them. The ideals of the nation were in danger and so they
fought, and the fact that they did so risk their lives sent
them back to their homes more loyal to Israel's ideals with
every occasion of their rising. The new soldiery were a Praetorian Guard. To whom were they subject? To the king; and
that they could be nobly loyal to their salt is proved by the
case of Ittai from Gath. But they were no integral part of
the state as such. So long as the king was loyal to the old conceptions and construed his functions as the minister of Yahweh
to his people they were quite innocuous. But what if he
changed? Did you not then run the risk of getting a kingdom
like one of the nations, an oriental despotism of the common,
dreary type? The prophets felt this.

The matter shows itself in another direction. The situation
demanded a new bureaucracy. Perhaps this is too large and
strong a phrase to apply to the simple arrangements of early
Israel. But there were new officials needed to carry on, espec-

ially Solomon's large works of building. One finds him appointing certain men over the levy and over the tribute and over the labour which he employed at Jerusalem. To whom were these men responsible? To the man who appointed them, and they were apt to conclude that any situation which continued them in power was good for Israel. One sees how all this, demanding new forms of taxation, new methods of administration, could not work with the old tribe and clan division of Israel. Solomon re-divided his kingdom for purposes of administration along lines which ignored the old clan divisions. One notes how, as soon as this was done, Jeroboam rose against him, and Jeroboam represented the popular feeling because he was the son of a poor widow in Ephraim. While Solomon was able to drive Jeroboam into Egypt, the rebellion against his weaker son began by the murder of Adoram who was over the tribute, i.e. the levy.

One can see how all kinds of influences united there: the human dislike of increase of taxation, the objection to centralization which involves the ignoring of the old methods of life, the sense that all this was turning the people into a kind of sheep driven by the king. That this religious motive, obscure but real, was present is shown by the fact that a prophet, Ahijah, supports Jeroboam.

Another source of finance was trade. Solomon stimulated trade with Egypt, dealt with Phoenicia, broke new ground in Arabia and Ophir (wherever that was) down the Red Sea by way of Elath and Ezion Geber. This was natural, because his great enterprises demanded money: and the situation had its advantages from the point of view of the larger outlook of the nation. But note the change it brought in the internal condition of Israel. The men had passed from the nomadic to the agricultural stage with little difficulty. The leaders in the one became leaders in the other. These leaders were amenable to the old, decent, seemly order. They lived in the community, influenced by the common spirit of the race. Their elders administered the law and were themselves responsible to the community they lived among. But the traders lived in the town, broken away from the prejudices and the sanctities and the traditions of the little community. What did they need to care? Compare the bitter complaints of the later prophets. It is the eternal danger of all finance. Of course it was not big in our modern way of thinking : but, in the conditions of simple Israelite life, it was big. And who does not feel it to-day, who ought not to feel it? We have to reckon with the existence of a body of men who care nothing about the traditions of Scotland, nothing about the beauty of Scotland, yet who have the fate of Scotland in their hands. To whom were these men in Israel ultimately responsible? Not to the community. They were ultimately responsible to one man who was at the head of everything.

Take again the rise of the temple at Jerusalem. The building of a temple at all was an effort at making worship more worthy and at keeping it in line with the growing wealth and higher conditions of the time. But it was the royal chapel, as much as the Cathedral of St. Mark's was originally the doge's private chapel. As one learns from the story of Athaliah, there was a direct entrance from palace to temple, and the king's bodyguard mounted guard both in the palace and in the temple courts, so much were the buildings part of a complex edifice. If you remember what I said about the king's bodyguard being largely foreigners, you will understand how some good people in Israel were as much shocked at uncircumcised Philistines keeping order in the temple as Christians used to be offended on seeing Turkish guards keeping order in the Church of the Holy Sepulchre at Jerusalem. Hence we find Ezekiel objecting to them and expecting their removal.

In connection with the temple it is significant to remember that it must have been crammed full of Phoenician symbols. Solomon had no workmen who could design and carry out such a building and was compelled to ask for help from Hiram of Tyre. Besides, just as Yahwism coming from the desert had no harvest festival of its own, which reflected its own conceptions of Yahweh's nature, so it had no art of its own, which should or could embody its distinctive principles. Hence the temple at its beginning may have been a danger and would have been a greater, had it not been the private chapel of the king, since, along with the art which was the expression of Phoenician worship, comes the risk of borrowing heathen conceptions of God embodied in these artistic symbols.

But a more serious danger in connexion with the temple was that its personnel fell under the control of the king and the early kings exercised their right without hesitation. One hears, for example, of Solomon deposing the old line of Eli and appointing a new high priest in the person of one Zadok. Why it was done we do not exactly know: but it was done at the initiative of the king. One notes that David appointed one or two of his sons as priests (2 Sam. 8 : 18).

No doubt it is an excellent thing when kings are nursing fathers to their kirks, but the situation is not destitute of its dangers. To whom were the priests responsible?

If we take our evidence from any quarter we please, we see the same thing. The centralization, which had been essential to the nation's existence, is throwing all power in the nation into the hands of the king. And remember that this is happening in a community where there is no clearly drafted, sharply defined law, to which the king is, equally with all his people, subject himself. Is it not the conundrum of all governments to get something above all men to which even the executive power is responsible?

One sees all these classes in the community, powerful classes in the youthful, incoherent community—the traders torn away from communal feeling and subject to no new authority: the royal officials, tax-collectors, army, priests, new and needed civic authorities. To whom were these last responsible? They were not elected by the community, nor in any way responsible to them: they were not always members of the community. They were responsible to the king. And the king was no longer in such close touch with the community as David and Saul had been. He was not there to satisfy a need of its existence: he inherited the kingdom and came to feel as though it were his natural right to hold it. Queer how the idea grows on men. Solomon already shows the taint in its beginning. David had the instinctive feeling of knowing how far one might go. He felt in his bones what his people thought. But then he had been born in Judah and knew its local pride and its local feeling. Through this he could measure all local pride and local feeling. Solomon was born at Jerusalem, a colourless place, neither Judah nor Ephraim—a dangerous place to be born. He was also born in the purple, a still more dangerous situation in which to be born.

Now, one must not fail to recognize that the kingdom with all its blemishes, which it was my business to emphasize, was an enormous benefit to Israel. In a rapid sketch like this, where one has to cover a great deal of ground, one must often be content to be impressionistic and paint in hard, sharp black and white, without shading off the greys.

It is noteworthy that the nation never of its own choice threw off the kingdom : and it is further significant that it put its Messianic expectation in the shape of a glorified return of its first king.

Apart from any other considerations, it was inevitable that the nation should change and it was no less desirable than it was inevitable. It must pass from the old condition of the peasant commune under the control of the village sheikhs into a more centralized authority and under a more defined law : and it was desirable that it should so pass. For, while the old conditions held many wholesome things, life was apt to become sheer stagnation among the practices of the past with no wholesome stirring of its fetid waters.

One feels all through the books of Samuel a state rising with its broader, stronger currents of life, with its wider outlook, with its hand on new forces and new difficulties. It was a great gain that men should have opportunity to feel, beyond the little corporation where all their narrow interests were centred, the pulse of the bigger life in Israel. It was a great gain that they should have opportunity to look even beyond Israel and, through Solomon's trade and his relations to Tyre, feel themselves in a way citizens of the world. And one feels the larger vitality, the larger unity, influencing the writing of the period. We are beyond the stories, gathered in the glens, of the heroes of Abiezer and Gilead, who rose and passed and sent on nothing. You now have the feeling of Israel for which each lives, and which takes to itself each man's contribution, preserving it, immortalizing it.

To take one or two points at random, one from the external life of the time, the other from the inward condition of Israel. There was deliverance from the hideous waste of the Philistine wars, where in time past men never felt as though the thing were at an end. Men breathed with the rich deep

4

breath of security and liberty. And there was an end to such
a practice as the blood-feud, which raged between the tiny
communes in Israel, setting valley against valley, before there
was such a thing as the king's court to which one might go
and bring it to its final end. Such a saying as that of 2 Sam.
14: 11 makes one feel the relief of many a poor soul in the
kingdom.

But the task of every advancing civilization is to see that,
with the advance that attends each new time, as little as
possible of the strength of the past should be lost and, in the
profit of a new period, as little as possible of what gave
stability and dignity to the past which is always dying away.

In the rise into sight of new material needs, in the appro-
priation of new material gains there is need for extreme
care that the very spirit by which the gain was made possible
should not be forfeited. The kingdom had been made possible
in Israel, not only because it answered the material wants, the
growing material wants of the community, but because it
promised to assure its spiritual gains. And remember, by
spiritual gains, I do not mean merely religion in its narrowly
construed sense, I mean such spiritual gains as equal protection for all and justice for the weak. If, in grasping the new
satisfaction of the material wants, it let slip the soul of the
community, if it began to erect itself as an end for itself,
and to seek its own selfish aims, it would lose the very thing
which made all the present gains real, or could guarantee the
possibility of further advance.

Hence it is perfectly natural that from this time you find
prophecy beginning to lift its head in warning against the
kingdom, the very institution which it had itself created. Prophecy had in charge, not the material wants, but the soul
of the community.

But, the moment you recognize this, you are compelled
also to recognize that prophecy is not the birth of the new
circumstances. For it brings to bear on the new conditions a
standard which it has learned elsewhere and it applies criteria
which the new men tolerate very badly.

To put it in our modern method of stating the position, the
prophets were asking for an ethical basis for the new kingdom. The old tribal organization did have such a basis in the

customary morality of the time, a basis which was shared by all, understood by all, acknowledged, though not necessarily submitted to, by all. The sheikhs in the gate administered such a system in conformity with such a morality. But the old tribal organization was passing away never to return : it could not possibly meet the new conditions of a new period. With its passing vanished also much of the old morality by which it stood. In the new world, which I tried roughly to sketch to you, the old morality was rapidly losing its hold on the leading persons in the nation who controlled the whole. The new thing had come. And what the prophets dimly and confusedly saw was that as yet it had no ethical basis and above all nothing which could control, and so guide, the strong, dominant masters of the state. And they also saw that without this the kingdom could not continue and had no right to continue.

Occasionally, as is natural with men in such circumstances, the prophets idealized the past, because it seemed to them to have exactly the elements which appeared to be lacking in their world. You find even so great a man as Hosea inclined to do this about the wilder period before the settlement in Palestine. But this tendency is to be seen most clearly in the Rechabites who were not content to idealize the past but who tried to turn back the clock and to bring the people back to it. Then they are apt to become, as the Rechabites did become, mere hopeless conservatives, trying to recall a past which could never come back. Yet what they admired and looked wistfully back to in the past was that it had this basis for a secure and happy future, and, in having this, had also what was distinctively Israel. And what the greatest among them wished for was, not to bring back the past, but to preserve and create in the present this element which could alone preserve Israel's peculiar heritage and guarantee its right to a place in its world.

As an illustration of what I mean, take the story of Uriah and the action of the prophet there. It makes the situation only more remarkable and more clear, when you recognize that it was not the king's sexual irregularity against which Nathan protests most vigorously. It is primarily his wanton interference with the rights of another man. In those days a wife, it is necessary to remember, was regarded more as a man's property than she is to-day. Nathan's parable brings out this element in the situation by making the robbery of the wife parallel to the robbery of the poor man's one ewe-lamb. To note this feature in the parable is to note where prophecy was making its protest and why it was stirred by this deed on the part of the king. After all, *qua* sexual irregularity this thing was no worse in a king than in a common man. The peril lay in the king's superior and irresponsible power against the rights of one of his subjects. And you should further notice that the subject in this case is not even a fellow-Israelite : he is a Hittite, who has no clan to back him and no law to which he can make his appeal. That against which prophecy raises its prompt and emphatic protest is lawless power, wantonly used.

Prophecy made this kingdom possible. Was it to be a kingdom of this type, a kingdom like those of the other nations? We of Israel are not as the other nations and our kingdom was meant to be different also.

Now turn to the account of David's flight from Jerusalem and Absalom's rebellion and see its character as a whole and whether I am not right in saying that it is one of the great pieces of the world's literature. I suppose I ought to say that no one can taste the full flavour of it without reading it in the original. In a measure this is true. The stuff is written in classical Hebrew and the writer knows how to use his own tongue. The phrases are pithy, compact, with every word telling. But Hebrew, because of its natural picturesqueness and its want of subordinate sentences, translates better than most languages.

The man, for example, had an eye which could see and a pen which could report the thing he saw. He can etch a character in a few sentences and leave it without any need for underlining or multiplying remarks. We know Absalom in a moment, when we see him at the gate of Jerusalem and watch him drawing the decent countrymen who are returning disappointed from court, because David in his weary old age is not exercising his function as judge. " Lo, thy matters are good and right," he says to the worthy man already flattered by the king's son taking him by the sleeve, " but there is no one to put thy cause through. If only I had the power as I have the will, there would be fewer wronged men like you to-day in Israel." Give me the job, in fact, and you will see the millenium. It is the perennial demagogue.

He could describe a man too; and describe him as he ought to be, by the thing he does in the hour which demands him. David is sunk in the harem, under the spell of Bath-sheba. The moment the rebellion breaks under Absalom, he starts awake. And when the situation seems desperate, everything rallies behind him. He steps naturally and inevitably into the front; and all the little shady people, who have been swarming into prominence, take at once the second place. Joab, with his clever trick of left hand stabbing disappears and with a few swift, unhesitating decisions, David orders his war, breathes courage into his broken ranks, knows what must be done. Everything owns its master and falls into line at once.

How he loved a man and how he could write about him tersely and without marks of exclamation. David came down on the day of his flight to the last house outside Jerusalem before the desert road to Jericho began, and there, taking his post by the wayside, watched the little company of royalists file past him. Among them his eye lighted on the foreigner, Ittai of Gath, and he bade him halt his troop. " Wherefore do you go also with me? You are a foreigner and you have to live by your sword. You came to me for what I could give you. And once the bargain was fair, for then I could pay you in money or in loot. But these days are gone and I am a broken man. I give you free discharge and you must seek new service." And Ittai looked him in the face and said, " As the Lord liveth and as my lord the king liveth, in what place my lord the king shall be, whether for death or for life, there also will your servant be."

And David looked him in the face and answered, " Go and pass over." There are times when it is something of an impertinence to thank a man : your only way of thanking him is to take him at his word and accept what he gives with a willing mind.

This thing happened : and the man who wrote it saw it happen and knew how to write about it with the seemly reticences with which a man ought to write about a great thing

like that. Such love David could win from men and such love
could he win to himself and keep.

Do you want a picture of a different type of man? Well,
he will give you that too.

Behold, there came out from Bahurim a man of the family
of the house of Saul, whose name was Shimei, the son of
Gera : he came out and cursed along the way. He also cast
stones at David. And thus said Shimei when he cursed :
" Begone you man of blood and man of belial."

" And there went over a ferry boat to bring back the king's
household, and Shimei the son of Gera fell down before the
king as he was about to cross Jordan. And he said unto the
king, ' Let not my lord impute iniquity unto me, neither
remember what your servant did perversely the day my lord
the king went out of Jerusalem, that the king should take it
to heart. For your servant doth know that I have sinned :
therefore behold I am come this day the first of all the house
of Joseph to meet my lord the king.' "

Do you not see the man grovelling on his stomach, the man
who knew the difference between one who has his face toward
and away from Jerusalem? You see him as clearly as Ittai.

These are the men who interest the author and whom he
describes in clean-cut brief phrases. I do not need to insist on
how they stand out for us. But quite as interesting and as instructive is it to recognize the situations which hold his mind
and appeal to him.

He gives a picture of David leaving Jerusalem—David and
Jerusalem, the scene of his proudest and most honourable
deeds for Israel, the place he has made for all time the centre
of his nation's memory and hope. And round him are a handful of loyal men, no more than a handful to remember the
things he did for Israel here. For he who builds on the favour
of the multitude builds on running water. David and Jerusalem. The city has meant this man's life work, what he spent
his sweat and blood to make a reality in his nation's life. And
now the man who holds it is Absalom, his favourite son, whose
ambition and cruelty he has already pardoned. He is calmly
planning the best way of proclaiming to Jerusalem his view
that his father is as good as dead by publicly taking over the
royal harem on the palace roof. In the palace itself Hushai

and Ahitophel are setting their clever wits to mine and countermine each other. On whether Hushai's advice or Ahitophel's be followed rests the fate of David, of David who made Jerusalem Israel's and built the palace and framed the nation for control of whose destiny the intriguers plan.

The man who saw this and set it down in such wise that after the lapse of 2,500 years we can see it too, knew the mutability of mortal things and saw on how small an accident the fate of a nation may at any given hour depend.

And one hardly needs to do more than mention the scene above the gate, where one stands beside the Hebrew outpost and sees the white spurts of dust rise behind the swift feet of the runner who brings the news of the battle. And in the room below all triumph is dashed out of the heart of the king who was not only a king but a father, not only a king but a life-weary old man. And he lets it all drop, all the success: "Would God I had died for thee, O Absalom, my son, my son." So life deals with us, giving what we have given our best strength to win and a little more which spoils the rest.

Listen again, if you would know the situations the author can picture and on which he desires to have our thoughts dwell. David is saying farewell to the men who have been faithful to him in his adversity on the east bank of Jordan. He would fain take one of them with him. "And Barzillai said unto the king, How many are the remaining days of the years of my life that I should go up with the king unto Jerusalem? I am this day four score years old. Can thy servant taste what I eat or what I drink? Can I hear any more the voice of singing man and singing women? Let thy servant, I pray thee, turn back that I may die in my own town by the grave of my father and my mother. And the king kissed Barzillai and blessed him: and he returned unto his own place."

The king's robes and the subject's concealed two old men who know that their chief business now is to get ready to die.

And David makes his way to Jerusalem, very weary. But he is a king and cannot act as though he were a private man. So Joab comes and drags him out to show himself to the people. Joab, of course, is perfectly right. It becomes the king to acknowledge the men who have delivered the kingdom and saved his life. And he goes, but with his heart dead within him. His success is dust and ashes. So life deals with us, the poor puppets of a little day. And so the weary, broken old man retires after his burst of energy to his recovered palace and his broken home to wait for the end.

This is great literature, but surely it is much more. What seems most significant in the whole account and in the way in which it is told is the calm, patient, objective method in which the whole ghastly drama is related, with no favour for David, with no bias against David. Thus it happened once in this our great life, where things do not come by chance. Remorselessly, with the dignity and firmness of a Greek drama of fate, it shows the man who has won through so many personal perils and has lifted his nation up into a new position before the world. He grows slack in his prosperity, first unable or unwilling to control his own appetites, then unfit to control his household which becomes delivered over to lust and hate and greed. At once he becomes unfit to control his kingdom, letting it drop through his lax hands into the power of any intriguer, who happens in this case to be his ambitious and unprincipled son. And the end of all this cannot be prevented by a sudden spurt of feverish resolution and a great effort at the close : the end of such things must be a broken house, a weakened kingdom, because it betrays a sapped confidence.

Contrast it with the earlier and later material available to us and how vastly it stands above them both. Anyone can see how much higher it stands than the stories in Judges or the hymn of Deborah. But do not fail to see also how much more powerful it is than the later pragmatism of the frame in which the stories of the book of Judges were fitted. There is a narrowness of view in the picture of the people sinning and suffering, repenting and being delivered, which does not apply at all in this account. You are in the hands of a man who sees things more clearly as they are, and who, being in touch with the realities of experience, sees how the events of personal and national life come, not by intervention *ab extra,* nor yet by accident, but by the sure inexorable law in the nature of things. The will of Yahweh is in this sure law which determines that righteous, clean and honourable living is in the nature of things. These are the methods of His government of this universe, which is in His hands.

Israel at this period was breeding men who could think, who dared to think, along these rich, fruitful lines. I have said that the immediate problem before the thought of the nation in its religious activity was no longer to reserve the allegiance of the nation to Yahweh, but to determine what was the character of Yahweh, which made Him different from the gods of the nations and which made Him worthy of a solitary and supreme allegiance. It was that they thought of Him as acting thus.

The matter is the more remarkable that the whole account is written without any outward sign of being a purely religious account. It has more of a secular air than the pious reflections of the introductory sections in Judges. But this only proves how the religious point of view saturates all the thought of the nation.

I have dwelt on this account at what may seem undue length, since it may appear a little apart from a purely historical study such as this, to devote so much attention to what may be called a mere literary product of the period. But I have done it deliberately. For one thing, a historical study is of little use unless it can let us see how the men of the time with which we are dealing looked out on life, what they thought of themselves and their nation and the tasks on which they were engaged. Now nothing can do this so well, not even the most careful tabulation of the historical documents which deal with the economic and warlike and external civilization of the time, as some documents which can show us the men thinking aloud on their function and their duty and their world. This is what this priceless document of old Israel does for us.

Besides, to pause on this product of Israel at this period of its history supplies a needed corrective. It is easy to estimate the period too low : and this has been done. Economically, financially, in all the outward gifts of civilization, it was low. Israel must have lived in houses where we to-day should only house pigs. Its towns were destitute of the rudiments of sanitation. It had no books, no newspapers, no system of education. It had not even a decent system of roads to bind the

4*

scattered villages together. And we, who are slaves to machines and drowned in what appear to us necessary adjuncts of civilization, inevitably come to think that the age which had only just passed out of the bronze age was itself at an immensely low stage. Yet it could breed minds capable of judging human life and capable of writing about the movements of human history with the justness and insight of these passages.

No doubt the Egyptians thought of the people who inhabited the hills about their coast road very much as the people of India regard the Afghans of to-day, turbulent nuisances who unfortunately held the passes between them and the further East. And yet they were on the road to a conception of history and life which makes them the masters of the men who despised them. It gives one furiously to think.

Eduard Meyer, the greatest scholar of the documents of antiquity, who brings to thought on Israel's output a mind which has an intimate knowledge of the products of Babylonian and Egyptian thought, makes a just and significant remark in this connection. He says how he cannot sufficiently admire the fact that Greece and Palestine alone wrote history, so different in essence from the dry annals of Babylon and Egypt, history with the movement of life in it and especially with the supple play of development in it.[1] We ought to recognize, and I have tried to let you see, how there dawns in Palestine, so far as culture outwardly is concerned, the lowest civilization of its time, a mental vigour and a moral judgment which set it far above everything which the time produced.

---

[1] *Die Israeliten und ihre Nachbarstämme*, p. 486.

4

AMOS

THE ORIGIN OF THE BOOK

E VERY reader of the Bible will recognize that Amos is
the first prophet whose sayings or oracles appear in the
form of a book. The prophets who preceded him, like Nathan
or Elijah or Micaiah ben Imlah, make their appearance in
the historical records of the nation, and then we are told of
the action they took in relation to certain events in that history and of the sayings they uttered in connection with those
public acts. Amos is not mentioned in the Book of Kings, and
all we know about him is derived from the book which bears
his name. It is natural, therefore, that many who read that
book take it for granted that it was the prophet's own composition. They think of him, probably when his life-work was
coming to a close, as having collected and set down in order
his oracles so that they might serve as his legacy to the following generations.

Now, it must be acknowledged that no one knows with
entire certainty how the book did come into existence. But
there are certain features in the book itself and in what we
know of the prophet's life, which make it highly probable that
Amos did not have any hand in writing it. One of these must
be apparent to any reader who attempts to make out its
meaning and to form a coherent idea of its general teaching.
That is the want of connection between certain of the oracles
of which it is composed. In some passages, for example, in the
two opening chapters, there is no difficulty at all, for the
oracles follow one another in a natural succession. But in
other parts of the book the author appears to start with one
subject, and then, without hint of any reason, to break off
and deal with another. He does not exhaust what he has to

say. Again, one may read three or four consecutive sentences
full of sap and meaning; but when one ponders them for a
little, it is not easy to see why they appear in the order in
which they do. They would be equally suggestive and pregnant if they were differently arranged. Nor does the arrangement of the book in chapters offer any light. The opening
chapter presents a unity, but it breaks off before that unity
has reached its conclusion in what follows. The seventh chapter, again, presents a single theme, since it tells of three visions
which happened to the prophet and culminates in the public
act which resulted from the conviction he drew from the
visions. But in all the other cases it is impossible to resist the
impression that the division into chapters is purely artificial.
It does not present us with successive stages of the prophet's
thought on the themes which engaged his attention. It is difficult to believe that, if the author had arranged his material in
a book, he would have failed so signally to bring out the connection of the things he had to say. We are all, of course,
aware that the ancient Eastern did not think precisely along
the same lines as the modern man of the West. But, with all
allowance for this fact, Amos knew his own mind better than
any one else and must have known how to bring out the connection which ran through all his thinking.

This lack of order, combined with other facts in his life, has
driven modern students to the conclusion that it is wisest to
think of Amos, not as an author, but as a preacher. There is
no exact parallel to him in our modern life, but what comes
nearest to him are the figures of some of the older evangelists
among the Friends. When he was about his ordinary business,
there arose in his spirit the conviction of some message which
he must deliver to his people. At once he left his home and
went, as he did when he appeared in Bethel, to some place
where he was sure to find an audience and delivered his soul
to the men whom he found there. But he never wrote down any
of these sayings, any more than our Lord committed his utterances to paper. What happened was that memorable sayings
in his oracles clung to the minds of the men who had listened
to him and were repeated by those who had been stirred by
his teaching. The fact that many of those momentous words
were uttered in a kind of rude rhythm made them more

memorable and made it easier for them to be handed on. They were afterwards collected at some date which it is impossible to determine, and were then fitted with the title which appears in the opening verse. Again, there is a certain resemblance here to what we possess in the Gospels. What is known as the Sermon on the Mount is a similar collection of the words of the Lord, lovingly put together for the use of the infant Church by the men who revered His memory. But that these were not all spoken at the same time is evident from the fact that several of them appear again, and, when they reappear, are supplied with a picture of the circumstances in which, and the persons to whom, they were originally spoken. A better translation of the heading of the Book of Amos might well be: A Collection of the Oracles of Amos concerning Israel in the day of Uzziah, King of Judah, and of Jeroboam, King of Israel.[1]

THE PERIOD

The Book of Kings has not much to say about Jeroboam II, in whose reign Amos did his work. He succeeded Joash about 780 B.C., and inherited the fruits of renewed vigour which had marked his father's reign. Since he reigned for an un-usually long period, 41 years, he was able to consolidate the kingdom and to give Israel a breathing time of peace, such as it had not known under several of the preceding kings. There was grave need for a period of recovery, because, prior to the reign of Joash, the kingdom had been profoundly shaken, both outwardly and inwardly. During the reign of Omri the country had been drawn into closer relations to its neighbours and had had to face dangers which arose from the designs of Assyria in the West. That king's able policy had helped to

---

[1]Any readers who may be interested in the subject are advised to secure T. H. Robinson's *Translation of the Book of Amos into colloquial English*, published by the National Adult Schools Society. I suspect that Dr. Robinson has carried the division into separate oracles too far, and that there is a real connection between verses where he sees none. I am also sure that he denies to the prophet several utterances which can be justly counted authentic. But there is nothing which can give the ordinary reader so clear an idea of the way in which it is now generally believed that the book came into its present form.

avert the peril, but no sooner was this overcome than a new one had arisen from the increased strength of a nearer neighbour, Damascus, which came under the control of the ambitious Hazael. The Syrian king attacked Israel. The weight of his attack was naturally directed against Eastern Israel where border wars of a peculiarly grisly character, of which Amos has given a vivid picture, wasted the country. The effort to maintain itself had strained the resources of the smaller nation and left it almost exhausted. What brought it relief was the recovery of Assyria, which, reviving its old ambitions on the West, attacked Damascus in the rear. The Syrians were compelled to leave Israel alone in order to meet the greater danger which was threatening on their eastern frontier. This condition of affairs had given Israel the opportunity to recover itself, of which Joash and Jeroboam made prompt and effective use. Jeroboam in particular had taken advantage of it to conquer Moab and to recover the lost territory of his people on the East of Jordan. Israel was restored to its old limits under earlier kings.

Another crisis, however, had arisen to trouble Israel's peace. This time it came not from without but from within. Ahab, influenced by his wife, Jezebel, who was the daughter of a Tyrian king, had permitted the worship of the Phoenician Baal in the kingdom. Whether the king had merely desired to permit the practice of this foreign worship in Israel, or whether Jezebel had aimed at the substitution of Baal for Yahweh, as the acknowledged national God, is far from clear. In either case the policy of the court was deeply resented by the stricter party in Israel. To them such a policy implied a departure from the fundamental principle of their religion— the absolute and undivided allegiance of the nation to its own God; it was nothing less than national apostasy. They could not tolerate that any altar, other than those created in honour of the God of Israel, should be allowed to pollute the holy land. The party found a leader in a young captain of the army, Jehu by name, then engaged in besieging Ramoth Gilead. Supported by them, Jehu, carried out a successful revolution, and, after butchering all the supporters of the opposite party, made himself king. The dynasty which he founded, and of which Joash and Jeroboam were members,

was committed through its origin to uncompromising loyalty
to the national faith.

The natural result was that in the reign of Jeroboam the
people felt more secure than they had been able to do for more
than a generation. Their sense of security was firmly based on
a double foundation. The new dynasty had not only won back
the old limits of the kingdom, but they had done this after
they proved themselves the loyal supporters of the national
religion. Under their guidance the people had shown their
loyalty to the God of their fathers and proved their obedience
to His claim on them. They had blotted out from the land
every vestige of the abominations of the house of Ahab. Their
new security and welcome peace were the reward for this
faithfulness; God had returned in favour towards a loyal
people. He had vindicated their cause in the sight of the
nations and shown Himself as of old their protector against
their enemies. In recognition of the mercy He had shown,
there was a quickening of the outward forms of religion in the
country. The altars smoked with sacrifices, and the people
were thronging to the festivals at the sanctuaries. Men in
Israel were satisfied with what they had done, and were persuaded that their present success was sufficient proof that
their God was satisfied with them. There was no limit to what
they might expect now. Anything further which their God
might do must only be a continuation of what had been so
greatly begun. The day of the Lord for Israel, any day which
might come to it from Him, could only prove afresh His good
pleasure with His loyal servants.

The nation was satisfied with itself and persuaded that its
God was equally satisfied with it. Now a nation which is in
that smug and dangerous estate stands in great need of a
prophet.

THE MAN

So far as knowledge of the circumstances and life of the
prophet is concerned, there are no sources on which we can
draw except the meagre hints supplied by the heading and by
his own utterances. These give no more than the dim outline

of one of the great figures which have often come out of the shadows to leave their impress on their time and on later time through their sense of the presence of God. But a few things are clear. Thus, in the case of a number of the later prophets, the name of the prophet's father has been handed down : Hosea was the son of Be'eri, Jeremiah the son of Hilkiah. Amos has no patronymic and bears no name except his own, so that he was a landless man who worked for others. His sudden emergence out of the desert of Tekoa brings to mind the description John the Baptist gave of himself : I am the voice of one crying in the wilderness. Here was another voice of one crying in the wilderness, and, like that of its successor, it was a voice, not an echo. Indeed it was a voice which was likely to raise many echoes.

When he came to Bethel, he told the priest there that he was a herdsman and a dresser of sycamore trees. The two occupations were not incompatible. For the pastures at Tekoa on the high land to the South of Jerusalem could only be occupied during the winter and spring, when the rains produced enough grass to feed a flock; in the summer heats everything was burned up. On the other hand, the sycamores bore a coarse fig which formed a food for the poor of sufficient importance for the trees to be classed in one passage alongside the olives. Yet the trees themselves needed attention only during the short season when their fruit was ripening, that is, at the time when the Tekoan pastures were bare. It was possible, therefore, for Amos to combine the two occupations, and eke out his livelihood in the two places. But the sycamores cannot grow on the Judean highlands, and, wherever they are elsewhere referred to, appeared as natives of the Shephelah, the maritime plain which runs along the Mediterranean on the East of Joppa. Since the herdsmen were not likely to have their permanent homes in the wilderness, it is further probable that the future prophet's abode was among the sycamores in the plain. He followed the sheep on their annual pilgrimage to the uplands.

The situation of his home gave Amos two things. It was probably on the march where Israel, the northern part of the Holy Land, and Judah met, so that a man who lived in it was helped to realize the unity of the nation which had split into the two kingdoms. Amos showed himself alive to this fact when he addressed his people : they were to him the children of Israel, the whole family which their God had brought up out of Egypt, the nation which He had chosen out of all the families of the earth. They were bound together by the ties of a common heritage and a common destiny. The God who had made them His elect people was coming to judge them both. Yet the man's home could not but give him a wider outlook. For along the maritime plain ran the great coast road which formed the principal corridor between Asia and Africa, between Phoenicia, Damascus and the Tigris-Euphrates valleys on the north and east, the Nile valley on the south and west. The caravans for trade and the armies in time of war followed that road and brought the men who lived along the Mediterranean into touch with the outer world. The peasants there had a wider outlook than that which was possible to the farmers among the hill-glens. The world which Amos knew, and on which he denounced the divine judgment in the oracles which compose his first chapter and the opening verses of the second, corresponded to the two places in which he did his work. Damascus, Philistia and Tyre sent out the traders whose caravans passed and re-passed along the trunk road : Edom, Ammon and Moab occupied the hill ranges and plateaux which filled the horizon of a herdsman on the steppes between Jerusalem and Hebron.

His manner of life supplied the images which he has reproduced in his oracles. His home had been a peasant's cottage, put together with rough, undressed field stones and daubed with clay, in the crevices of which other tenants lurked. He has described a man who took refuge from a bear in one of these houses and added that, even as he leaned panting in fancied security against a wall, a snake bit him out of one of those crevices. Damascus, he said, has threshed Israel with threshing instruments of iron. He had seen the sheaves tossed loose on the threshing-floor and had watched while the oxen dragged the heavy sled, faced on its lower side with flints or studs of iron, across the harvest which it ground into fragments. The remnant of Israel, again, after the Lord had finished His work with His people, was to be like the shin-bone and the tip of an ear which a shepherd gathered in the morning. So the herdsman at Tekoa, when he went about his work at dawn, had come upon the scene of an evening tragedy, where a lion had selected his victim. So he had stooped carefully to gather and carry to his master the proof that the mutton had not found its way into the pot of the shepherd. It is only necessary to contrast his language whenever he came to speak about towns in order to realize where the man felt himself at home. All his vivid phrases disappeared at once, to give place to what is stereotyped. He denounced woe on several of these, but repeated with something of reiteration that the fire should devour the palaces thereof. The towns to him, as to many like him, were chiefly places where rich men lived.

A peasant too he was in his knowledge of what it is for which the common man, whose contentment in the end makes the glory or the shame of all the civilizations, supremely cares. Amos knew, and showed that he knew, how native to their minds, not needing to be taught because God had been beforehand with that revelation, were justice and mercy. He was conscious of how they judge ultimately all the institutions which govern them, the great men who undertake to lead them, and projects which are designed to guide them, by whether they bring or do not bring justice and mercy down to the huts where poor men lie. Let judgment roll down as waters, and righteousness like a perennial stream, he cried aloud. For, where these things failed, there was in his verdict, which is the verdict of all his like, a famine which was worse than any possible hunger for bread, a thirst which was more insistent than any thirst for water.

HIS CALL

To this man, not ill-equipped in some respects for the work which he was to undertake, however imperfectly equipped in certain others, the word of the Lord came. From a rather clumsy expression in the heading to the collected oracles it would appear that the revelation came to Amos while he was actually herding his sheep in the steppe at Tekoa. So he belonged to the company of those who, like Moses in the wilderness of Midian and St. Paul in his eastern retreat, discover in solitude the instant presence of God and the task which is henceforth to claim their entire life. Like them too he never looked back but from that hour became one of the happy company of those to whom life has become high and simple, because they see in it a single purpose and have found their way. Yet he himself did not give this information, nor has he offered the least hint as to how the divine word came to him or how he knew it to be the word of very God. In that he was like many others who are not given to self-inspection or troubled with thoughts over the source of their convictions. What interested him was not how the word came, but the end for which it came and what it behoved him to do because of its coming.

There never seems to have been any hesitation on the part of this prophet such as is reported in the case of some others : there is no hint of a struggle in his mind, prompted by self-distrust or sense of personal unfitness, far less by any fear of consequences. This was the word of the Lord to him, and there was only one thing to do with it. As he himself expressed the matter afterwards : when a lion has roared out of a thicket, who can keep his nerves from twittering; when the Lord has spoken, who can help prophesying? This attitude of mind marked, to be sure, his strength : it marked no less surely his limitation.

He has, however, told one thing about his early experience, when he first realized his call to speak in the name of God, but before he had taken up his public rôle. Since it shows the prophet's thought of the God in whose name he was to speak, it deserves closer examination. There came to him two visions, the meaning of which could not be mistaken. Once a cloud of locusts swept down and devoured every blade of grass in the fields; again a fire appeared so fierce that it licked up the great deep and threatened the land, which was the home of man. That was to be the burden of his message. The Lord was at hand, and the day of His advent must be a fearful looking for of judgment which should devour. The instant response of the new prophet was a prayer of intercession; " O Lord God, I beseech Thee, forgive : how shall Jacob stand, for he is but small?" Not only did he plead for his people in its littleness and its weakness, but he believed that his prayer prevailed. The Lord repented and said, "This shall not be". Only when the same message was repeated in a third vision did Amos desist.

The desert colloquy between the prophet and his God which is overheard between the sudden raising and the dropping of the veil deserves to be remembered in any estimate which is formed of Amos. When we read his accusations of his nation in the name of its God, and hear his denunciations of doom, falling like the blows of an inexorable fate, his message is apt to appear monotonous and even one-sided. The relation between God and Israel seems to be reduced to that between judge and criminal, where the accused may expect strict justice but no more. It is necessary to remember then that behind the arraignment of the people lay this scene. The first instinct of the prophet, when he learned that his message must be one of doom, was to intercede. Nor is that all which the passage suggests. If we should interpret it as no more than the spontaneous reaction of an individual prophet, it would reveal merely the temper of Amos and his unwillingness to believe in such an end for his people. It ought to be recognized that the petition which Amos offered to his God was offered in his capacity as a prophet. Throughout the Old Testament it is the constant privilege of every prophet to intercede for individuals or for the nation. These men, who were nearer God than common men, who knew His mind as other men could not do, whose function it was to reveal His purpose to Israel, prayed for the nation to which they were sent. They dared to do it, because they believed in One who would listen to such prayers for mercy. They knew that mercy was ultimate in the purpose of their God. When He punished, it was to prepare the way for men's return to Him. He resorted to chastisement, only when other means had failed, but He was ever ready to forgive those who returned to Him.

When the third vision had convinced Amos that every other means had failed, he ceased from intercession and went out to announce the advent of the Lord in judgment.

THE SCENE AT BETHEL

Probably the nearest parallel we can find to what was happening at the leading sanctuary in Israel was the mediaeval practice of combining at some famous shrine a holy day in honour of a saint, a fair for transacting business and a junketing. To realize its background and its atmosphere a Scotsman can hardly do better than re-read Burns' *Holy Fair*. While, however, the place and the day gathered a somewhat motley crowd drawn by very different motives, the centre point was the altar where the officiating priest offered sacrifice and where the worshippers brought their gifts, their tithes, their thanksgiving and free-will offerings. That was the reason why we frequently read of the prophets resorting to these centres. They were sure of finding an audience there, and an audience which was interested in religion.

Into the middle of such an audience, engaged in the offices of their religion, and before the altar where the priest was conducting sacrifice Amos strode, and announced that He in whose honour the service was performed was about to bring both Church and State in Israel to a common ruin. His appearance naturally created a sensation. Amaziah the high priest bade him notice that what he was saying was rank sedition, and that in the interests of his own safety he would be wise to seek asylum across the frontier. At the same time the priest sent a hurried messenger to Jeroboam, warning the king as to what had happened. Neither king nor priest was likely to have forgotten that the dynasty had won the throne through an outburst of religious enthusiasm. What had raised it might readily bring it down.

It is easy to pour contempt on the priest for the action which he thus took, but it is also a little cheap. For it is legitimate to ask what else Amaziah, who was charged with the duty of keeping seemly order at a sanctuary, could have done. To dismiss the matter in this perfunctory fashion is simply to shut one's eyes to a perennial difficulty which has always attended a phenomenon like prophecy in connection with religion. Is the individual with his personal conviction always right and is the recognized order of things always wrong? Is there no room for authority in matters of religion?

It may help to bring the large question involved more clearly to mind if we attempt to conceive a parallel case in our own time. Next year, before the General Assembly proceeds to its ordinary business, its members will gather in the High Kirk of Edinburgh to celebrate Holy Communion in order that they may be better prepared for the work which lies before them. Any year an unknown figure might stride up the aisle and, taking his stand in front of the Communion Table, might declare it to be the purpose of Almighty God to bring both the General Assembly and the British Parliament to their swift and fitting doom. The first thought which would rise in the minds of all who were gathered there would be that the man was of disordered mind and that this was a case for a doctor. What is of even more significance is that in nine cases out of ten the instant verdict would be correct. It has pleased God in this our strange world to leave it difficult for men to determine at once when they are brought face to face with a prophet and when they are dealing with a charlatan or a lunatic. All those questions as to how the word of the Lord came to Amos, as to the test by which a man may convince himself first and the world afterwards that it is the very word of God and not the imagination of his own heated brain, are broached at once.

Amos did not attempt to answer them then or at any time. He had his limitations. Instead he replied to the priest : " I was no prophet, nor was I the son of a prophet, but the Lord took me from behind the feeding sheep at Tekoa and sent me here with a message which I can only deliver ". Because it was not his message which he brought, but the divine word, no regulations, even those of a royal chapel, could stop it. The priest was not trying to silence a man, he was attempting to stifle prophecy. It would be as practicable to attempt to stop a burst reservoir with a man's naked hands.

When God had a message for Israel and the world, He took a herdsman of the hills. It was possible, even easy, to silence the messenger : but when he was gone, God could find another, as unexpected and as disturbing as the first. What was impossible, even at a royal chapel, was to evade or turn

aside the divine purpose which was afoot in the world. For
the judgments of the Lord were abroad in the earth, and He
meant that Israel should know that they were, and why they
were, drawing near. He would not fail to find a messenger.

This attitude on the part of Amos implied that prophecy
was inevitable in Israel. It was the very nature of the God of
Israel that He was self-revealing. He made known His will
through His deeds in the world. Now He sent the rain, and
again He withheld it; now the land was ravaged by locusts,
and again it was covered with crops. No man in that period
believed that these matters were governed by natural law,
which was fixed in its processes : everyone saw in them the
acts of those superhuman powers which controlled the lives of
men. When drought came, the gods were angry; when the
watered fields bore abundantly, they were satisfied. But, while
other men must dimly seek to know the mind of those dread
powers, to Amos Israel was not left at the mercy of mere
guesses : " Surely the Lord will do nothing without revealing
His counsel to His servants, the prophets ". Again, since the
destinies of all the nations were in the hands of God, the
events of their changing history served to make known His
purpose in the world. He brought the Syrians from Kir and
the Philistines from Caphtor as surely as He had led the house
of Israel out of Egypt. But the Syrians now occupied Damascus and the Philistines possessed the cities of the maritime
plain, and neither nation knew why they were there or who
had brought them. They were satisfied to believe that they
had won their lands by their own prowess, and convinced that
what they had so won they might use for their own ends. The
border-wars of the one nation might be as pitiless as Syria
chose to make them : the only check they acknowledged was
the thought of what best served their own interests. The
Philistines might enslave a group of villages and sell their
people into captivity : what alone controlled them was
whether it was profitable to exhaust the source of future supplies of men. But Israel knew that it was God who had given

them the land of the Amorites. For He had sent to His people prophets who made them realize the divine aid without which they would still have been in the wilderness, and the divine end which they must serve in the land of His gift. Israel to Amos was in the hands of a self-revealing God and was moving on to the realization of a purpose which was divine in its origin and in its end.

In this the prophet was only expressing an idea which runs through all the Old Testament. Nowhere in it can be found the idea that any true knowledge of God has been reached through man thinking out for himself the problems of the universe and thus arriving either at a conviction of the divine existence or at a personal relation to God. Everywhere it is God who takes the initiative, either by communicating Himself to men, or by instituting a relation to them. In the record of Israel's history, God spoke to Abraham and entered into covenant with him, He appeared to Moses in Midian and entered into covenant with Israel. In the Psalter it appears again : " He made known His ways unto Moses and His acts unto the children of Israel" (Ps. 103). In neither instance is the statement put forward as a dogma which men must accept; it is simply stated as a fact. To its authors and readers the Old Testament was not the story of man's search after God, but the record of God's approach to man. Equally sure were they that He had not withdrawn Himself beyond man's reach. He had revealed Himself and especially had made Himself known to Israel. But here, again, the modern idea that the Semitic peoples have a peculiar genius for religion was utterly alien to the men of that world. Instead they dwelt continually on the failure of Israel to recognize the greatness of the knowledge they had received. To them the selection of their nation for this privilege was due to the inscrutable will of God. But from that time they became the sphere of the self-revelation of God.

It was this last truth which Amos saw more clearly than the rest of his own generation. He believed, as all his people believed, that they became a nation when they were brought out of Egypt, and that the signal action which turned them from a gang of slaves into a people of free men was due to the mighty hand and the stretched-out arm of their God. But

he saw with unfaltering clearness that Israel had not been
redeemed for its own sake. It owed its existence to a great
act in which God had manifested His purpose in the world,
and what brought it into being must continue to be its
strength and its guide. Otherwise it forfeited its right to be
the people of God. Therefore to him the supreme sin of Israel
to which he was sent was that they longed to be rid of the
divine voice : "Ye gave the Nazarites wine to drink and ye
said to the prophets, prophesy not". The messengers of the
God who made them a nation had begun to weary them. But
they could not thus easily be rid of the divine purpose with
them. God, the self-revealing God, could not leave them
alone. He was coming, but this time in judgment.

THE ELECTION OF ISRAEL

The conviction that God had made known His mind to
men and that their faith was not merely the reflection of their
own desires or fears has always been a mighty force in religion. It has supplied the nerve of some of the great movements
in history. The men who held it have won a new confidence
and a new strength. It gave unity and meaning to their world,
when they could believe that it came from the hands of God
and that He had not left it to itself. As there was a divine
mind which had conceived it, so there was a divine purpose
which controlled it. Nor had men been left to search and
grope in order to discover, if they might, its hidden end, for
out of the thick darkness God had spoken to them.

As their universe yielded its meaning so their individual
lives, which had hitherto seemed trivial and brief and in-
consequent, won a new significance. The men themselves were
no longer flotsam, at the mercy of changing circumstance and
driven hither and thither by their own sudden appetites. There
was a way for their feet to walk in, there was a work for their
hands to do, there was an end which they could follow and
even attain; and these were appointed for them by God. When
they took their lives from His hands, they were themselves
taken up into His mighty purpose and at once found themselves. They were the servants of His purpose, and to realize
it gave singleness of end instead of inconstancy, and a patient

endurance. God could use their lives : He meant to do so, since He had stooped to make Himself known to them. They had become His elect.

Such men were also conscious that they were no longer alone, bound to their fellow-men merely by the ties of nature or common interests. Ties of that character were at the mercy of circumstances, and were liable to be broken by the conflicting interests and the restless passions of those who entered into them. Now men were linked together by a common faith and served together an end which was not of this world. Their fellowship was one of the spirit. Therefore it was not confined to the present, but made them realize their brotherhood with those who had served the same end before them and with those who would serve it in the future. They belonged to the company of those to whom God had revealed, to whom He might reveal, Himself.

Accordingly St. Paul's favourite word for the little communities whom he gathered round his Gospel was the elect of God. They were saints, not in virtue of anything which they had done to deserve the title, but because of what God had done for them. He had been pleased to reveal His Son to them, and in that act had chosen the men out of the world : They were His elect people.

What the New Testament said about the Church, the Old Testament tried to fit into the narrower frame of the nation. In the thought of the earlier time Israel had become a nation, because its God had manifested Himself in the world for its sake : He had heard the cry of His people and had come down to deliver them. He had taken the people which He had redeemed into a peculiar relation to Himself which was guaranteed by the covenant into which He condescended to enter with them. Since He Himself was different from the gods of the nations, the relation into which He brought Israel set it apart from all its world. The nation which He had chosen in which to set His name knew Him, as the others could not. Therefore Israel was God's peculiar care, and He could not wholly forsake it : for Him to forsake it would be to forsake His declared purpose toward it. The other peoples of the world might go their own wild way, but Israel was secure in the keeping of Him who had made it His own,

Their sense of a common heritage had bound them into a closer unity among themselves. Israel was a brotherhood, since it was united by more than the ties of a common blood. The promise of God had been given to the fathers, it was made sure to the living present, it could not fail their children. They stood together, linked by a common destiny and separated from all the world. They must live together, as befitted men who were conscious of their unity. The sense of this bond among Israelites showed itself in their law. It forbade the nation to treat a Hebrew slave in the fashion which was permitted if the man had been a heathen : it forbade a Hebrew to take usury from his fellow-Hebrew, though he might take all he could get from one who did not belong to the race. As Israel's religion was national, so was its ethic : God had chosen one people and set it apart in a world which did not own the same obligations. The whole people would have understood and agreed with Amos when he said in the name of their God : you only have I chosen out of all the families of the earth. Israel was the elect of God.[1]

But for a nation to believe that it has been peculiarly favoured of God may become the worst of all dangers. To know that it has been set apart from all the rest of the world may breed arrogance and contempt for other men : and to believe that God has thus separated it may only serve to justify its attitude. To be convinced that its God had brought it into a peculiar relation to Himself and cared for it may issue in the confidence that He will protect and favour it, whatever it may become. The future could only make more patent the special favour which God had shown to Israel, and that favour must be of the character which Israel desired and its world could appreciate. The conditions of the time were such as to make that temper more prevalent among the people. They had vindicated at some cost the cause of God by making sure that He alone was worshipped in the

---

[1] It is not without interest to compare the pathetic modern efforts to make a nation something more than a bundle of atoms, united by race, or by history, or by common dangers, or by common interests. Realizing that only a spiritual bond, born of a common faith, can unite what is otherwise a sand-heap, several of them are attempting to conjure into life such faith. So when men have rejected a God whom they serve, they create a god after their own image who will serve them.

Holy Land. They were thronging to His altars and giving Him what was His due in his sacrifices. Already He had approved their zeal by giving them what all the world must recognize as the evidence of His favour, for they had been able to win back all the land which He had promised to the fathers. They could expect only good at the hands of God. The future was bright with the assurance that He would deal favourably with them.

Amos came to remind them of the character of the God they worshipped. He was the God of righteousness and loving-kindness, and He had chosen them to be the sphere of this self-revelation. His day was at hand. He was coming to visit His people, and that meant to test and try their ways in the light of what He was and of what He had declared them to be. He had created them to serve His purpose in the world, but was it being fulfilled among them? They were tired of His messengers and only wanted to be left alone. They were multiplying their sacrifices, but men brought to the altars the proof that they were wronging their neighbours. They were not living as befitted men who were nearer a God of righteousness and love. God had chosen Israel out of all the families of the earth: therefore He would visit upon them their iniquities. The nation wanted to be let alone, to enjoy its new security and to expect more good. Because, said Amos, the God of Israel is what He is, and because He is self-revealing, He will never let us alone. In their present temper the day of the Lord must be darkness and not light.

THE NATIONS

While, however, Israel was the peculiar sphere of the divine self-revelation, that did not mean to Amos that God was indifferent to the life of the other nations. Not only did He have the Philistines and the Syrians under His control, moving them like pawns on the vast chess-board of the world. He had also in some measure made His will known to them. They had not, like Israel, received law or prophets, but they were not destitute of some knowledge of Him who controlled their fate. Their knowledge was sufficient to bring them in as guilty in the day when God came to judge the world. He had revealed Himself so clearly that He had the right to judge it.

In the oracles which have been grouped together at the beginning of the book Amos envisaged the Semitic world which surrounded Israel, and, as he passed it in review, he denounced judgment on it in the name of the God of Israel. Two things stand out in the catalogue. On the one hand, there was no loyalty or honour among those peoples : Tyre had broken the brotherly covenant and Edom had pursued his brother with the sword. The cement which holds human society together, a man's faith to his word, was gone, and nothing was left to lend cohesion to the heap. On the other hand, and more prominently, the nations were destitute of pity. Amos spoke of the ferocious border-wars in Gilead, where Damascus slaughtered women and men in order to annex a strip of territory. He recalled how Philistia had emptied a village and left it a waste, in order to make some money. He ended with Moab, where a king had carried his vendetta beyond the grave, for he had burned the bones of a neighbour into lime. The act had not even the poor excuse of being profitable : it brought nothing but the gratification of hate.

The world, as Amos saw it, was moral chaos. Because it stood for nothing which was enduring, it itself could not endure. In the day when God came to judge His world, it could only pass away like an evil dream which had too long troubled the lives of men. When God arrived, and the world of seemliness and order which was His order emerged, the dream must simply pass away, for it had no hold on reality. Only that which belonged to the divine held any power of endurance.

Yet the ground on which the prophet in the name of his God doomed the nations was not the law of the two tables, which had been revealed to His own people. It was something which antedated Horeb, belonged to man as man and had been made known to all mankind, so instinctive was it and so compelling in its native truth. Amos was feeling after the conception of a law which did not embody itself in a contract, because it was before every contract, because it was the invisible, yet necessary, basis of every contract. He had risen to the idea of a law which all men must acknowledge,

because they were men, not because they were the chosen
nation, and which was bound up with the very constitution
of this world. Without it the world went back to primaeval
chaos. There was a relation, unacknowledged but real, between God and humanity. Because He was by His very nature
self-revealing, He could not leave men alone.

It was an amazing conception to come from one who was a
herdsman and a dresser of sycamore trees, and it forms his
great contribution to religion. The limits of this lecture make
it impossible to develop at all adequately the amplitude of this
feature of Amos' teaching. but it may be possible to suggest
two directions in which its influence appeared.

MONOTHEISM

Thus it contributed more than anything else to make the
unity of God primary in the Hebrew faith. That the prophet
was a monotheist can be seen from the other features of his
teaching. He believed that the God of Israel controlled the
forces of nature; He could withhold the rain or send it as He
willed : He could command a fire which devoured the great
deep. Equally Amos believed that the God of Israel determined the fate of other nations than His own people. But it is
possible to bring analogies to this teaching from the religions
of Egypt and Babylonia; it is even possible to say that the
idea of the divine unity was widely broached in the eastern
world of that time. To conceive of one supreme deity instead
of the crowding gods which engrossed and bewildered the
minds of men was a natural thought to arise in' men's minds
as soon as they began to think at all. The rise of the great
empires, which were then beginning to consolidate into one
the petty kingdoms, was fitted to support, if not to suggest,
the same situation in the government of the world. To acknowledge one supreme sultan on the throne of the universe
was to own a single allegiance, and to bring a unity into its
concerns. It satisfied the thoughtful mind.

All that was wholly foreign to Amos's thought on the subject. He saw a world which was made one in the moral purpose of Him who controlled it, and who was bringing it to
its sure issue. Whatever conflicted with this was doomed. It

might maintain itself for a little time, but it was bound to collapse sooner or later, because it had no hold in reality. The one enduring reality was the will of God, and He would not suffer His world to reel down into chaos. Because He had His own purpose to fulfil through it and His own end to which He would bring it, He could not leave the world alone. In His own time and in His own way He would intervene in order to bring it back to the right course. The God of all seemliness and good order would in His day appear to destroy that which had only led to confusion and to set up in its place that which was after His mind. Amos's monotheism was essentially religious in its origin and in its character. As such, it was no speculation of the type which was engaging the minds of a little circle of thinkers of Babylonia or Egypt: it was a conviction which was based on faith in a self-revealing God. Because it was this, it could rise in the mind of a herds-man and dresser of sycamore trees, who was not brooding over the mystery of the universe, but was living by faith in the God of his fathers. Because too it was essentially religious, it did not remain the property of a little clique of theorists. It could go abroad into the world and be welcomed by all who held the same faith. It could become the property of all who were like-minded to the prophet, for it was born out of the common faith which they and he held, and it was fitted to stay up the hearts and to strengthen the efforts of all who shared its initial conviction. The result has been that Israel has made this part of the prophet's teaching its own and has never let it go. The Jew has never evolved much of a creed: indeed his faith must often be the source of despairing wonder to all who cannot understand how religion can ever exist with-out a coherent system of theology. But he has always held fast to one dogma, for which, however narrowly he construed it, he has even been prepared to die. He owes it largely to the work of a prophet who made monotheism an essential part of his religion.

UNIVERSAL RELIGION

In another direction, however, through the attitude he took to the nations outside Israel, Amos was preparing the way for something greater, greater perhaps than he himself realized. His conviction that Israel held a peculiar relation to God so that it was the elect nation did not to him exclude the fact that God held a real relation to the other peoples of the world. It was not the same relation as that into which it had pleased God to admit His own people, but it was equally real. For it was based upon the same firm foundation as the covenant with Israel : it was the outcome of the nature of God, who could not hold aloof from any of His creatures. He had made Himself more clearly known to some men than He had to others; but even those others were not entirely destitute of a knowledge of His will. The knowledge which they had, inadequate though it was, was real within its limits. It was also due to revelation, for, to the Hebrew thought of that time, all knowledge of the divine will was only possible through God's communication of Himself.

Some who read this may justly object that it is at least remarkable to find that the only use which Amos made of the relation which he thus conceived to exist between God and humanity was that he counted it sufficient to bring in the heathen as guilty in the day when God visited His world. A relation which only served to justify doom may well appear to be a somewhat barren thing. Yet it must be recognized that the same thing may be said about the prophet's message to his own people; its chief burden was to proclaim judgment on Israel for its breach of the covenant. The reason for this attitude, both to Israel and the nations, is to be found in the three visions which came to Amos immediately after his call; the content of all three was that the world was ripe for a judgment which could no longer be delayed. He conceived himself to be sent out in the capacity of the messenger of that which was on its way, in order that the men to whom he was sent might not be without a warning of what was at hand. What is true there about Amos is in a certain measure true of most of the prophets of the Old Testament. They abound in denunciation of the sins of their nation. So largely do their oracles deal with the topic of judgment that they are apt to appear a little monotonous to many modern readers. If we would escape from this impression, we must pierce behind the stream of recurrent judgment and try to realize the positive elements which it contained. What did it imply as to the character of Him who brought the judgment and as to the character of those on whom it fell? What was there in the nature of Him in whose name His servants spoke which made it inevitable that He reacted against the foulness of the nation and the world? He alone of all the gods of the nations reacted against disorder and pitilessness and want of faith, so that, when His messengers inveighed against these hateful things, they were insisting on what He was.

So the seed of a great ideal lay behind Amos's judgment of the nations. To him the coming catastrophe was no natural calamity, the inevitable collapse of a civilization which found no place for good faith or pity; it was the direct intervention of God who thereby removed what prevented His purpose from having its way in the world. The nations as well as Israel were included in the scope of the divine counsel and must have their share in all which it brought; they could not be shut out in the day when God revealed Himself. Nor could Israel shut itself away in a proud isolation, as though it alone was the object of the divine care, or as though the world in which it lived had no place in His mind.

Amos did not develop the ideal which had dawned on him, above all he did not attempt to relate it to his conviction that God had revealed Himself in a peculiar way to His own nation. One who had begun life as a herdsman and who had become a revival preacher was not exactly fitted to follow out the implications there or to develop a coherent system of thought. But it was there in the oracles which his disciples reverently collected and, like every rich and fruitful ideal which has been once lodged in a religious community, it could not die. The world of men could not be cut up into separate compartments. For it was one in the purpose of God who controlled it and who by His nature could not stand aloof from His creatures. There was the germ of the conception of a religion which was universal, not national, in the prophet's thought of his God.

5

5

HOSEA

The Period

THE death of Jeroboam II was the signal for an outburst of sheer confusion, a condition of confusion from which Israel never recovered. This coincided with a grave change in the outward conditions of the nation, namely, the recovery of Assyria from its temporary collapse before the power of Armenia with its resultant effect in leaving the Empire free to resume its forward movement into Syria. It coincided, that is to say, with the new vigour in the Assyrian Empire, rather than resulted from it. For the collapse of Israel was so sudden and so complete, and in particular it antedated by so long the actual contact of revived Assyria with Israel, that one is compelled to the conclusion that it was, if not entirely due to, at least accompanied by, grave inward corruption, and that the approach of Assyria supplied little more than the touch which is enough to start decay in a pear that is already rotten ripe.

Now, seen from this point of view, the collapse of Israel confirms for us Amos's estimate of the conditions existing among his people, and enables us to believe that the prophet was right in the main in his severe strictures. It serves also to confirm Hosea's view, which in a certain measure is even darker than Amos's. Such men's witness always does need confirmation. As the prophets are not absolutely reliable witnesses to the details of history, one welcomes confirmation of the ugly collapse of the state after Jeroboam II.

Tiglath-Pileser III (745-27 B.C.) was one of the great world conquerors. For some six years he was busy settling accounts with the hillmen on the east and north of Nineveh and repairing the confusion into which Assyria had fallen as a result of their attacks. Then, about the close of the year 740, he resumed the Assyrian push for the west and succeeded in making Arpad in North Syria tributary. So formidable was he that Rezon of Damascus and Hiram of Tyre sent him tribute. As his communications were secure through the submission of Damascus, he next subdued Hamath *c.* 740 or 739. His closer approach to the coast brought him nearer Palestine and we find Menahem of Israel paying tribute. Through this campaign Assyria not only reached the Mediterranean but touched and threatened Egypt's sphere of influence. Thus the two great empires were brought face to face. Palestine as the connecting link became the sphere of intrigue between the two world powers both of which were scheming for influence.

But, just as the statesmen could not ignore the presence of Assyria on their borders, as little could the religious leaders. For one point of Assyria's policy was that it required from every state which entered into alliance with it or which was subject to it recognition of its supreme god. So far as we know, the measure was not religious in its motive. It has rather interesting analogies to the practice of the Roman Empire in deifying the Emperor. I have never been able to believe that the intellectual society of Rome, with men like Tacitus and Cicero and Pliny among its members, ever took the business seriously as though it really meant that the emperor was a god. What they deified was the Empire in the person of its head. The incense thrown on to the altar before Caesar was a form of allegiance to the Empire. All the nations which were polytheistic and all the men who did not take their religion seriously accepted this with a shrug of their shoulders. But Rome to its mingled astonishment and disgust ran up against the prejudices of the Christian Church which did take its religion seriously. In exactly the same way, Assyria ran up against little Israel which under the guidance of its leaders took its religion seriously. The result is that from this time we find Israel never submitting to Assyria, continually rebelling against it in spite of the appalling consequences of such rebellion. Only when Judah came under the power of the Persian Empire do we find the little nation taking a different attitude toward its foreign masters. The reason is obvious. With the accession of Cyrus we see for the first time the appearance of an Empire which we would call civilized, an Empire, that is, which did not think its subjects were there to be exploited, but tried in its own way to admit them to be partners in a larger entity. Immediately on his accession Cyrus issued an edict which meant toleration for religion in every corner of his far-flung Empire. Sheshbazzar brought it to Jerusalem and actually laid the foundation stone of the new temple to Yahweh. From this time the Jews became loyal.

Now, what I should like you to notice is that this new condition of affairs with all the difficulties it brought was not due to any overt act on the part of Israel. Assyria was there with its ambitions and its overwhelming power on one side : Egypt with its ambitions and its natural fears on the other. Between them lay Israel, and no action on its part could alter the situation. What it had to do was what we all have to do in this world at times—determine what we ought to do in a world which is not our creation.

The influence of these intrigues and counter-intrigues of the two great Empires shows itself in the utterances of the next great prophet to whom we have to turn. For it is to the balancing between the rival promises and threats of Egypt and Assyria and to the consequent division of his nation between rival factions with the danger to its own distinctive life which for him was bound up in its religion that Hosea seems to refer in 5 : 3; 7 : 11; 8 : 9; 12 : 1. Again it is the penalty which must result from this faction rivalry which he appears to denounce in 9 : 3, 6; 10 : 6; 11 : 5. One only records these utterances in passing in order to illustrate how the events of the time were having their effect on religious men. The question remains to be asked as to the grounds on which the prophet based his objection and what were the spiritual results he dreaded.

This brings us down to 738 when Menahem paid tribute to Assyria. To this 2 Kings 15 : 19 ff. refers : the Pul mentioned there was Tiglath-Pileser III. It is probable that the submission of Menahem was secured by the Assyrian King sending a detachment south after his capture of Hamath. It would need no more than such a detachment, since, on the evidence of the Jewish historians, the Israelite king, so far from opposing Assyria, was relying on Tiglath-Pileser and supporting himself on the throne by this extraneous authority.

Now, with this shift in the world's politics as the background, take the record of the kings who followed Jeroboam II. Out of the six rulers four were assassinated and one died in captivity. The summary in itself, even without commentary, is eloquent of the disturbed conditions in which Israel found itself.

We must, however, glance at the details. Zechariah, Jeroboam's son and immediate successor, died by a conspiracy after a reign of no more than six months. Since the man could not have had time in the brief period to rouse such violent opposition as was able to organize itself and pull him down, the conclusion is that some discontent which could not come to a head under the strong hand of the father saw its opportunity under the son and broke out before Zechariah could seat himself firmly on the throne. The fact is to me another evidence that the priest at Bethel had a justification for his action, when he sent the special messenger to court to warn Jeroboam about the appearance of Amos with his seditious preaching. Even at the close of Jeroboam's reign matters were uneasy.

Shallum, the leader of the rising, was able to maintain himself only for a month. This again demands explanation. What is clear is that the conspirators had not the country behind them, but that the business was rather of the nature of an intrigue which failed. What is *possible* is that the intrigue had been fostered by Egypt, for we find that Menahem who deposed and killed Shallum and who was the military governor in the old capital, Tirzah, was definitely anti-Egyptian. He supported himself by the help of Assyria, sending tribute as we have seen to Tiglath-Pileser at Hamath. This policy kept him in power for the rest of his life.

When, however, his son Pekahiah succeeded in 735, the other faction saw its opportunity and took it. Pekah ben Remaliah was anti-Assyrian. He murdered Pekahiah and entered into league with Rezon of Damascus and we find him later trying, in league with Damascus and Phoenicia, to force Judah under Ahaz into a coalition against Assyria.

Now it ought to be possible to recognise from this sketch the general situation, if it were only to measure by it some of

Hosea's oracles. These kings who follow each other in quick succession are to us names and no more. They stand for nothing of any abiding value. Sometimes they seem to stand for less than nothing, since one may suspect that some served no more than their personal ambitions and personal interests which are a minus quantity. Even when some of them represent a policy, it is the mere policy of deciding whether it would be better for them and their state to become an appanage of the Assyrian or of the Egyptian Empire. Actually we find Hosea having a good deal to say about the kingdom. In one case he sums up the matter in a somewhat significant phrase. Speaking in the name of Yahweh, he says: " Ye have made for yourselves kings, but not by Me." It is as though he would say, Kings and kingdom came into existence to serve the nation and enable it better to serve its God. They were summoned into being to fit Israel better for serving its supreme King. They stand now for nothing real, nothing which holds of the eternal.

One can see how the prophets experienced a revulsion of feeling against what the kingdom had become and how this might easily pass into a revulsion against the kingdom in itself. That is why I am inclined to set in this period the account in Samuel which takes this attitude to the kingdom. It was the expression of this bitter experience of the way in which the kingdom, as a matter of fact, had disappointed the high hopes of the men who founded it for other ends and with other views.

Devout men might uneasily feel that the result of the kingdom had been to entangle the people in this world of human ambition and to make them forget the greater interests and issues for which the divine election of the nation stood. It is understandable even that there might rise an honest difference of opinion on the question. Some men might say that the kingdom was a creation of the faith, that it was an institution which was a means for maintaining the faith. It must at all costs be maintained. Other men might declare that it was a mere creation of the faith and that now when it was threatening the purity of the faith, it were better away.

THE BOOK

The gravest difficulty which meets us in the Book of Hosea is simply this, that the text is the worst preserved in the whole Old Testament. In certain passages it is not possible to make sense out of it at all without having resort to conjecture. I could wish that sometimes the R.V. translators had had the courage to say that their rendering was purely tentative. In these circumstances a teacher is torn in two directions. He is tempted continually to justify some position which he holds by entering into details which it is difficult for his students to follow. And, when he refuses to do this, he is troubled by the shame of the scholar in operating with a text for basis which he cannot lay before those whom he asks to follow his conclusions.

One thing, however, I should like to say, because I think you could all follow it with a little closeness of attention, and because it has a bearing on a larger matter than the mere Book of Hosea. You cannot have failed to note, even in glancing over the book, that the first three chapters which contain the story of the prophet's relations to Gomer and its application to the condition of Israel are quite different in character from the rest of the book. The other chapters contain a collection of oracles : these contain an incident with the allegorical application of it. Well, let me add to this what you could not learn from merely reading over the book that the text of the early chapters is much better than that of Chapters 4-14. Probably their form led to this. It was easier to keep the correct text in one case than in the other. Possibly even Chapters 1-3 may be the nucleus of the whole, taken from a different source, some account of the prophet's life and fortunes, while Chapters 4-14 are the collection of his great sayings.

Now, inside Chapters 1-3, there are three passages which have roused suspicion. The first is the opening verse. There we find Hosea's activity dated by the reigns of certain kings of Judah and the date is the same as that which appears as a heading to the Book of Isaiah. Yet, since Hosea worked in

North Israel and since his writings must have been collected
there, it was not natural to date his book by the reigns of
kings in Judah. And this is not all that serves to suggest that
the title of the book had been added at a later date and is not
wholly relevant. For the prophet's activity is referred to as
belonging to the period of only one Israelite king, Jeroboam
II. Now, this is so inadequate as to be misleading. Hosea may
have begun his career in the reign of Jeroboam, but, as we
have already seen, he refers in his oracles to incidents and
conditions which belong to a later time. Even if he began his
work under that king, he must have done the more important
part later. But again, we find in 1 : 10–2 : 1 E.V., three verses
which have always aroused surprise. They occur immediately
after the woes denounced on Israel through the symbolic names
of Hosea's three children, Jezreel, Lo-ruhamah and Lo-ammi.
And they deliberately reverse these three woes. But, in deliberately reversing them, they hopelessly interrupt the connections.
For 2 : 2 begins again with an interpretation of the first three
woes and an allegorical application of these to the condition of
Israel. And not only do they thus interrupt the natural connection, but they anticipate the conclusion of the whole allegory in 3 : 4 ff., where Hosea sums up finally what is the
purpose of God's dealing with Israel. The verses are justly
suspect.

And yet again these verses of the conclusion 3 : 4 f. raise
their own difficult questions. Hosea has said in 3 : 3 that
Gomer was isolated with a view to her moral improvement—
" Thou shalt abide for me many days and be no man's wife."
She who has abused these relations should be apart from
them, destitute of them for a period. We expect then to hear
that Israel, who in the allegory is Gomer, should be also
isolated for a period with no relations to Yahweh whom she
has betrayed. Consequently we are not surprised to read that
the children of Israel should remain without sacrifice and
without *mazzebah*, without *ephod* and without *teraphim*—
all means of intercourse with Yahweh or with Baal. But what
has the mention of kings and princes to do with this? Nor
are we surprised to read that in the end Israel, purged and
solemnized by her experience, should return to Yahweh with
a right mind in the consummation. But why should the child-

ren of Israel be described as returning to David their king?
What has the Davidic kingdom to do in this connection?

Now, the usual explanation of these three different sections
is to regard them as additions from the exile, that amazing
period which seems to have been what Voltaire said about
Habakkuk, *capable de tout*. Yet the explanation breaks down
in every case. Thus it fails to explain why the man dated by
the kings of Judah and put in an incorrect or imperfect date by
the kings of Israel. In connection with 1 : 10-2 : 1, it ignores
the terms of the promise, that, "in the place where it was said
to you, ye are not my children, it should be said, ye are the
sons of the living God." Evidently to men who wrote this
clause Israel was still living in the place where its doom had
been pronounced. Finding again the statement that Israel
should go up from the land, and recognizing that this will not
fit the condition of the exile, it boldly changes the text and
reads " the lands " with no authority except the need to make
it fit a theory. Yet the land from which the people are to go
up is the same place where the doom is to be reversed, that
is, Israel is still living in its own land.

In connection with the final verses again, it is possible to
say that, when Israel seeks David its king, the meaning is that
the nation should seek Messiah. David, then, is the symbol of
the Messianic hope. But how about the princes of the earlier
verse? What have princes to do with Messiah? And if we
take the king and the princes of the earlier verse in their
natural sense, we must take David their king in the same.

The explanation I would suggest is as follows. Hosea was a
North Israelite prophet. His oracles were collected and preserved there. But at some time they must have been, not only
transferred to Judah, but adopted and accepted by Judah. It
is from Judah and through Judah that we have received the
book. When was this done? It must have been done before
the exile. In my judgment it was done during the period of
Josiah. Josiah was attempting to undo the work of Jeroboam
I and to unite the derelict province of Israel with Jerusalem.
One of the means he took to effect this was to bind the two
people together by their common religious tie. He made Jerusalem the only centre for worship in the country and by
destroying the altar at Bethel compelled the Israelites to come

5*

to the temple. But he also gathered the religious literature of
the north and incorporated it in that of Judah. Among the
rest was brought over the Book of Hosea.

Naturally the book received a new heading : it was now
dated by the period of the Judaean kings. And, since the men
knew generally that the northern prophet was a contemporary
of their own Isaiah, they set him down to the some period.
But this will not explain why Hosea is falsely or inadequately
dated by Jeroboam alone. The LXX. shelves that riddle. For
the LXX. connects the date under Jeroboam directly with v. 2
and says that Hosea's first revelation came under that king,
precisely as we read in Amos that he received his first revelation when he was among the shepherds in the reign of
Jeroboam two years before the earthquake. The new editor
took this date to refer, not to the first oracle, but to them all
and made Jeroboam parallel to the three kings of Judah.

But he also inserted the little section 1 : 10-2 : 1. Then we
understand at once why we should hear about the place and
the land. Israel is still living in part in its own land. And
where the doom was uttered, there it is to be reversed. And
from this land where the people are, the people shall go up.
The word is the technical word for going up in pilgrimage.
The nation is to go up to Jerusalem now in the day of its
renewed fortune. Before they so go, they shall appoint themselves one head. The programme is the programme of the
Josianic reform : the ideal of a nation united politically and
religiously under one political leader and in reverence at
one sanctuary.

The same thing explains the curious phrases about the king
and princes and David their king in the last verses of Chapter
3. The time of Israel's trial and abandonment is the time
during which it has lived under Assyrian domination without
a king and princes of its own. But this is all past. And in its
place has come the day when the entire nation shall unite
under the old Davidic king and seek Yahweh its God in the
centre of its cult. What Hosea saw to be the outcome of the
consummation, when men sought Yahweh in repentance, is to
his later editor the outcome of the hard discipline of years
already past. Now, when the brighter future is dawning, the
nation shall be one in outward and seemly order with its

national and historical king, with its own worship of Yahweh, the God of the fathers.

But, while we have to acknowledge that the book has received a certain amount of revision when it was thus adapted for use in united Israel, we can be confident that Hosea began his activity under Jeroboam II. And further we can be tolerably sure that most of the prophecies, if not all, were not later than 734. For in one or two passages Hosea alludes to Gilead as still in the possession of Israel, for example, 6 : 8; 12 : 11, and does not leave the impression that any catastrophe had befallen that district. Now in 734 Tiglath-Pileser III swept away into capitivity the inhabitants of the district beyond Jordan (2 Kings 15 : 29). It is possible that the book is composite. First came Chapters 1 and 3, telling the story of Hosea's call with the account of his experiences in connection with his marriage, which, as I hope to point out, is integrally related to his call. Along with this would naturally go his exposition in Chapter 2 of this marriage experience of the prophet in the form of an allegorical reference of it to the relation between Yahweh and Israel. After this comes a collection of loose, undated prophecies, about the date and reference of which we must conclude from their contents. The main period then of the prophet's work will, as Driver concluded,[1] be between 743, when Jeroboam II died, and 734 or 735. And this is the period which has been rapidly sketched above. Only I should add that we must not pronounce that no oracles can date later than 734. My reason for differing from Driver is that, while the references to Gilead which he has adduced are enough to prove that the oracles in which they occur must have been spoken before Tiglath-Pileser's campaign, they do not prove that no oracles were spoken after that time. The difference between us is really on the question of how the oracles came to be collected. He thinks of them still as pretty long and almost speaks as though they were put together by the prophet. I can only see in them much briefer oracular utterances and am quite sure that they were not collected by Hosea himself.

There are several passages which have been rejected, partly

---

[1] Driver, *Introduction to the Literature of the Old Testament,* 9th ed. p. 302. Driver dates Jeroboam's death in 746. [Ed.].

because they interrupt the course of the thought, partly because they imply a line of thought alien to Hosea's prophecies :- 1 : 7; 3 : 5 about David their king; 1 : 10; 2 : 1; 4 : 15 ff.; 6 : 11; 8 : 14; 14 : 1-9.

As to their rejection on the ground that the sentences break the course of the thought, what has already been said on the fact that there is not a course of thought is enough to warn us against being too ready to apply such a criterion to sentences which have always been recognized as strung together in the loosest connection.

And for the theological portrait of Hosea, which leads especially to the rejection of 14 : 1-9, that connects itself with questions which arise also with reference to Amos, that is, it is based on the impossibility of the early prophets uttering anything except words of doom, or on views as to the early prophets being primarily concerned with what the events of their time must bring to pass or with what Yahweh is capable of bringing to pass.

Apart from Chapters 1-3 which form a connected narrative with a definite prophecy based on that, the book consists, as Jerome saw long ago, of a series of broken, abrupt, ill-connected even unconnected statements, full of flashes of insight, unique in style among all the utterances of the prophets, bearing often the stamp of authenticity on their face. Jerome said, " *Osee commaticus est et quasi per sententias loquens,*" meaning exactly this composition in broken detached clauses. Dr. Driver sees in this style " the expression of the emotion which is stirring in (the prophet's) heart : his sensitive soul is full of love and sympathy for his people; and his keen perception of their moral decay, and of the destruction towards which they are hastening, produces in consequence a conflict of emotions, which is reflected in the pathos and force, and ' artless rhythm of sighs and sobs,' which characterise his prophecy."[1] I have neither desire nor intention to deny the truth of this : but I think it worth while to maintain that we have not the right to take it for granted that the sayings are in our hands as they were originally uttered. And the form in which they have come shows rather what we might expect if we clearly recognize how we have the broken utterances of all that a people

[1] Driver, *loc cit.*, pp. 305-6.

remembered of the sayings of one of its great men, one of the greatest men who were ever sent to alleviate and to give meaning to a hard time in a nation's life.

Perhaps, in closing this brief review of the book, it may be worth while to direct the reader's attention to a division of the material from Chapter 4 to Chapter 14, which is to be found in Driver's *Introduction to the Literature of the Old Testament*.[1] Dr. Driver considers it possible, not merely to divide the long series of oracles into sections, but even to assign to them tentative dates. Personally I cannot feel satisfied with any division of the material. It seems too loosely hung and amorphous to be capable of such division and still less to be tolerant of fixed dates. But I may be unduly influenced by my conception of the prophecies as consisting of short, unconnected oracles. Others may find Driver's division of the material valuable and suggestive. At least a different point of view is offered here, a different method of approach to the study of the book and a different angle from which to look at it all. And this is always valuable.

THE MAN

About the personal life of the prophet we know nothing at all, except the name of his father from which we can conclude that he was a man of some position, and the tragic story of his family history which has been incorporated into the book. But we are able to conclude from the whole tenor of his oracles that he was a man of the north country through and through.

Immediately before the little state came to an end, when it was in its death-throes, torn by dissension within and attacked by its great enemy from without, it gave voice to this great utterance, one of the greatest and most deservedly influential products of all its history. It is as though, before it vanished from the stage of history, and from independent life as a nation, Hosea gathered the best it had produced, the outcome of the travail and the hope of its past, and handed this on, its contribution for the help of the following generations.

[1] Driver, *loc cit.*, pp. 303-4.

And so again, when Judah in turn came to be on its deathbed as a political force and a national entity, Jeremiah came to gather up its contribution to humanity and to say— this is the salvage from the apparent wreck, this is what we hand on for perpetual memory.

Still later, when the whole Jewish polity was drawing near to the tragedy of the year 70, when the temple was on the point of disappearing before the flame of Rome's war, never to be rebuilt, a greater than Hosea and Jeremiah rescued the precious heritage of the past.

It is a striking fact that we have these three successive voices coming from the three crises in the national life. And what makes the fact more striking is that each of the three builds on, and is intimately associated with, his predecessor or predecessors. Jeremiah is saturated through and through with the principles and teaching of Hosea, as over against those of Amos. And Hosea is precisely the prophet of the old economy from whom our Lord quotes with the greatest freedom and with whose spirit He seems to have felt Himself in the closest sympathy. I mention this not merely as an interesting fact. Interesting facts are often dangerous, when they are merely accidental and do not lead us to a fundamental principle with which they are in relation. Now, the three facts which I have cited seem to stand in integral relation to a common principle.

In each of the three cases, it is when the outward form, the national casing of the religion, is breaking up that the great voice appears, seizing the permanent and non-national features of the past, preserving them as the enduring element out of the past and handing them on as salvage and inspiration for the future. All the three are beyond the national limits and are dealing with the eternal and universal factors in this faith.

When he is set in such a great succession, Hosea is recognized as at once the most suggestive, the most spiritual and therefore ultimately the most influential voice from the Old Testament. The fact only makes one regret the more that his actual messages have been so badly preserved, alike in themselves and in their historical connection. Not only are the eleven chapters (which follow Chapters 1-3) made up, as I have already stated, mostly of fragments of great utterances flung together without connection and without apparent effort to provide any, but also we are unable to tell where they were spoken and to whom, what prompted the prophet to say exactly the things he did say, in what historical circumstances and under what conditions they seemed to Hosea the needed things for his nation's life, over against what movement inside Israel's mind they were set.

Occasionally, as in the case of 8 : 9 to which I have recently referred, we may be able to see behind the prophet's words rival political factions fighting like vultures for posses-sion of the derelict carcase of Israel. Often we can learn, from the references to the rival schemes of pro-Egyptians and pro-Assyrians, how fiercely the intrigues were carried on from the one side or the other. But how these party moves affected the minds of men in Israel, how they touched the way men actually lived, how they influenced the way they prayed, we do not know. And, when once we recognize that the prophets were closely related to the concerns and life of their time and were speaking words which were meant to tell on these, it is not difficult to realize that we may occasionally fail altogether to appreciate a reference and so, failing to appreciate the reference, may misinterpret the whole.

I have said that Hosea is unquestionably a man of the north country with the intimate and loving knowledge of one who knows its habits, who shares its traditions, who feels the pulse of a common life flow through him, who realizes that these traditions and this common life have moulded him and given him at once his most personal and individual outlook and yet his Israelite outlook. Nothing shows this to me more clearly than his liking for place names, names which he introduces without halting to explain what they mean to him or what they stand for in his people's life. He does not need to explain, because he is talking to men who can supply the reference for themselves. He talks about Gilgal and Shittim and Tabor, as a Highlander might talk about Culloden or Glencoe, or a south country Scot might mention Flodden or Bothwell Brig. Which of us, when we are talking among our-selves, feels it necessary to add anything to any of these names?

It is true that Amos writes, using place-names in a general way. He speaks of how Israel came up out of Egypt and took the lands of the Amorite. He speaks of men who poured southward on pilgrimage to Beersheba, and he can set us into the middle of a festival at Bethel. But even we know about the Exodus: we know why men chose Beersheba for their pilgrimage: we understand why Bethel became the centre for Israel's worship. These places all appear in the historical records of the nation.

Hosea's knowledge is intimate and personal, not based on books but on observation. Because of this he sometimes eludes us altogether and we have no idea as to what the names he uses refer to. His exact meaning escapes us, because the places and events of which he speaks have not found their way into the histories. Gilead (6: 8) is a city of them that work iniquity. What gave the place this infamy? The priests (5: 1) have been a snare in Mizpah and a spread net on Tabor. Mizpah we know from the story of Jacob and Laban: but nothing in that story connects it specially with priests. As for Tabor, was it a shrine, that a priesthood was connected with it? If it was, what kind of net did the priests spread there? These places evidently meant something very definite to the prophet and in the time to which he spoke. But they mean nothing clear to us. They reflect features in a life which has passed without a record.

There is another feature in Hosea to which I must refer and that is his knowledge of, and the close relation of his prophecies to, the Code of Deuteronomy. The prophet knows the law-book intimately, so intimately that its ideals are often reproduced in his addresses to his people. This means that Hosea was a more cultured man than his predecessor. Probably he could read. Or, if he had not read the law of his time, he had heard it, when it was read at public services in his time. And he had done more than gather its casual commandments: he had assimilated its temper and made its peculiar and distinctive outlook his own.

One may indeed say that his prime aim is to take the leading demands of this book, namely, that Israel is to have no other God than Yahweh, and to turn it from a mere law laid on the nation *ab extra* into something with more spiritual content. The demand to worship only Yahweh rests for him on the character of his God. If Israel could only realize what its God is in His nature, it would be incapable of worshipping any other. Accordingly he is continually insisting that Israel shall know Yahweh as one who proclaims that its defection from Him is due to an utter failure to realize what He has been to it.

One sees further the intimate knowledge Hosea has of the life of His nation in the way he can refer to his people's worship. Amos showed in a vivid way the excesses which went on at the shrines and scourged the public vices there. But Hosea writes as one who had taken part in some of the great festivals and he sees them from the inside. He has listened for example to the stories which were told there, for he gives in 12 : 3 ff. a story about Jacob such as was probably told at Bethel with its historical associations with the patriarchs. It is the story of the midnight wrestling at Jabbok, but, as Hosea tells it, it does not exactly agree with the story in our Genesis. For Hosea has not read it in a book : he may have heard it as a boy, when he made pilgrimage to the shrine. He quotes it as he knows it, and the fact that his version differs slightly from the version we have in Genesis incidentally helps us to understand why and how our present stories show variant forms here and there.

He is not content like Amos to tell that men sang songs at their festival times, nor to say with Isaiah that men sang them to the tones of the lute. For in 6 : 1 ff. he quotes one of those hymns taken from the lips of the men whom he had heard singing it. The lilt of it in the original Hebrew is unmistakable still across a couple of thousand years. One can hear the broad Hebrew vowels and mark the rise and fall of the adoring chorus. But one can notice more : one can see in it a more primitive type of religion than what became the official type in Israel. The fact is hidden from us Scotsmen, because the hymn has been turned into one of the finest, if not the finest, of our Paraphrases.

> *Come let us to the Lord our God*
> *With contrite hearts return:*
> *Our God is gracious, nor will leave*
> *the desolate to mourn.*

Our hearts, if God we seek to know,
    shall know him and rejoice;
His coming like the morn shall be,
    like morning songs his voice.
As dew upon the tender herb,
    diffusing fragrance round;
As showers that usher in the spring,
    and cheer the thirsty ground.

But we did not notice the fact that the Christian poet in para-
phrasing has transformed the whole character of the poem,
infusing into it ideas which are Christian and remote from
every pagan association. Thus there is nothing in the original
about contrite hearts, while the whole emphasis of the para-
phrase is laid on this. Further, the Christian poet has dwelt on
the dawn and the dew and the spring showers as reviving,
refreshing, renewing. This is not the emphasis in the original
hymn. The emphasis in the Hebrew hymn is on the sureness
of God's coming, on its being sure as the dawn, calculable
with its two days or three as the spring showers. Yahweh here
is closer to nature than to moral processes. He does not promise His return on repentance. Men calculate His return with
the same sureness with which they count on the dawn which
shines on just and unjust alike.

Read it so and it is not one of the hymns which have come
down in the Psalter, official, accepted, stamped with the syna-
gogue's approval. It belongs to a coarser faith, rooted in the
soil, when nature and God were closer to each other and when
God's return to bless His people was as independent of Israel's
reform as the rain which falls on the sinner's fields as liberally
as on those of the righteous. So men sang about the day of
Yahweh, peasants from the hills of Ephraim, elders out of
the towns, priests at its shrines.

And because it was this, borrowed directly from their lips,
Hosea follows it immediately with a summons to repentance.
For he is in charge to say that Yahweh's coming is not like the
day-dawn, but does distinguish between just and unjust, nay,
has this for its principle, to make precisely this distinction.

The song is like a curtain lifted for a little so that we look
out into the kind of sensuous religion which the prophets
needed to fight.

Also Hosea seems to me to have been something of a town-dweller or a man from some village of North Israel. Amos came from the hills and the open plain, and his speech betrays the man of the open air. To him Yahweh speaks in the thunder that mutters in the south-east over Jerusalem before the cloud bursts on the top of Carmel. He has seen the vineyards, the fig trees and the olives stripped by the scourge of the worm, has watched when the rain failed a village. When he wants to speak of judgment on a town, he wants concrete images in which to express it. He says, Fire shall alight on its palaces, and he says this over and over with monotonous reiteration.

Hosea is different. He knows the life of towns so well that it is natural for him to take his figures from this familiar life. To him Ephraim is a half-baked cake (7 :8), burned on the one side, raw dough on the other. You have all been reared on machine-made white bread and you may not fully appreciate the figure. I was reared on bannocks of bran meal, bannocks of barley, and I have not forgotten how, when the firing had been a failure, one's teeth crunched through the burned side to stick dolefully in the sticky, ill-baked dough on the other. The princes of Samaria, again (7 :4), are like bakers, and they treat their pet schemes as bakers treat their bread in the leavening.

Israel was a child, and like a child Yahweh taught Ephraim to walk, holding him under the arms, as a woman holds up the uncertain feet of her boy (11 :3). Ephraim is a heifer broken to the plough, steadily tramping over the harvested grain (10 :11). Judgment, when it comes, springs like the lush growth of weeds that bury the furrows to which men have committed their grain, an unwelcome crop but the hardiest (10 :4). The farmers in the plain of Esdraelon and among the wheat fields of Samaria knew this to their cost. Ephraim shall be like a morning cloud, vanishing at sunrise, like the early dew which dries as though it had never been, like the chaff tossed wide by a gust of wind from the threshing floor, like the smoke from a cottage chimney.

> *The reek of the cot hung ower the plain*
> *Like a wee wee clud in the warld its lane.*

But a breath of wind is enough to scatter it (13 :3). These are the figures which come naturally to Hosea, sometimes, like those at 13 : 3 tumbling over one another on his tongue as they crowd out from his imagination. They are figures from the homely life of hamlets where men live and children are born and the harvest is reaped. He has others which are not so much his own, for they reappear in other men's writing. These were so much his own that no other man borrowed them. They would have been out of place, not familiar in the new surroundings. And they reveal, especially when one unites them with the other characteristics which I have noted, the manner of man he was, a man who loved the life of men and fell in easily into the kindly work of the world of which he felt himself a part, a man who loved the orderly life of nature, its drying dew as the sun rose, the cottage chimneys smoking when the cakes were baked for the cottagers' breakfast, a man who delighted in the tilth and the fields bearing their burdens of grain and loved to see the trained cattle doing their darg at the orderly life which maintained them and their masters alike, a man too who loved not only life in general and its gracious simple services, but who loved his own nation with a passionate affection, who knew its legends and felt their appeal to him, a man who felt himself a part of the world and especially of this little world of Israel into which his God had put him. It had made him what he was : its thoughts were familiar to him : its outlook was his : its ideals had become part of his intellectual and spiritual outlook. He was part of it, by no mere accident of birth. He was part of it by virtue of its having reared him and contributed to his mental outlook. All its life poured into him, making him, moulding him, colouring his personality, so that he could no more deny his heritage than deny what his eyes saw. He was no cosmopolitan but an Israelite through and through, conscious of the special contribution Israel could make to the world's thought and not delaying to compare it with the contribution the Philistine or Syrian could bring. Even when he became a prophet, he remained an Israelite. It is through no accident that we do not find in him, as we find in Amos, an attempt to estimate the relation between the outside world and Yahweh.

Yet he became a prophet. If I am right in construing his

attitude and his initial outlook, you will recognize how it was not, as it were, a natural thing for him to become a prophet. It cost some men little to become prophets, especially prophets of woe. One can conceive that it cost Amos not a very great deal to thunder denunciations against a life which he did not love, because he did not feel himself part of it. Those palaces were remote things to him, phrases or shells. When they disappeared, he lost little or nothing. The fire might devour the palaces thereof. It did not touch the open desert.

But Hosea must have found it difficult to conceive all this life, every part of which he loved, every part of which had contributed something to him, as doomed. And so it needed a special experience, a very special and terrible experience, to make him a prophet. And this experience, which, evidently because it was so greatly needed, has been so fully recounted to us in his book, is what we must try to look at, before we seek to ask how he approached his life task as a prophet.

HOSEA'S MARRIAGE

There is a type of man who finds it hard to believe in the tragedy and evil of this world and hard to pronounce utter condemnation on it, not because the world has dealt tolerably well with him, nor because he finds it hard to conceive a world which has given him some comfort as only fit for condemnation, but because he loves men and everything which men do. The world to such men does not hide its inexplicable quality and its hideous side, but even with these things he realizes a certain sympathy. They are all parts of a life to which he feels himself to belong and with which he dare not become utterly impatient. He finds it hard to believe that life may not renew itself and shake off what hampers and pollutes it.

What awakens such men rudely to a realization of how deeply the canker has eaten into the world and life of their time is to have the part of their nature by which they are most closely linked to their fellows, their affections, wounded to the quick.

This was what happened to Hosea in the unfaithfulness of his wife. The account of what happened may be read in his book and need not be elaborated here. It is necessary, however, to touch on one point. It seems a blunder to suppose that the man believed himself commanded by Yahweh to marry a woman who was of notoriously lewd character. Dr. T. H. Robinson, in his book *Prophecy and the Prophets in Ancient Israel*[1] has not hesitated even to say that the woman Hosea was ordered to marry was one of the q*e*dheshoth, that is, one of the public prostitutes at an Israelite shrine.

I am not able to oppose this on the ground that one must count it incredible or impossible for an Old Testament prophet to have believed that he was divinely ordered to do such a thing as this. It is always dangerous to determine *a priori* what men may or may not have conceived their God to have ordered. Men have held that their God ordered as strange things as this would have been.

The reason why one should reject the idea is that, if we so interpret the relation between Hosea and his wife, this is, if we suppose that he married a woman whom he knew to be lewd in character and loose in conduct, the entire analogy which the prophet sets up between Yahweh and Israel, which is conceived as parallel to the relation between husband and wife, falls to the ground. If a man married a woman of notoriously loose character, he had no right to expect that from that time she would show a sudden faithfulness to him, of which her whole previous life showed her to be, and helped to make her incapable. And, if Yahweh chose Israel, already proven disloyal, and made her His bride, He had equally no ground for His anger, if the nation proved itself as disloyal to Him as it had already done to others. The point of the analogy surely lies in the idea of the virgin simplicity of girl and nation, which has been crowned by the gift of trust and love by man and by God, but girl and nation have been too frivolous to understand how great a gift has come into their hands. It is the more extraordinary to find Dr. Robinson advancing his theory because he sees so clearly that this is exactly Hosea's contribution in the matter of religion.

As we saw in the temple hymn discussed above, the nation said, Yahweh's choice means that we can count on Him with

---

[1] Pp. 75-76. Cf. Oesterley and Robinson, *An Introduction to the Books of the Old Testament*, p. 350.

the certainty with which we can count on the sunrise or the recurrent spring rain—whatever we may be. Yahweh's choice, said Hosea, implies the urgency of a great moral wonder, the wonder of God's trust.

Hosea married a girl whom he loved and who loved him so far as was in her nature. For a time they were happy in their mutual affection and in their home where a child was born to them. But when love entered its claim, when love demanded loyalty, she failed not only him but love's self. She proved, to use our significant phrase, a light o'love, a woman who could not see or could not bear the grave demands all love makes on the moral nature.

Of course this broke up the home, not only outwardly but inwardly. The woman left him for another man: this was the outward break. But she had left him before she had sought the other man: she had no longer been his: this was the inward. The end for her was the natural end of such a light o'love, that the man who took her for their mutual enjoyment left her when pleasure was dead. She drifted down to misery and ruin.

Hosea was left, it seemed at first to him, with nothing but his ruined home and his deserted children. But presently he found that he was left with more, with his old love which refused to die. This woman, who had once been more to him than any other woman, could not even now be nothing to him. They had lived together: the children were hers as well as his: their lives had intertwined so intimately that she could not be torn out of his life. And so, when she was cast off and lying a derelict in life's road, he went to seek her. He could not reinstate her simply as his wife. What had made the old relation true, that she and he were all the world to each other, was gone, never to come back. They never could be that to each other again. Yet she could not be like any other woman to him. She could not even remain nothing to him. Love meant loyalty to Hosea. And he gave her back what he could, not the renewal of the past, because the past was past, but all which was possible. He protected her, watched over her, set her beyond need and shame in the hope that even yet she might learn something from the dolorous past and become something of what she had once been to him.

And then, as in a flash at first, more and more clearly as
he groped among these astounding, heart-shaking experiences,
the man began to see what this meant as to the relation of
God to Israel. Yahweh chose Israel in her virginal simplicity
when He brought her out of Egypt. Why Yahweh chose her
he does not know, any more than he knows why he chose
Gomer bath Diblaim, any more than any man knows why
one woman is all the world to him. Yahweh gave His name to
Israel which became the people of Yahweh. He brought her
into His home in Palestine and gave her a place in the sun,
a place of His choosing. He guided her life and safeguarded
it by the great institutions through which it could be wisely
and worthily expressed, through the priesthood and the kingdom. These natural things in a nation's life were its God's
gifts to enable its life to embody itself in fitting forms and
manifest all its richness before the world. One cannot help
noting there too the difference between Amos and Hosea.
The prophet of the desert regarded prophecy as the one means
of divine revelation to Israel. The prophet of the cultured land
recognized God's hand in the more constant things, the more
apparently natural gifts of seemly government and practical
guidance of daily life. God's guidance of Israel to the one was
spasmodic, to the other was constant.

Israel took the gifts, but failed to understand their meaning. Being light o'love, it could not see that what moulds men
is not outward gifts, whether dealt liberally or in smaller doses,
but the attitude men take to the outward gifts, recognizing
whence they come and what they imply. Above all, what
determines the moral nature is the attitude men take to the
things which have come to them for nothing, the gifts which
are wholly beyond their desert. To take what came from the
grace of God, without realizing that it was the mere evidence
of a bigger thing behind it, the grace which prompted it, was
to have the outward husk, but no more. Israel was very content with its land, pleased and satisfied with its dignity as a
nation. Even so a girl might play with her wedding ring and
preen herself in her wedding clothes and finger the outward
signs of her new dignity as a married woman. But that love
means loyalty, and that loyalty is its crown, was hidden from
her. That it demands as well as gives, that in its demands and

through its demands it gives its best, that through claiming all we are and all we have in order to recognize and return it, that it makes us new and makes all life new to the new eyes which see it, that it sends new valuations into everything : all this was hidden from her wayward and undisciplined heart.

To Hosea it is all obvious : religion to him is dependence on a care which has been unmerited and self-surrender to a God who has dealt generously with men. Quite naturally he cast his thought of the relation between Israel and Yahweh into the metaphor or analogy of the marriage relation which had meant so much to him. From his time idolatry, as whoredom or adultery, became lodged in the religious language of Israel, to be expounded into details which occasionally as in Ezekiel and the glossator on Jeremiah became offensive to good taste. To Hosea, it marked how *the* sin of Israel is disloyalty to the generosity of God.

YAHWEH AND ISRAEL

The analogy of husband and wife, however, does not adequately express all that is in the prophet's mind about this relation. A wife stands in too independent a position towards her husband to represent what Israel has received from Yahweh. There was a period of the wife's life which was out of all relation to her husband : there was no period of Israel's life which was out of relation to Yahweh. The time when she became a wife marked, it is true, the period when her life flowed into richer channels. But to Hosea, Israel did not exist as a nation and counted for nothing in the world before Yahweh made her his own. Hence the prophet uses the analogy of the child (11 : 1), which could not even have staggered to its feet and learned to walk without the guardian care of God. Yahweh gave Israel being when it was in danger of being submerged in Egypt. He supported and guided its tottering feet across the desert. Without Him it would never have been a people. Israel for Hosea owes everything to its religion, its self-consciousness as a nation, its sense of having any place in the world, and any function to fulfil there, its power to occupy the place and fulfil the function. There was nothing

in its distinctive life among the other peoples of the world
which did not draw its inspiration and its reality from its
relation. Hence the forms into which its national life casts itself, not merely the priesthood which administers its religion,
but the priesthood which administers its law and justice, the
kingdom which controls and embodies its national consciousness, are different from those of all the other nations, for they
are inspired by the same spirit which gave it life at all, the
spirit of its distinctive religion.

The analogy of the child's relation to its father bulks much
less in Hosea's prophecy than the other analogy of the wife's
relation to the husband. The reason is simple. The analogy
of the marriage relation does not express so well the idea of
dependence on God, but it expresses better the idea of self-
surrender, the spiritual and moral respect which is due by the
nation to the grace of its divine benefactor. There, of course,
it fell in better with his primary function as a prophet, to
drive home upon a slack generation, which construed God's
faithful care as a guarantee of their national existence, no
matter what they were, how the best gifts were only appreciated through a worthy respect. There, also, the analogy fell
into line with the experience, which, if it did not make him a
prophet, filled his prophetic mission with a new content. But
it embodies most of all his prophetic conviction, namely, that
the ethical and spiritual life is the answer man makes to the
gifts of God. The measure of a nation's, as of an individual's,
initial soundness is the attitude it takes to what has come to
it from the divine generosity. The measure too of its growth
in moral stature is the extent to which it consistently construes
what such generosity demands and, through demanding, as
consistently gives.

You will notice how this implies a slightly different attitude
to the historical revelation from that in Amos. Amos began
from the relation Yahweh holds to all the world. So doing,
he could think of the coming of the Philistines from Caphtor
alongside the coming of Israel from Egypt. He could set the
transgressions of the nations alongside those of Israel and
could regard both as equally transgression against Yahweh.

Hosea, on the other hand, emphasizes the uniqueness of the
life of Israel, based on the uniqueness of its relation to

Yahweh. To him there is nothing comparable with this in the life of the surrounding nations. Hosea's prime interest is not a theoretical relation which Yahweh, because He is God of the world, must hold to all the nations of the world, with which relation you must then correlate any specially intimate relation into which Yahweh has entered with Israel. His religion is at once a warmer thing and one which sits closer to the facts : it is warmer, because it sits closer to the facts. What interested him first and engrossed him afterwards, was the historical religion in which he had grown up, which had made his nation what it was, which had given it a different genius and a different outlook on life from that of all the other nations among which it lived, and which alone could give any body and content to the vague generalities into which the thought of Yahweh's relation to the world and to all nations is apt to tail off.

One can see the different attitude of the two men in the title they use as a name for God. Amos speaks about Yahweh Z^{e}bhaoth. This probably means Yahweh who is Z^{e}bhaoth, Yahweh who subsumes into Himself all there is of spiritual force behind the world, in principalities and powers both in earthly and heavenly places. As such, the title agrees with the prophet's thought about God's activity. Hosea, on the other hand, has only one name for God : he calls Him Yahweh, giving Him a name which was a personal name, and above all the name which only Israel used and which only Israel could measure through its historical revelation. As such, He was Israel's Maker, 8 :14, Israel's God, 9 :1. The deeds of Yahweh on which the prophet dwells and the only one on which he dwells are His deeds for Israel and towards Israel. Thus He called Israel out of Egypt, 11 :1; he taught them to walk, 11 : 3; He gave the nation its land, 9 : 3, 15; He gave the priests their law, 4 : 5, which, of course, one must recognize as meaning a wider thing than the mere sacrificial torah. Everything which gave solidarity and continuity to the life of the nation was of His institution. When the priest rejected knowledge, Yahweh rejected him from being His priest, 4 :6. The offerings these prescribed were Yahweh's offerings, 8 : 13. The prophets were Yahweh's messengers, 6 : 5. The kingdom was of divine institution and, as such, was meant to be an expression of the divine will, for the blame cast on the realm is that its people "have set up kings but not by me", 8 : 4.

It is an historic revelation, embodying itself in concrete, tangible things which Hosea sees and seeks to measure. We are what we are, he would insist, as individuals and as a nation, because of what Yahweh showed Himself in the past towards us, not merely because of what Yahweh in the secret of His being must be, nor even because of what He has always shown Himself to be to the whole world. When I set the matter thus sharply and set it in contrast with the position of Amos, the weakness is that one thinks of the opposition as conscious or even intended. But one must not think of Hosea as denying the other truths or even having any distaste for them. Only these to him are not the truths which have determined his people's national life and made Israel what it now is. Nor are these facts which bring Israel in as guilty before God and make the situation so desperate in this hour when Yahweh is about to reveal Himself anew in the world. Therefore we do not find Hosea introducing, as Amos did, the heathen nations as recognising, far less as approving, the righteous acts of Yahweh's judgment in connection with Israel. These have not the criterion by which they can measure Yahweh's conduct towards Israel and as little can they, therefore, measure the character and the depths of Israel's sin. Only those who know what Yahweh's love has been can know what Israel's ingratitude has been. For the former do not know the intimacy of the relation into which Yahweh has brought His people to Himself, and, not having this knowledge, they cannot appreciate how far short Israel has fallen of the great possibilities God set before it.

God, then, made the people a nation for He gave it a land, a law, a priesthood, prophets. These outward things were the means He employed to make it what He desired to make it, not merely a nation, but the nation of Yahweh. The people was Yahweh's bride to bear His name confidently before the world : and all the manifestations of its varied national life and rich natural energy were the means, or were meant to be the means, through which this unique relation, which expressed eternal truth, was to be made manifest to the world of men. Hence the people's history, since the great day on which Yahweh chose it, was no mere casual thing, but it expressed an eternal fact; it was the story of God's love for Israel. The motive for this love of God, which brought Israel into being, could not be found in anything which Israel was or had done, for Israel was not till God's love summoned it into being, and it had never shown itself conscious of the greatness of this to which it owed its being. The motive for this love lay in the infinite purpose of God, outside of time and unconditioned by time. Because it was this, it expressed something which was as unchanging as this out of which it came. It expressed something abiding and real, because this which had called it into being, the divine purpose, was the one thing abiding and real in an unstable universe.

Because Hosea saw the history of his people thus, in the light of a vast purpose, which created it for a great end, and which continually guided it to an end too great for it to be able even to conceive, its history became to him symbolic. Behind the transient things of its life lay something which was not transient, and which had used this nation to express itself in the world.

I think it is wise to try to realize something of what such a position means and of what it implies, because it has a quite definite bearing on the attitude we take to all the prophet's historical allusions. Every fact, however apparently trivial, in Israel's past became new and charged with fresh significance. For it ceased to be merely the record of the effort of Israel : it was the expression of an eternal idea. Behind it lay a spiritual reality and through it wrought an inner compulsion. Through each of those stages of the nation's fortunes, which might be regarded merely as the casual events of a people's changing life, the eternal purpose of God was manifesting itself in this world of things. For in each of these was bodied forth something of the relation that existed between Israel and its God. The break away from Egypt, through which Israel was born, was the act in which Israel's distinctive character as the people of Yahweh was made clear.

If, then, Hosea, as he does, warns the people against returning of its own accord to Egypt, 11 :5a, or if he represents Yahweh as threatening that it should be brought down again into Egypt, 8 : 13, it is unwise to conclude too readily that the prophet is thinking about a physical exile, which is to be brought about by the domination of Egypt over Palestine. Nor is it safe to conclude that the main key to the explanation of such statements is to be found in the close study of the shifting international politics of those uneasy days. It is wiser to keep before us that Hosea may have had in his mind a much wider question. He may mean that matters are to go back to the position in which they stood, before Yahweh chose the people at all, and before the people stood unique among the nations as the bride of God. Its failure to respond to its God's summons is to result in the removal of its privilege. Instead of standing out free, distinct, characteristic, with a life of its own, because that life is the proud gift of its God, it is to sink back submerged in the grey mass of heathenism out of which Yahweh once brought it.

This consideration only becomes more weighty when we look more closely at the way in which Hosea actually speaks about exile. We find him prophesying exile, sometimes to Assyria, at other time to Egypt. What did he mean? Do the two prophecies reflect a different political outlook on the part of the prophet, according to whether he was now impressed by the hopelessness of setting up resistance to the colossal and growing power of Assyria, or again had become convinced that Assyria would not be able to resist when once Egypt began to put out its strength? Possibly : but in that case it becomes difficult to understand why he had the right to blame the politicians who, uncertain between the two great powers to the south and east, wobbled hopelessly in their views of the line the nation ought to take. The prophet seems to wobble as badly as they do.

It becomes especially difficult to interpret the prophet along these lines, since, as in 9 : 3, he seems to speak of exile to both places at once. How could the little nation be overrun by both the great rivals for the hegemony of Syria and overrun at the same time?

If, however, he thought of exile as a religious idea, that is, if he regarded the exile of Israel from Palestine as the expulsion of Yahweh's bride from the home to which He brought her, the matter becomes clearer. It really was of no significance to the prophet where it was carried into exile or what nation possessed it. The significant thing to him was exile as such and what it connoted. It connoted its rejection by God.

Hosea prophesied, 9 : 17, that Israel should become landless wanderers, masterless and forsaken among the nations. Again, the emphases of the prophet show what was in his thought. To be landless was to be expelled from the home to which Yahweh brought them. To be wanderers and masterless meant to be destitute of His guidance and control, the guidance and control by which they once learned to walk and learned where they were to go. The things Yahweh gave to make them unique in the world were to disappear. They were to lose precisely those characteristics which gave them distinction and to sink back into what they were before Yahweh chose them. They were to be " among the nations."

Again, the prophet said that, since they had chosen the Assyrian to be their lord instead of Yahweh, the Assyrian should be permitted to work his will on them, 11 : 5. But that does not mean necessarily exile at the hands of Assyria. It means that, when a nation surrenders its own distinctive life, it becomes the plaything of circumstances, submerged in the world of colourless common-place, from which only the guidance of Yahweh could draw it to a distinctive place.

Take Hosea's attitude from another side. He thought of Israel as constituted through an act of God for its salvation. Hence he saw the community as having one supreme task to fulfil, and he saw this task to be its response to the supreme love for it, and trust in it, which its God had shown. This gave him a profound thought of the reality and effect of its sin. But especially he saw that its sin was one in principle, however varied might be its forms. He cannot therefore speak, as Amos could, of three transgressions of Israel and of four, definite, calculable transgressions which could be set on a list against the definite commands of Yahweh. All the individual and concrete sins of the nation sprang from a common root, unfaithfulness to the love of God which had given it everything.

To Hosea the unmerited love of God to Israel was a source of perpetual wonder. Therefore Israel's sin of ingratitude for this unmerited love was a source of as constant amazement.

He could not fathom it, this whoredom which was found in
Ephraim, 6 : 10. For to him it implied profound ingratitude,
" I have strengthened their arms, yet do they imagine mischief again *me* " (7 :15). It implied too an unfathomable
folly, " Ephraim is like a silly dove without understanding "
(7 :11). But above all it was treachery. " Ephraim compasseth
me about with falsehood, and the house of Israel with deceit "
(12 : 1).

The men whom Yahweh had chosen out of all the world
to know Him were ignorant of the nature and the purpose of
Him who had thus selected their nation. Yet their ignorance
was wilful, and, because wilful, was worthy of censure.
Yahweh accused them on the ground of their ignorance
(4 : 1), because what caused their ignorance was the perversity
of their conduct (4 : 11 ff.). Hosea is no intellectualist. To him
ignorance is failure to respond to the intimate claims of the
spirit, failure to realize how the one real response to love is a
life devoted in all its manifestations to the love which has
brought it into being and which has given it its distinctive
characteristics.

But, because Hosea is no intellectualist, is on the contrary
a great ethical teacher, because too he sees that the distinctive characteristics of his nation's life rest on its calling by
Yahweh to serve His ends, and hence that its institutions and
its policy must be framed to embody and to serve the purpose
which called it into being, he is no political statesman, but is
emphatically a religious teacher. And even those judgments
in which, at a first glance, he might seem to be speaking of
merely political questions can be shown to aim fundamentally
at a religious end and always to have a religious source. Thus
he returns again and again to the complaint that, in the time
of its national peril and perplexity, the people was relying on
political alliance. Once in 7 :11, it is true, he seems to write
as though it were the inconstancy of the people in relying,
now on Assyria and again on Egypt, and the futility of such
political inconstancy which roused his anger against the
nation's purblind leaders. And in the sketch of the political
history of the period we have seen how natural it was that
the troubled times should give rise to precisely this type of
weathercock policy. We can measure also how hopeless it was

to try to fight against it. After all, it was inevitable that, in a
weak state placed between two powerful neighbours, which
for their own security were trying to establish themselves in
the middle region between them, some men should see their
national safety to rest on relying on Egypt, while others insisted on holding by Assyria. It was inevitable too that such
opinion should fluctuate according to the varying fortune of
Egypt and Assyria respectively. It was equally inevitable that
one party should be dominant now, and the other hold the
upper hand later. We are there wading in the shifting sand
of human politics. And in our profound ignorance of the political factors of the time, and of what might be politically wise
at one period or at another, it would be fatuous to determine
what was wisdom and what was folly.

But since a weathercock policy, however natural, was hopeless, it might be enough to conclude that the prophet, looking
on from a serener height, was trying to bring his bewildered
compatriots to see it, to take one definite line and to hold by it.

But other passages in the book warn us against this easy
solution, for they clearly prove that Hosea would have been
equally ill-content, if the people had sought to maintain its
distinctive life, by relying on a single ally. His condemnation is
launched, not against their variation in their alliance, but
against their having sought alliance at all. When Ephraim
went to Assyria, it is as though he had hired lovers (8:9):
that is, it is a sign of disloyalty to the one Lord of the nation
to depend on Assyria at all. Again (5:13), when Ephraim
saw his sickness and Israel his wound, then went Ephraim to
Assyria and sent to the great king[1] That is to say, instead of
seeking the true healer, they turned in their recognition of
their need of help, to a fake source of succour. Alliance with
the foreigner aggravates a disease which only Yahweh can
cure.

What Hosea clearly means is this, when Israel turns for aid
in maintaining its distinctive life in Palestine to alien help,
and when accordingly it comes to hold its land and its freedom and its position at the will of another nation, it must serve
the bidding of its new master. And from this moment, in this
deed, its unique character, as holding everything from

[1]Read *yisra'el* for *yᵉhudhah, malki rabh* for *melekh yarebh*.

6

Yahweh, and therefore as holding it to serve the purposes of Yahweh, was *ipso facto* lost. As he expresses it in another place (8:8), Israel becomes at once through this deed mixed among the nations. It has lost its distinctive character, as depending on Yahweh alone, and is at once merely one among the many. It now seeks the same ends as the other nations, instead of reserving itself jealously to serve its peculiar ends, the ends of Yahweh. Or again, 8:8, " Israel is swallowed up : now are they among the nations, as a vessel in which there is no pleasure ", that is, a vessel in which Yahweh can have no pleasure. In that passage it deserves close attention that Hosea is not uttering a prophecy : he is describing an actual condition. He does not say what will or must happen to them, if they follow a certain course. This is the thing which has happened to them. And what caused it is their act in asking for assistance. When they hold the land at another's will, they are inevitably bound to do the will of their new master. And, so soon as this happens, they have lost the distinctive character of being Yahweh's bride, whose task and whose pride it is to serve no other will than His.

If we grasp this problem with all it implies, we see at once how and why it is a matter of indifference to Hosea whether Israel seeks help from Assyria alone or from Egypt and Assyria alternately. It is reliance on any external power which he rejects, because reliance on an external power means serving its will and submitting to its direction. We can further see it is a matter of indifference whether Assyria is able to protect those who have sought its help or merely exploits those who trust in it. Hosea is not dwelling on the ultimate and external consequences of such a step : he emphasizes its internal and immediate results. Israel, in electing to serve the foreigner, has made itself the servant of the will of the alien instead of the servant of the will of God. What Assyria may choose to do with it does not interest the prophet particularly. What does interest him intensely is what Yahweh must do with the nation which in this act has proclaimed itself to be no longer His loyal lover, but which has hired lovers.

It is, of course, true that this may imply no more than the recognition on Hosea's part that political alliance in those days had a deeper implication and a wider result than it has in ours. Here, as in so much else, we often fail to appreciate that alien and distant world and how much its life was a unity, not broken up into economical, political, artistic, religious spheres. Alliance with a foreign power to-day, like our own nation's former alliance with a power such as Japan which does not share our faith, leaves the inner ideals of our own people and of the Japanese uninfluenced except superficially or at most in subtle and very indirect ways. But at that time dependence on the foreigner brought with it a direct recognition of the religion of the superior state which had thus been acknowledged as the protector of the weaker. We find Ahaz at a slightly later time putting himself under the protection of Assyria and at once sending back from the place where he acknowledged her Assyrian suzerain the pattern of an altar on which, after it was erected, he himself constantly offered sacrifice. From what is known of the practice of Assyria it is clear that Ahaz was not wantonly moved to flatter his new ally and protector by acknowledging the ruler's faith, but that he was required to do this as one of the conditions for receiving Assyrian support. This might account for Hosea's dislike of alliance with the power in the east, since we must remember that the prophet belonged to North Israel and the time was not far distant since Ahab's alliance with Phoenicia had had very baleful effects on the purity of Yahwism. Yet it must be acknowledged that it will not account for his equal dislike of alliance with Egypt, the other power in the southwest.

But, if we allow that this side of the situation had a good deal of influence on his attitude, that only serves to set into clearer light the fact that the prophet's objection to foreign alliance was a religiously motivated one. In my judgment the dislike of the Egyptian alliance proves that the objection in his mind went deeper than dislike of the risk of being required to acknowledge a foreign god. He contemplates Israel's dependence on Assyria with disgust and horror. It was an offence in his eyes to acknowledge the help of an alien state at all, because it, with all that it implied and brought with it, was disloyalty. The going to Assyria is what Hosea calls whoredom.

What now are we to say about such a position as this?

How can we, I mean, translate it into terms that correspond in any way to our own attitude and our thought to-day? Are we to conclude that Hosea was merely a species of dreaming enthusiast, who did not face the actual world in which men live, where they are required to do their work, where they have to patch up some working arrangement which will serve as a temporary shelter for bewildered men in their short earthly pilgrimage across time?

It would be the conclusion to which I should be driven if it was the prophet's business to give his generation guidance about political things. In that case he was demanding from his people an independence of attitude which was impossible in a world where Assyria was their neighbour.

But suppose one should conclude that his mind is moving along a different plane from that on which men were content to live then, on which they are trying to be content to live now. It is possible that his mind was filled with the conception of a kingdom which was unlike the other kingdoms of the world, which owed its being to sources beyond this world. He may have been demanding that this kingdom must, in the recognition of what constituted its source and its distinctive character, dare to draw its sanctions from, and rely for its support on, other sources than those of this world. He may have seen that if such a kingdom, with such a source and living by such sanctions, entered into tangling alliances with powers of a wholly different type, which stand for other ends than those which are its own, it must be infected with their aims and hopes and turned away from its own peculiar purpose, which is its own. That purpose is its own precisely because it has come to it from no other source than God.

So to interpret that purpose is, of course, to acknowledge that Hosea's great pregnant ideas do not deal with the world of practical political relations at all but with the world of religious ideas : but then that is what he claims to know—the mind of God about things. And, certainly, so to interpret it gives a logical coherence to the course of the prophet's thoughts. It also brings it all into relation to the religious thinking of our own generation, for there are men still who hold strongly Hosea's primary conviction that there is an attitude to the world which men gain through the gift of God.

And they too draw his conclusion that all entangling alliances with powers which own other sanctions and seek other aims only blur the sharpness of the distinctive character of the religious life. They say that the Pope's alliance with Austria did not help to make Christianity stand out the impartial arbiter which it might otherwise have been, that the German Church's alliance with Prussianism did not exactly add to that Church's vision of the eternal things, that an alliance with Socialism or any other 'ism may help to win temporal gains at the cost of a clear witness to the affairs of eternity. They are even able to say that Judaism did not do least for the world and did not contribute least to its life, when it ceased to fight for political power with the Maccabees and, instead, concentrated on the things of the spirit.

There may be some among you who see no difficulty here at all. You may be of those who believe it possible to impose on and demand from an Empire like our own a certain line of high moral conduct such as is natural to men who profess and call themselves Christians. But you will bear with men like myself who cannot help remembering that the Empire is not made up of Christians alone, but of Mohammedans and Brahmanists and Jews as well, all of whom have a right to have their convictions recognized. And even inside Britain there are many who, Christian though they are, construe their Christian duty very differently and have a right so to do.

Can you ask from a community, constituted on this basis, living in a world which is in great respects unchristian, conduct which you expect from, and have the right to expect from, convinced Christian men? Was this thing which Hosea was asking from Israel, what Israel, as it then stood in the world, could give? As I construe him, he was asking from empirical Israel what only a spiritual Israel could do and offer. And it is precisely this element in his thinking which makes his prophecy so amazingly difficult to fathom. Part of his obscurity is due to the uncertainty of the text. But perhaps the text was badly reported. That may have been because the men who quoted it did not fully realize its import.

Part also of his obscurity is due to the mere fact that he was out seeking a new road along a hitherto unblazed trail. He was out on a new road where no one had led the way before him : and, as is inevitable for all men in such circumstances, his thoughts come brokenly, in great flashes of insight, without exact coherence.

But in great part the obscurity is due to the fact that Hosea was trying to force his new thoughts about what Israel was and about its function in this world into a frame which was far too narrow for it. He was still embarrassed by the effort of attempting to identify the kingdom of his inspiration with the actual physical kingdom of Israel. He was asking for empirical Israel what the nation in which he lived could not see, and what, even if it had seen, it could not do. Time was to prove that what he aimed at could not be realized in Samaria with an army and a court of politicians busy about alliances with Egypt or Assyria, even with a priesthood busy with sacrifices at Bethel. He was out for a church, a body of men held together by a conscious conviction, not after a nation, held together by the accidents of history.

HOSEA'S VIEW OF RELIGION

One may see how Hosea's thought was moving on a different plane from that on which a man moves who is only thinking of a kingdom based on circumstance and race and maintained by outward institutions. His idea of sin, as that which broke the relation between Israel and God, proves how spiritual all his thought on the subject was. I have already said how he does not speak of three transgressions of Israel or four, things which can be catalogued, and therefore things that can be checked and even removed by an outward authority. Even as his idea of religion is self-surrender to a grace to which one owes all, so his conception of sin is not that of offences, but of failure to offer such a self-surrender. As such, it is of its nature inward, incorrigible to police regulation, incapable of being reached by ordinary means of discipline. Justice of a sort can be attained by careful regulations but loyalty of heart can be absent under all the regulations. Without loyalty of heart the regulated life is in vain.

Hence it is true to say that to Hosea the one sin is idolatry. But one must be careful to recognize that he insists on more than mere formal acknowledgment of Yahweh alone. Idolatry means that the root of all evil is forgetfulness of the true God, is an initial religious failure. Of course with Hosea's intense realization of the closeness of the tie which exists between Israel and its God goes monotheism. Such a self-surrender as he demands with such a resulting loyalty of spirit can only be given to One and can only be given once. Hosea does not reach his monotheism through seeing but one purpose which all the world must serve, the will of God: he reaches it through realizing a care, a redeeming care, which is unique. A god, who could be what Yahweh has been to Israel, is one. So Hosea is not merely a monotheist: his monotheism is touched with the passion of emotion: he opens the long Jewish polemic against idolatry. The root of all Israel's sin was in that day when it fell into idolatry, its hateful faithlessness to Yahweh (9:10). It found Israel like grapes in the wilderness, so fresh to the thirsty wanderer, but they came to Baal-peor and consecrated themselves unto *habbosheth*, that is, to Baal.

But out of the same position springs his polemic against image worship. He is the first to object to the representation of Yahweh under these outward emblems. One cannot say that Amos ever objected to the images at Bethel and Dan under which Yahweh was worshipped. It seems as though, so long as Yahweh was worshipped under these images, he was satisfied. But Hosea is not content: his gorge rises at the idea of men kissing calves (13:2). The text is not sure, but fortunately the sense is: the point lies in the contrast between men, conscious, intelligent, reasonable men and the emblems under which they remain content to represent God. "Of their silver and their gold they have made to themselves idols that they may be cut off: He hath cast off thy calf Samaria. This thing is only from Israel: a workman made it and it is no god: verily Samaria's calf shall be smashed" (8:4-6).

"The inhabitants of Samaria shall be in terror for Bethel's calves: it too shall be carried for a present to Assyria, as a present to the great king" (10:5ff). This, which came out of Israel's mind, which bore the print of Israel's workmen, this over the safety of which men could tremble, this which could be used as a bribe in the pressure of a political necessity: this was not God who could carry Israel like a nursing mother:

this was Samaria's calf. God to him was so great and wonderful in thought and reality, so rich in content, so abundant in self-revelation, so close in His relation to him, that it became not only inconceivable, not merely incongruous, but positively hurtful to go on representing the deity in the form of a calf. The figure must correspond with the reality and, if the reality were too great for any figure, it were better to have none. The outward forms of religion must represent something of the intimate spiritual relation which true religion means.

Now, gathering all this together, think what this whole attitude implies. The essence of religion consists, according to Hosea, in self-surrender to the will, and submission to the mind of God. Israel's national life was to embody that relation, and to embody it in its outward concrete forms of kingdom and priesthood. Embodying its distinctive national life, all these forms were to be different from those of the nations round her. Lest she should lose this distinct national type which came from and through her religion, she must be content to cut herself off from alliance with any of these other kingdoms.

Inside, her life was to be governed by *hesedh,* which implies that Israel was to be like a family. It is interesting and instructive to note in this connection that the prophet in 4:2 speaks about sins against *hesedh* in terms which suggest that he was already acquainted with the second table of the Decalogue. He reproves sins on that second table. And hence some men are able to urge, not without justice, that some such Decalogue as appears in Deuteronomy must have been already existent in his time. But, however that may be, it is of interest to note that Hosea does not base his appeal and rebuke to his people on any written law which is already known to them. He bases it rather on the fundamental relation of Israel to God and on the resulting relation between fellow Israelites which flows from the fundamental relation of Israel to God. He bases it in fact on those profound and simple convictions which must be the common property of any people, before a code which seeks to embody and to enforce these principles can have any power over them. And, because this is so, his statement goes out into regions

which could never be satisfied by such a law as the Decalogue. Gripping first those grave and simple relations of Israel
as holders of a common tradition and common life, as bound
by service to common ideals and common aims, he cannot be
satisfied with forbidding one thing here and another thing
there which conflict with such a community of life. He can
only be satisfied when he has found what will embody and
deepen those relations to Yahweh and those relations to one
another, which make up Israel's community of life. He must
try for something in Israel which is not content to repress
everything that disturbs or mars its rich and full life. He must
long to see instituted something which shall maintain those
principles that alone can make Israel's life sweet and strong.

Fundamentally, that is to say, Hosea's principles imply far
more than a Decalogue which forbids, which is negative,
which says and must be content to say " Thou shalt not ".
For his ethic is positive, claiming some means by which the
principles that make Israel's common life full shall be expressed and shall maintain and deepen the whole national life.

HOSEA'S CONCEPTION OF THE CHURCH

One can see how such fundamental convictions were bound
to give Hosea a new attitude to Israel's cult. Now what I
desire to impress upon you in connection with all this is that
it is a self-consistent system based on one or two great convictions about God and about the relation of Israel to God.
Grant the postulates of faith which lie behind it all and the
rest comes inevitably and naturally from it. But it is such a
scheme of thought as could not be reached through any political programme. Not only was it impossible of attainment by
any political programme, but it was impossible to exact or
expect from empirical Israel, as Israel existed then. It could
only be expected or exacted from a body of men who held the
same convictions about God and life and duty as seemed
self-evident to the prophets. One only needs to think of existing Israel with its mixed northern blood, its restless uneasiness over its foreign politics, with the squalid history beyond
it which I have tried to sketch to you, to realize how hopeless

6*

it was for the men who had control of the state even to understand what Hosea was driving at.

This man was speaking about a spiritual community and he was, in the irony of circumstance, needing to say such things to a community which stood on a wholly different basis. I do not know whether he saw it or not, and I do not much care. But in his fundamental convictions he has moved away from national religion. He is insisting on a temper of mind and on a consequent course of duty which no nation, *qua* nation, could be expected to cherish and to fulfil. Yet he is embarrassed by needing to express his new thought in the terms of his own time, according to which Israel as a people stood in a peculiar relation to Yahweh.

Even already the people to which the prophet spoke, and of which he was so proudly conscious that he formed a part, included very diverse elements, some borrowed from the world outside. It was easy to require of all these men that they should enter the congregation of Israel by submitting to circumcision, by attending the three annual festivals, or by sacrificing at the Yahweh shrines. But it was impossible to make such men share in the real inheritance of Israel's past in the way in which Hosea conceived that. Far less was it possible to make them share his conception of the relation which had lent the past its lustre and which constituted Israel's claim to a peculiar place in the world.

To the ordinary Israelite the kingdom which he loyally served was an institution which served to represent the national unity and which asserted the national independence, but which, even because of this, needed to enter into some relation to the external world round about it. Or it was the means of maintaining some decent order inside the nation with the resulting need of accommodating itself to the condition of the people's moral development.

To Hosea Israel was an expression of the mind of God which maintained His standards in this world, and which, because its business was to maintain these standards, must stand jealously aloof from the rest of the world, lest through close contact it should be brought to lose what it was its glory to hold. Well, I think we can see that it was only the individual who held these convictions and the society constituted of individuals who shared these convictions and who envisaged their life-tasks as such, who could fulfil so great a function in the world, or who could be expected to do this.

Hosea's ideals, whether he knew it or not, were breaking with the national Israel and were leading out sooner or later to the conception of a church which is a body of men who are united, not by the accident of birth, but by their community of conviction and by their share in a mutual duty. This body of men has to recognize that, just as it stands for ideals which do not come to it from the world in which it finds itself, but from above, so it owes its being and its origin, not to the accidents of time, but to the act of God who called it into being to serve His will in time.

One must, I think, always recognize this fundamental thought in seeking to measure the prophet's thoughts. He was asking from Israel, as Israel then was, what Israel in its national character was incapable of rendering. His thoughts were his own, singularly new and piercing, rising from his own personal intercourse with God. They came from the inspiration of the Eternal. But he was trying to pour them into the moulds which came from the forms of thought of his own time. The new wine was bound to burst the old bottles. And, if the new wine was not to be spilled and wasted, new institutions in Israel, capable of retaining them, were absolutely necessary. Now Hosea, like his predecessor, expects the intervention of Yahweh, which is His self-manifestation. God is about to reveal Himself in Israel and before the world. Both of them agree in the belief that this self-revelation must imply primarily judgment 'in Israel. But the two prophets approach the question from totally different standpoints. To Amos the judgment of Israel is only part of the judgment which the divine self-revelation brings on the whole world. Israel is more severely and first judged because it is possessed of larger knowledge : but each is judged according to the knowledge it has enjoyed. Hosea is a particularist, not interested in the world and its relation to Yahweh. Hence he has no judgment of the nations. And his judgment of Israel consists simply in the revelation of the facts of the case. The relation between Israel and Yahweh has ceased to exist : Israel is not any longer faithful, and, not being faithful to its

husband, has no place in his house, as it has no place in his
heart. The judgment is merely the revelation of this fact, and
the resulting conclusion. Since Israel has no place in Yahweh's
house, it shall be swept out of the land, without king or priest,
sacrifice or law. This is no judicial act, exacting retribution
for an outraged law. It does not even exact retribution for an
outraged affection. Yahweh does not reveal Himself to
demonstrate His rights or to vindicate His character before
the world. In His self-revelation the realities are laid bare:
and one of these is that the nation which was His in the relation of loyal love has given its heart away from Him. The
home which was Israel's home as Yahweh's gift and all the
privileges which came to the people as Yahweh's bride cease
at once in this great hour of divine self-manifestation. Hosea
does not dwell upon or elaborate what the new time is to bring
in as a new order. In some respects he is as silent as Amos
about the future beyond judgment which is to be ushered in
by God's supreme act of self-revelation. And he is always as
unhesitating in his insistence that the fate which was to befall
the people was irreversible.

In one place (6 : 1-3), he appears to suggest that if they but
repent, the disaster may be turned back from their doors.
But, as I have already pointed out, these verses are a repro-
duction of one of the temple songs which did not speak about
repentance at all and which, because it did not speak about
repentance, Hosea must follow up with a summons to repentance. But, while he asks for repentance, he does not suggest
that the doom can be reversed, if the people should repent.

Rather we find that, so sure is the fate which is to come
from Yahweh, that Hosea, as he watches in misery over his
people's condition, can only pray that the fate should be as
speedy as it is sure. " Hither," he cries, " hither, O Death,
with thy plagues; hither O Sheol with thy destruction " (13 :
14). St. Paul, who quoted the chapter from the LXX version,
not from the original Hebrew, is responsible for our modern
interpretation of the verse as a defiance of death— " where
O Death are thy plagues?" But this merely cuts the verse in
two, and makes the first half hopelessly contradict the second.
For the concluding clause " repentance is hidden from mine
eyes ", that is, Yahweh's eyes, proves clearly what was in the

prophet's mind. The sense of the whole verse is perfectly consistent, so soon as one recognizes the force of the conclusion.
" Shall I ransom them from the grip of the grave, shall I
redeem them from the power of death? Nay, but hither O
Death, with thy plagues; hither O Sheol, with thy destruction;
repentance is hidden from my eyes." It is Yahweh's repentance or change of mind which is spoken about, not repentance
on the part of the nation. He is resolute in His purpose toward
them. Since this was so, since this was the immitigable purpose of their God, there was left only one mercy which the
prophet could request. " May the children on whom this ruin
was to fall be few in number! Give them, O Yahweh, what
shalt Thou give them? Give them a miscarrying womb and
dry breasts " (9 : 14). No other prayer could express so
plainly or so terribly how grave was the end which Hosea
foresaw as sure to come upon his people.

Yet even in this passage, where Hosea had declared that
" though they bring up their children, yet will I bereave them
that there be not a man left " (9 : 12), he added, in v. 17,
that the outcome of their God having cast them away shall
be that they shall be wanderers among the nations. Evidently·
there must be someone left to be a wanderer. What this seems
to imply is that the destruction of the state shall be absolute,
sparing none, but the destruction of the people need not be
complete. For the doom pronounced over them is the same
as that which is uttered in 12 : 10, " I that am Yahweh Thy
God from the land of Egypt will again make thee to dwell in
tabernacles as in the days of high festival," that is to say,
matters shall revert to their primitive condition. For one notes
there that Chapter 9 begins with the declaration that Israel is
to be cast out of the Lord's land, which was the home to
which Yahweh brought His bride. And again one notes that
in 12 : 10 Yahweh is characterized as Thy God from the land
of Egypt. The sense, when one takes the two passages together,
is that Hosea wishes to emphasize that the present relation
between Yahweh and Israel is to be declared at an end. It was
really brought to an end when Israel became unfaithful.
It is to be declared at an end, when Yahweh expels from
his house the nation which has no real claim to be there.

Matters are to revert to the position in which they stood

when Yahweh at the beginning made Israel a nation. He has given them great gifts which have constituted their national life in its distinctive characteristics, gifts which have also revealed what is His mind toward them. They have failed to understand and to respond to these gifts of privilege and of affection. Therefore Yahweh withdraws them, and brings matters back to their first condition.

What is left when the nation is thus restored to its primitive state? Nothing, except what made them a people at the first, the unmerited and free grace of their God. But that is left. Hosea had found that his faithless wife broke her marriage vows and failed in allegiance to her husband. She could not remain his wife. There was no bond between them any more, except that he could not remain indifferent to her. He had loved her: they had lived together: She was the mother of his children. Even when she had profaned all the sanctities which made their common life together real and beautiful, he could not remain indifferent to her. She was different in his eyes from any other woman in the world; and he could not live as though that were not true. He must do something which expressed that fact.

God's act in intervening to redeem Israel had not been a mere casual fact in a world which was bound together by mere contingency. It implied something of an eternal character because God had done it. He had, as it were, committed Himself in His deed, and could not go on to do something radically different. His further acts toward the people must be consistent with his initial deed.

You will note how Hosea, like Amos, bases on the conviction, common to prophet and nation, that God had chosen Israel. But the two prophets, each from his own point of view, give ethical content to what had become to the people a source of confidence that God would be with them, whatever they might become. Amos, the stern moralist, makes it the basis for his contention that God could only remain with Israel if Israel was faithful to God, even as two men could not walk together except they be agreed. Hosea, as usual, looks at it from the divine side and recognizes that God cannot, even in the case of Israel's failure, leave the nation alone. He must do something further for its redemption. One may say that Hosea was working at the tremendous problem in the Catechism's question and answer about Effectual Calling.

It was not mere national pride which made the finest and noblest spirits in old Israel cling to the idea of the election of Israel. It was not even the idea of Israel having been chosen for special duty and for special service, true though that idea was. It was the belief that Israel had not made itself what it was before the world. The nation owed its being to the grace of its God, and that grace continued to abide with it even in its sin.

It will be observed that Hosea has no doctrine of the Remnant. Yet this conception appeared in the prophetic thinking as early as the time of Elijah, and we have noted how, though Amos made no room for it in his teaching, it might well have found a place in his idea of God's will with and for His world. We shall see that it appears with large consequences and still larger implications in Isaiah. Why should it be absent from Hosea, especially since it might well apparently find its place in his thought of a grace which cannot be denied its way? Simply because the prophet approached the whole question of religion from his own individual standpoint. To Amos who conceives God chiefly as law-giver, to Isaiah who thinks of Him almost entirely as king, the obedience men render to the law or to the king is the primary element which makes them. What such men do, what they fulfil in obedience to the demands made upon them, lifts them out of the vain show of things, sets their feet on what is enduring and brings them in to have their part in a world which does not pass away. They have constituted themselves in a certain measure as belonging to the eternal order. To Hosea, on the other hand, who sees Israel to have come into being through the divine grace, it is not what man does which constitutes him of the eternal order: it is what God does. He is nearer St. Paul's world of ideas in this matter : we are saved by faith, and that not of ourselves : it is the gift of God. In the thing which God has done toward man, precisely because it is God who does it and because therefore it cannot be mutable like man's changing purposes, man finds his guarantee as to what God must always do. In that God once intervened to make Israel His people lies the assurance that He cannot leave them alone, cannot simply stand by and suffer them to fall back into the grey world of heathenism from which He brought them.

There had been something of the divine nature revealed on this side of time in the simple deed by which Israel was made a nation. Israel's life was symbolic. Therefore in the humble but wondrous processes of Israel's history, in the slow, tortuous, various means by which a nation came into being, in the institutions which represented its unique life and served to mark it off from the rest of the world, in the pieties and reverences which gathered round its sacrifices and centred in its humble homes there was present something which was not of earth, something which was of eternal significance, something which could not pass away as though it had never been.

Love, unmerited and free, prompted Yahweh to build up this little people and to desire its broken response to His loving-kindness. And love must govern all His succeeding attitude toward it, for the end of God's work is one, though the methods must change. You see how, in the language of his own time, or, to put it in our modern phraseology, under the categories of his own time, Hosea is feeling out after the conception of evolution, of life not being a succession of casual events, far less a revolution of the world on itself. It is the slow emergence of the fundamental thing which brought it into being, the coming into expression of the love of God.

One can see it from another side. I have pointed out how Amos never threatens Israel with Assyria, because he wishes to thrust forward into the foreground what prompted the threat and what governed its certainty. That is to say, it was not the greed of a neighbouring nation which was destroying Israel: it was the just anger of God. So Hosea never speaks of Assyria either. A chastisement which came from Assyria had nothing behind it. But a chastisement which came from God had a purpose behind it, and a purpose which could not be exhausted in ruin. God's primary and eternal purpose had been revealed in creation, the creation of this nation. It could be satisfied with nothing less than its re-creation. Hence in Chapter 11 Hosea insists on how Yahweh tried kindness with Israel, and how, since this failed, He has been compelled to change His method : because of this His compassion has been turned to anger(v. 8.) But while He has changed His method God had not changed and cannot change His nature and the purpose which is born out of His nature. He has only changed His method.

Hence it is fundamental to Hosea's entire attitude that the punishment which is to befall Israel is pedagogic. This does not mean that the punishment is to be mitigated or can be turned back. It is both fearful and sure. How fearful and sure we saw. But all its end is only fulfilled, when men have learned its end in the counsel of Yahweh. And they can bear its present incidence the more patiently when they believe that its meaning is not exhausted in ruin.

Yahweh was about to bring His people back to the very foundations of its original position. It should become anew a nomadic folk, landless, kingless, without outward forms of worship. But its original position was its first beginning. And to be brought back to its original position by Yahweh means the possibility of a new beginning, if the people can take heart and learn through its tender and bitter experience what its God means toward it. If, therefore, the people can learn from its discipline and cast away its reliance on tangling alliances with alien powers, on its own strength and on its false worship, Yahweh will again be to it all that He has been in the past.

You find exactly these things insisted on and expressed in 14 : 4 ff. These verses are generally rejected as additions belonging to a later period. But the reason which has prompted their excision is the *a priori* dictum that the early prophets can have no mission except one of doom. We may allow this to be true to the extent that the doom they all predict is one which is irrevocable and which no repentance on the part of the people can now turn back. But this does not carry with it the conclusion that the prophets were unable to look beyond a doom which was sure. They could do this, because they began, not with Assyria, but with Yahweh. Because Hosea began with the thought of Yahweh as one to whose love Israel owed its very being, he above all others could conceive love as that to which Israel should owe its renewal.

Hence I would insist that the chapter, with the exception of

v. 10, is wholly in agreement with Hosea's attitude. You will find an admirable definition of it in Principal Smith's study of Hosea. Let me merely add to this by pressing on your attention one or two other points in it. I need not repeat how well its general teaching agrees with the prophet's fundamental conceptions of Yahweh's nature. But I would urge how clearly it agrees in its details with his previous teaching. Thus the three sins which vv. 4 ff. represent the people as repudiating, after they have learned from the divine chastisement, are precisely the sins on which the prophet had dwelt in his castigation of their earlier temper. Alliance with alien powers, which changed the unique spirit of the nation, confidence in its own strength which implied and deepened its failure to acknowledge an entire dependence on Yahweh, false worship which led to, and confirmed, false conceptions of Yahweh's nature—these were, according to Hosea, the causes of Israel's downfall, and these are the things which Israel is here represented as repudiating.

There are even two smaller indications which point in the same direction and which may deserve to be added. There is the vague description of their idolatry, " neither will we say any more to the work of our hands, ye are our gods." That is not the kind of thing which was the favourite theme of the later glossators. But in its very vagueness it wholly agrees with the attitude of Hosea, who never clearly shows whether he means by idolatry the worship of Yahweh under the form of the calves at Bethel and at Dan, or the desertion of Yahweh altogether to worship alien deities. We know that he blamed both, but we do not know which he counted the outstanding sin of his own time. The same vagueness which characterized their sin characterized also their repentance.

And finally you should notice that the power which is here represented as an ally, from which Israel is seeking assistance and through dependence on which it was likely to lose its special character, is Assyria. We know that Hosea blamed all such alliances, whether contracted with Assyria or with Egypt. And we may conclude that when here he specifies Assyria he chooses as illustrative of a tendency the power to which they were most likely to turn. But no glossator could possibly have selected Assyria for this purpose. From the

time of Ahaz onwards, that is, from the time immediately
after Hosea till the outward collapse of the Jewish state,
Assyria was the enemy and impossible as an ally. The selection of Assyria betrays the contemporary hand.

HOSEA AND THE CULT

I must now say something about Hosea's attitude to the
cult. And here again, as in the case of Amos, it is not easy to
define precisely what attitude the prophet took to the cult
of his people. That he was alive to its significance and to the
power which its representatives held over the people's life is
very clear. One only needs to notice the frequency of his
references to the priests in order to recognize this. Again
it is possible to conclude from his quotation of the sanctuary
hymn and from his reference to one of the sanctuary tales
about Jacob that the public services had played a considerable and real part in his life. And further, he speaks as though
the priesthood, a right type of priesthood, and the kingdom
with a worthy representative on the throne, were the two
leading gifts of Yahweh after He had settled Israel in its land.

Hence one is not surprised to find him saying that Israel is
to remain many days without the outward forms of worship
(3 : 4), that this destitution is a sign of the divine anger. The
verse is one which has been often and curiously misunder-
stood. It states that the Children of Israel are to abide many
days without sacrifice and without *mazzeba* and without
ephod or *teraphim*. I have already given you reasons why we
cannot retain mention of the king and the prince. On the
one hand, one finds the conclusion confidently drawn that,
because Hosea includes the *mazzeboth* and *teraphim* along with
sacrifice and *ephod*, and with no more word of blame for the
one than for the other, these semi-heathen emblems were
counted perfectly legitimate in the Yahweh worship of the
prophet's day. Therefore, it is further said, since Deuteronomy
forbids the use of *mazzeboth* at Yahweh altars, the law must
be later than the time of Hosea. But one must note the connection in which the prophet sets the words. He begins with a
statement of how he treated his faithless wife. He brought her
back and said : " Thou shalt abide for me many days, thou

shalt not play the harlot and shalt not be any man's wife." The woman is to be isolated from all intercourse with men, licit or illicit. She is to be for some time alone with her own past and her own thoughts.

And Israel, when Yahweh restores her to Himself, should abide for many days, isolated, without intercourse with Yahweh or with the other gods. And Hosea sets down the ordinary means by which the people's intercourse with Yahweh has been maintained, and joins with each the means by which its idoltary was practised. Sacrifice and the *ephod* represent the licit means of worship : *mazzeba* and *teraphim* the illicit. And Israel for a time is to be deprived of both. It goes back to the beginning before these had come to be a help or a temptation to it.

On the other hand, the verse has been contrasted with v. 5, where it is said that afterwards, after the discipline of isolation, after the time of reflection and repentance, Israel shall return and seek the Lord. There it is said we find no mention of sacrifice or *mazzeba* or the rest. All we find is the conception of a people which seeks God. But again, that ignores the peculiar sense of v. 4. In its time of discipline Israel is to be without sacrifice or *ephod,* or, as we should phrase it, its old means of grace. It is not yet fit to appreciate or use these. They can only come back with healthful life to a nation which has learned to seek Yahweh.

And again we have a suggestion, though it cannot be said to be more, in 14 : 3. Repentant Israel is bidden : " Take with you words and return unto Yahweh " : it is to say, " take away all iniquity and receive us graciously : so will we render as bullocks our lips." Unfortunately the text of the last clause is gravely uncertain, for LXX, and Syriac both read, " so will we render the fruit of our lips." Probably this is the correct rendering. But at least one has there the thought that the people, when it returns, finds it natural to bring something. When it has nothing else to bring, it brings words. But something the glad and grateful heart must bring.

You see at once how such a conception fits in with Hosea's fundamental thought of religion as self-surrender to a God who has shown Himself generous.

How deeply too Hosea was convinced of the need for a

cult we can recognise from one feature of his prophecy which has been strangely ignored in this connection. For he definitely attacked the worship of the golden calves which Jeroboam had instituted in the nation. You will notice that he singles out there, not the cult in itself as the object of his attack, but one feature of it, the use of this particular emblem as a representation of God. It is a remarkable fact in connection with his polemic that he nowhere appeals to the law of the Decalogue or declares that Israel through this act has broken the fundamental condition on which its covenant with God was based. He speaks rather with disgust of sane and reasonable and reverent men making use of such an emblem to represent their deity—as he says, kissing calves. He talks about them as having come from the hands of a workman, made by the hands of those who afterwards adore them. He speaks about their principal value consisting in the metal of which they were made, so that they might be sent as a bribe to the king of Assyria. This was no fitting emblem of God, the God who called His son out of Egypt, who led it like a child through the desert, who gave it its land. This was Ephraim's calf.

But the chief feature to which I would draw your attention is that there you have a man who sees the value and importance of right emblems and worthy outward forms in men's worship. He shows that through his disgust with unworthy forms and emblems. He knows how inevitable some form is to the rituals and acts through which men think about their God. And he would have these befit and so deepen the thoughts they have come to have of their God. He may not need what they bring, but they need to bring it. For their gratitude must find embodiment and expression.

Hosea's theology was capable of giving a rationale for sacrifice. Unfortunately we do not know how the people of his time thought about the sacrifices which they offered. We know that they did offer sacrifices, and even to a certain extent that they made a distinction among them, assigning some as thanksgiving, others as vows, still others as piacular sin-offering. But this does not matter very much. What does matter is the ideas which they attached to the sacrifices they brought, what effect they were supposed to produce on the

God to whom they were offered, what effect they produced on the men who offered them and what was considered necessary in those who thus brought them.

Robertson Smith thought it possible to discern the fundamental idea which lay behind, not merely the Hebrew sacrifices, but all Semitic sacrifice in general, the practice of the *sh'lamim,* the peace-offerings, where God and men shared in the sacrificial victim. And he thought that the act of communion was thus fundamental to Old Testament and even Semitic teaching. Apart from any other consideration, this breaks down on the central position given to the *'ola,* whole burnt-offering, where the worshippers had no share at all. Certain men emphasize the fact of the ritual of blood reserved for God and make the piacular virtue of the sacrifice initial and fundamental. This breaks down on the fact that, in the case of poverty, a sacrifice of atonement might be offered without blood. No one explanation will satisfy. There are crossing and intercrossing lines of thought in the great sacrificial rites. In my judgment sacrifice cannot be said to spring from one simple and common root. The idea that it does rises from the false idea that the primitive man in his first broken ideas of things is simple and clear in his thought, and the confusion springs from later sophistication. Yet primitive man is anything rather than simple. Simplicity is the outcome of hard thought. It does not spring up from the ground at all, but must be toiled for. We are likely to be more correct if we think of the men in old Israel who brought their sacrifices having no clear ideas on the questions in connection with them which have just been mentioned. They brought them, because it was the custom, and they found help through them without very clear ideas as to their meaning.

Now, what Hosea's theology supplied was one clear thought on the meaning of sacrifice. It was a gift, the gift of grateful hearts. Men brought it as an expression of what they felt to be God's due from His people. They gave Him what He claimed and what they acknowledged He had a right to claim. And this we can say, namely, that the idea of a gift in connection with sacrifice came to bulk more in the conception of old Israel from the time of Hosea. One finds this view running through the Psalter.

There is, however, another side of the sacrifice on which we can recognize that Hosea produced a deep influence, and here perhaps it was more connected with the piacular or sin-offering. To understand what I mean you should recall what I have already said about Hosea's idea of sin. He could and did reduce sin to one common root, disloyalty. All the other forms of sin sprang from this, that men failed in loyalty to their God. Well, on the one side, that meant that the prophet could make and press one demand, even repentance. Instead of asking that men should mend this way or that, that they should cease to do this evil or that, he bade them return in one supreme, one single act of repentance to Him from whom they had wandered. From this initial act all other right doing could spring. Without this initial act any other form of improvement was only patchwork at best.

But, just because a right repentance could be so fruitful, it was essential. Nothing else could be put in its place. And I think we can see from that temple hymn he quoted and which he followed with a demand for repentance, that he found the sacrificial system of his time not insisting on this initial act of repentance. The priest was commanding the sinner or the man who in any way desired the divine help to bring his sacrifice. Possibly there was even a tariff, such as appears in Leviticus, according to which the character and quantity of the sacrifice was calculated, so that more was claimed from a king or a prince or a priest than from a common man.

But there was no corresponding or adequate demand for repentance. The rubric Hosea quoted, you will notice, made no such demand. It is not difficult to realise what such a practice would inevitably lead to. The sin-offering would be construed as a *quid pro quo,* by which the sinner offered his satisfaction to God. The sacrifice would come to be construed like a tariff, so much sacrifice for so much sin. And men went home after it no better men.

What Hosea demanded was a closer union between the sacrifice and repentance. And again I think it is possible to show that from his time dates the beginning of those great confessions which appear in the Psalter and which were spoken, either by the officiant or by the offerer, in connection with the sin-offering. You may well recognize, cannot but recognize, the limitation of what was done there. No rational was offered for the meaning of sacrifice in itself. There was no attempt to explain why God required a sacrifice and especially why in certain circumstances He required the outpouring of the blood of the animal at the altar foot after a certain ritual which the priest carried through.

I take these rubrics which accompanied the sacrifices to have been the work of the prophets like Hosea in connection with the cult of Israel. And the men were not theologians whose task it may be to provide such a rationale. They were men who were seeking to purify and raise the practical worship of their people. What they saw was the danger of repentance and sin-offering falling apart with all the ruinous consequences which such a division was bound to bring about in the moral and spiritual life of their people. And they combined with the offering an act of penitence on the part of the offerer. We may conclude that, if they thought of the connection of the two at all, they thought of the two acts as equally essential to a true act of worship. The altar was the meeting place for the two. And God who demanded the sacrifice equally demanded repentance. Without it no sacrifice was valid.

6

ISAIAH

THE BOOK

WHEN we come to Isaiah, we come to a situation totally different from that found in the books hitherto engaging our attention. There it was possible to tell you how certain verses were denied to the prophet, but to leave the bulk of the book to your examination. Here we have not a book, but a collection of booklets, ranging over a period which descends as late as the time after Ezra and Nehemiah.

It is necessary to occupy a good deal more time than has been previously given to the somewhat arid question of introduction. I cannot, of course, go into great detail. Probably the wisest method is first to separate out the sections which can be safely ignored for our present purposes as certainly non-Isaianic.

I need not labour to prove that the second half of the book, from Chapter 40 onwards, has no connection with Isaiah of Jerusalem. But, to confine ourselves to Chapters 1-39, even a cursory reading of the last four chapters, 36-39, is enough to show that these practically repeat what is already contained in 2 Kings 18: 12 ff., 19, 20. The two accounts are not identical, but they clearly come from a common source; they at least use common sources of information. And these must have been certain annals connected with the kingdom, as contrasted with materials written in order to introduce a reader to the history of prophecy. One recognizes that best, if one contrasts these chapters with certain other chapters such as 7 and 8 in the book of Isaiah, which also are concerned with historical events. Those earlier chapters relate the historical events, merely for the sake of letting us know what the prophet said and what action the prophet took in connection with this series of events. The later chapters, on the other hand, make the fate of the state and the capital and the king the primary concern, and Isaiah is introduced merely as a subordinate actor in a much larger drama. Hezekiah and the kingdom which he controls are the primary objects in the view of the writer, though Isaiah occupies, as he could not fail to do, a significant position. This section reminds us of the chapters in 2 Kings which recount Ahab's advance on Ramoth Gilead, where Ahab is the central figure, though Micaiah ben Imlah is a strong factor in the situation. The chapters, accordingly, appear to me not to have been written primarily for their place in the book and were therefore borrowed from another source by the man to whom we owe our present book of Isaiah, because they had a good deal to say about the prophet. This view, of course, does not deny them a very considerable value in our study of the prophet. All it emphasizes is that they do not form so integral a part of the book as the other chapters. So far as concerns the light they throw on Isaiah's life, their independent character lends them an added value, since they show us Isaiah from a different angle. The conclusion lies close at hand that the story of the incident was not written for our book of Isaiah, but was extracted from some other more secular authority and inserted here.

Again, immediately preceding these historical chapters, come two, 34 and 35, which in language, spirit and historical outlook are closely allied with what is named Deutero-Isaiah. It may not be so easy to place them as it is to place the longer collection. But I should not hesitate to count them as exilic in their origin.

And, further, we must count chapters 24-27 to be a late apocalypse. Speaking of them purely from the point of view of the ideas which they express I would urge that, while the ideas of this apocalypse are closely linked with the fundamental teaching of Isaiah, they are the outcome of that teaching and the result of later reflection on what this fundamental teaching implies. The contention, that they are later in date than the book to which they have been added, is confirmed by an examination of the language used. The argument for their later origin is cumulative.

This leaves chapters 1-23 and 28-33. Here we come at once on a body of material, chapters 13-23, which can be grouped together as oracles against or concerning foreign nations. In determining the authenticity of these, we are in a better position than we are in connection with some others, since the historical criterion can be applied with tolerable certainty. For the oracles about the nations contain here and there hints as to the position of these nations relatively to Judah or of Judah and the neighbouring nations relatively to Assyria. You will recall how the fact that Assyria was regarded as a possible ally in Hosea Chapter 14 was enough to show that the verse could not easily be regarded as a late addition, since, very soon after Hosea's day, Assyria became the great enemy and finally the destroyer of the Northern Kingdom. The use of some similar criterion helps us in connection with certain of these oracles. It is impossible, e.g., to retain Chapter 13 and the great part of Chapter 14 as belonging to Isaiah's period, because there Babylon is evidently the oppressor of Judah and has long been the oppressor of the Southern Kingdom. Now the only appearance of Babylon on the political stage during Isaiah's life-time is in the role of a possible ally, since we find Babylonian ambassadors at Hezekiah's court trying to influence the king to support a league engineered from Babylon.

Judging from the point of view of historical knowledge which, it is fair to remember, is by no means perfect or complete, we may retain among the collection of oracles, chapters 14: 24-32, 17, 18; and with less certainty but yet with probability chapters 20 and 22.

But this collection of oracles on the nations once stood by itself. Its incorporation into the book which bore Isaiah's name was an afterthought. And it was not baldly stuck on, but was woven into its surroundings. What preceded it was rounded off by the addition of a final oracle which betrays close affinities with exilic material. We must write off 11: 11 ff. and Chapter 12 as containing nothing genuinely Isaianic. This leaves us with 1—11: 10, 28-33 with the oracles on the nations which are Isaianic.

These are the broad lines on which we can partition the book, and so far procedure is pretty clear, and, above all, we are operating with definite criteria, historical or otherwise. When, however we come to closer analysis of what is left, the matter is far more difficult to disentangle with any certainty. For we come at once into the region where subjective criteria play a larger part. Men's preconceptions as to what was the function of a prophet at any time, and in particular as to what was the function of Isaiah in his particular time have a great deal to do with the results which are offered.

Still dealing broadly with the material, however, we find in chapters 6, 7, 8 and even 9, a series of historical narratives which are similar to the historical narratives of chapters 36-39 in certain respects, but in certain other respects very different in character. They are similar in that they are cast into historical form. They are different in that Isaiah is there the commanding figure and the whole account centres in what Isaiah said and did on the particular occasion. Something is introduced as to the historical setting of the narrative and the period of Isaiah's history to which it refers. But these details are reported only so far as they throw light on the attitude of the prophet and help to make clearer the course of what he said on the occasion. It seems probable that these chapters once formed part of a little work which might be entitled *The Life and Utterances of the Prophet Isaiah* with the emphasis laid on the utterances. And, as these chapters begin with Isaiah's call, i.e. as they begin with the incident which made him a prophet, which one might have naturally expected to find at the beginning of the book called by his name, the probability is that this narrative or document once existed independently of the chapters 1-5 which precede it and stood by itself. With this book we may associate such a chapter as 20. It too gives the historical setting, but only in sufficient detail to make a little clearer what was the meaning of the word for the sake of which it was set down here. Because the chapter deals with the fate of Egypt and Ethiopia, it has been removed from the little book of which it may once have formed part and placed among the oracles of the nations which have been collected into chapters 13-23.

Now it is very difficult to mark off the limits of the little book cc. 6-9 ff. Not only does the narrative merge into oracles;

it was written for the sake of the oracles : it was preserved for the sake of the oracles, to remind men of what Isaiah said. The historical introductions were put at the beginning of the oracles and hence one can tell where they began. But as nothing was added at the end, it is difficult to tell where the book ended and whether material which is at present closely connected with it originally belonged there.

But further, the book has also been put together in a way which we should count casual. Evidently the writer had a number of sayings which were attributed to Isaiah, which he believed to have come from Isaiah, and which he wished to incorporate. About some of these he knew the circumstances which called them into existence and so he gave his state-ment of those historical events with which they were con-nected. But you need only read Chapter 7 through in order to see that he had certain sayings which were lying loose, as it were, unconnected with any events. But these he was anxious, rightly and naturally, to keep. So he placed them in positions which seemed to him to refer to the same subject. Chapter 7 contained the prophecy of Immanuel about the coming of Immanuel in the end of the days i.e. in the con-summation or the day of the Lord. At its close, it is very instructive to remember one finds a whole series of verses, vv. 18, 20, 21, 22, 23 which all begin with the formula "it shall come to pass in that day", or "in the same day". Obviously the man had a number of utterances of Isaiah referring to the end or the consummation and he put them here where a great oracle dealt with that event. These also, one may sum up the end of the chapter, are sayings of the prophet about the consummation. But, seeing that, one must be on one's guard against taking it for granted that these other sayings were originally so closely connected, as at present they are, with the oracle to which they have been appended. They have not the historical event, which called out the first of them, in common. They have only this in common that they too refer to the time of the end. The same phenomenon appears again at the close of Chapter 8. It is difficult to know with anything approaching certainty where the oracle connected with Maher-shalal-hash-baz comes to an end. The original oracle, as Isaiah delivered it, has been preserved practically as the prophet uttered it—at least there is no reason to think otherwise. But to it have been added other sayings of Isaiah, several of which have no genuine connection with the circumstances which called out the Maher-shalal-hash-baz oracle. They were added there, because, to the collector, that seemed an appropriate place for their being included. And so in several other cases it is wise to keep before one the possibility that certain oracles are strung together because of some connection which was only patent to the thought of the man who brought them together. One has always to count it possible that the oracles were originally much shorter and more pithy than they appear when printed in our lengthy and careful present chapters.

Then, again, one has, for example, in chapters 1-5, and 28-33, (quite apart from isolated verses which may have been incorporated there) collections of dicta, bare oracles with no historical setting. These belong to all periods of the prophet's life: they have been put together by later men in utter disregard of chronological order. Whatever principle governed the collectors in their arrangement of the oracles they possessed, chronological order had no influence on them.

An oracle, like Chapter 28 : 1 ff., which implies the continued existence of Samaria, finds place after the vivid picture (10 : 28 ff.) which represents the victorious march of the Assyrian army to the crown of the ridge dominating the approach to Jerusalem from the north. Yet the idea of the unhindered approach of such an army to within striking distance of the capital was prompted by the collapse of Northern Israel and the capture of Samaria. Again, an oracle, which is clearly early, like Chapter 2 : 6 ff., is put after a view of the situation in Chapter 1 which represents certain parts of Judah as overrun by, and in the power of, the enemy.

Do not imagine that I am finding fault with the arrangement of the book. The chronological order of prophecies is not the only, nor is it necessarily the best, order in a book of sayings. It is perfectly legitimate for any man to attempt an arrangement of such oracles by subject. My sole reason for drawing attention to it is that, since to the modern student the chronological order is of some significance, you must not be astonished if I seem to pass from point to point in our study of the book.

I have thought it best to try to group the material round certain periods, the leading periods in the prophet's life, and so to make clearer the picture of the work he did in and for his nation and the way in which his own thought grew in relation to the situations which he was required to meet.

There are then four main periods of Isaiah's ministry.

(1) From the death of Uzziah to the beginning of the reign of Ahaz.

(2) The Syro-Ephraimitic invasion about 735.

(3) The period for which the centre of interest is the fall of Samaria in 721 which produced a profound impression on the Judean state and on all men's minds.

(4) The time of Assyrian domination which culminated in the invasion of Sennacherib in 701.

Menahem paid tribute to Assyria, and had apparently been able to maintain himself, after the deposition of Shallum, by the help of Assyria (2 Kings 15 : 19). He seems to have been a military governor of the old capital Tirzah, v. 14; and it was natural for him, as a military man, to admire the powerful, centralized force of Assyria and to recognize its remarkable efficiency. He may even have learned from its methods of government.

At least, having the support of Assyria behind him, Menahem was able to maintain himself for ten years and to keep Israel in subordination to Assyria. He not only maintained his own power, but handed on the throne to his son Pekahiah who reigned for two years. Against him, however, Pekah, son of Remaliah, another army captain, rose and made himself king about 735. Pekah may have been anti-Assyrian from the beginning, may have represented the faction which favoured an alliance with Egypt and may have risen in the name of the party advocating this policy. Or he may have come to power through his own ambition and through the vague discontent of his people, and may afterwards have been drawn into an alliance against Assyria, and the more easily so drawn, because a policy differing from that of Pekahiah naturally appealed to him. Either explanation of his conduct is equally natural. All we know with certainty is that he did break with

Assyria. But it is wise to recognize that we do not certainly
know why he took the steps he did.

We know certain facts about this period, broad facts: but
we know nothing of the motives which prompted and brought
about these facts. And I should like to put you on your guard
against accepting men's theories about the motives along
with the broad facts. We do not know the inner life of Israel
at this time, and whether there was or was not a sense that,
through Menahem's submission to Assyria, the distinctive elements of Israel's life and Israel's religion were being swept
away. Men guess at these inner motives, but they do it without knowledge. And then we all, supplying our interpretation
of certain movements, cannot avoid mixing it up with our
statement of the facts. You who only get the facts at second-
hand are apt to take it for granted that these facts imply,
and only imply, the motives which are suggested. I want you
to try, in judging men like Pekah and Ahaz and others, to
use your own commonsense and to keep an open mind.

Now we know that Tiglath-pileser from 737-5 was kept
busy in the east. We further know that Rezon of Damascus
and Pekah united against Assyria and were joined by the
Philistine towns, Askelon and Gaza, and even by Tyre and
Sidon. Whether Pekah rose before the coalition was formed,
as a result of the schemes of Damascus, basing on the anti-
Assyrian faction in Israel, or whether, having murdered
Pekahiah, he felt driven to join the coalition, we cannot tell.
But the coalition was formed, and an effort was made to
force reluctant Judah into union with it.

In Judah Jotham had succeeded his father Uzziah or
Azariah about 736. Samaria and Damascus moved against
him, but he died before any decisive result was reached and
was succeeded by Ahaz. This brings us to the Syro-Ephraimitic war and the rise of Isaiah. In connection with this, I do
not want at present to deal with Isaiah's attitude or to touch
on his message. One can see that more clearly, I fancy, if one
puts it by itself. Only I wish you to recognise the political
situation as it concerns our estimate of Ahaz, since our
estimate of Ahaz and his position has a good deal to do with
the question of how we interpret Isaiah's attitude and resulting message.

Now here is the situation. Ahaz not long on the throne, found himself faced by the hostile combination of Israel backed by Damascus and the Philistine towns. They wish to force him into an alliance with them against Assyria. His people are appalled : as Isaiah puts it, the hearts of the people were swaying as the trees of the forest are swayed by the wind. Little wonder! Experience had proved their inability to stand against Israel alone; what chance had they against Israel backed by these forces?

Ahaz judged that, if he fell in with the demand, it was practically all up with Jerusalem's independence. The control of the national destinies passed out of their own hands into the hands of these alien courts, and he and his people were simply pawns to be moved hither and thither at the will of these greater powers.

Further he seems to have judged that Assyria was by no means played out, but was able to assert itself still in the west. In fact he judged that Assyria was the stronger political force of the two, a judgment which history in a few years was amply to vindicate. It was natural, and to my mind legitimate, for him to say that, if Judah must be dependent on somebody, it was better for it to be dependent on the distant power, which, because it was distant, would interfere less with Judah's peculiar institutions and its peculiar life than close neighbours would. He determined to back Assyria rather than cast in his lot with the coalition.

Now, we are told that, by so doing, Ahaz introduced Assyria as a factor into the west and gave Assyria an excuse for interfering sooner or later with the life of Judah. This is plain nonsense. It ignores the obvious fact that Assyria was already not merely a factor but was the leading factor in the west. It was because Assyria was such a tremendous factor in the west that the coalition was hammering at the gates of Jerusalem. These powers would never have taken up the attitude they did to Judah, had it not been that Assyria was pressing close at their back.

Further, to say that by his action Ahaz gave Assyria an excuse for interfering in Palestinian politics is to credit Assyria with the need for finding an excuse. So to speak and think is to misunderstand the old Semitic world. Assyria needed no

7

other excuse to interfere anywhere than what was supplied
by its own ambition and greed. It had already interfered
wherever its own ambition and greed seemed to make it
worth while to interfere. If it had not interfered with Judah,
it was partly because the coalition was barring the way, and
partly because it was not worth while.

The coalition seems to have counted largely on the impotence of Tiglath-pileser with his hands tied by his eastern
troubles. Perhaps too they had hopes from Egypt. But in 734
the Assyrian turned fiercely on the west. He was able to mask
Damascus—at least he did not capture the town—and to
push forward against Israel. He captured Galilee and overran all Northern Israel beyond the plain of Esdraelon, 2 Kings
15 : 29. Thereafter, according to his own account, he turned
southward and, passing Samaria, took the two Philistine towns
Askelon and Gaza. The only explanation I can offer for such
a method of campaigning is that he was aiming at shutting
off all communication on the part of the league with Egypt.

Thereupon he turned on central Israel. Pekah was murdered by his own people, and the faction which favoured
dependence on Assyria set up Hoshea 734-3, cf. 2 Kings 15 :
30. After a two years' siege Damascus fell in 732 and its
people were deported. About this time Ahaz appears at the
court of Tiglath-pileser (2 Kings 16 : 10-16), and is said to
have sent back to his High Priest the pattern of an altar, with
instructions that a similar one should be set up in the temple
at Jerusalem. I have already alluded to the incident in dis-
cussing the message of Hosea. It appears somewhat improbable that what prompted the king's action was a purely
aesthetic consideration and that he, in an hour big with the
fate of his kingdom was eager to have a pretty addition to
the temple furniture. The greater probability is that the altar
was made after the Assyrian pattern, because it carried with
it the acknowledgment of the deity. The suzerainty of Assyria
brought with it a public recognition of the worship and the
power of the alien god.

Immediately after 732 when Damascus fell, Tiglath-pileser
was again busy in the east and was forced to leave the west
to itself. He died in 727 without having returned to this
scene of his conquests. The death of a king has always meant

more in a pure autocracy like that of Assyria, and especially in a military autocracy, than it does under a constitutional monarchy.

No sooner was the great conqueror gone and his strong hand off the reins of power, than Samaria began to stir afresh. There is reason to suspect that this new movement in northern Palestine was stirred up by Egypt. At least this is sure, that it coincided with an increased power which obtained in Egypt. A new king, Shabaka, who came from Ethiopia, had seized the throne and had brought a new unity and vigour into the kingdom. This inspired the desire to extend Egyptian influence into the border province of Syria.

Thus we find that Hoshea of Israel was persuaded to enter into alliance with Shabaka or So, as his name appears in 2 Kings 17 : 4. We also know that Hanno of Gaza, one of the towns in Philistia which were leagued with Pekah of Israel and Rezon of Damascus against Assyria, returned from Egypt about 722. All this makes one suspect that Egypt had its hand in this whole business and was stirring up Palestine and Syria for its own purposes. The conditions in Egypt itself which led to the rise of Shabaka are unfortunately far from clear, and so are the conditions which he instituted when he had seized the throne. But enough is known to make this suggestion not improbable.

Assyria crushed the rising. Hoshea was captured by Shal-maneser, but Samaria put up a desperate resistance in spite of the fall of its king. It was only taken after a siege of two or three years by Sargon in 722. According to Sargon's inscriptions 27,290 of the inhabitants of Samaria were deported after his victory

ISAIAH : INTRODUCTION

It was among such circumstances that Isaiah came to his work and tried to fulfil it.

Who he was, beyond the fact that his father was Amoz, that he was married, that he had at least two sons, and that he was an inhabitant, if not a native, of Jerusalem, we do not know. That he was city-bred, if not city-born, there can be little doubt. His thought moves continually round the Jerusalem he knows, its temple, its citadel, its annual pilgrimages, its thronged streets, its towers and walls and water-supply. He is at home among these things. Yet it is well to recognize that to be city-bred did not mean then what it is apt to mean to-day. No town in Judah is large enough to crib a citizen's imagination to the limits of its streets, and least of all Jerusalem. For the capital sat like old Edinburgh, a little city, high-perched, leading the eyes of its inhabitants beyond itself. One who knew it later talked about it as a place of far distances : and the phrase sets one aspect of the city vividly before us, reminding one of George Street with its glimpses of the Firth and the lands of Fife. As little did a town of those days in Palestine give the sense of being self-contained, which is apt to crib the imagination of a man who to-day lives among streets. A modern city is so large and its supply is carried out so methodically and so much out of sight that we do not need to remember, and so become apt to forget, our dependence. We remember it so little that we may come to imagine that the country depends on the town. The produce of the villages came to be marketed in the open squares of Jerusalem. The peasant woman with heavy baskets and the asses with laden panniers were familiar sights, necessary sights, reminding Jerusalem that without the villages it would starve.

Isaiah lived within sight of Olivet with its terraced oliveyards, within reach of Hebron and its terraced vines. He mixes with pictures of the riot in the palaces of Jerusalem the song of the vineyards (5 : 1-5), which is copied from a harvest-home chant and which still keeps the cadences of its origin. He utters woe on those who add house to house : and the extreme woe is that the seed of an omer should yield an ephah, that is to say, when he describes the failure of men's hopes, he turns naturally to the failure of the crops. The life about which he spoke and to which he spoke was in Jerusalem, but it was a Jerusalem still conscious of the processes of nature on which it all depended and of the outer world beyond the walls which is so liable to disappear as an influence upon the thoughts of modern men.

Only he is conscious, in a way in which, and to an extent

to which, Amos never showed himself conscious, of the need
for human organization and human civilization to build up
the frail structure in which men live together for their mutual
comfort and support. Amos is the peasant, living remote from
towns, self-centred a little, self-reliant more than a little,
either ignorant of, or wilfully ignoring, how much even the
loneliest man in Israel is made by the action and reaction
of the forces among which he lives. Hence Amos can view
with comparative equanimity the collapse of the outward
things on which he has never fully realized his dependence.
But Isaiah was city-bred and knew what social life is and
what it implies. He knows, and lets us see that he knows,
what it means when the force of law grows weak, when children are the governors and women the rulers of " my people ",
and when the leaders cause the common folk to err and lead
them off along strange paths, 3: 12. The faithful city becomes a harlot, when princes, who should represent law, are
themselves the rebels against law, so that the fatherless are
not judged and the cause of the widow is not considered, 1:
21 ff. He realizes profoundly that, in this perplexed life of
men, law is the one protection of the weak, and, when it is dis-
regarded, every defence is gone and life becomes a scramble,
where the weak will always go to the wall. Justice may be
merely a convention, and when it comes to be expressed in
human statutes, may err badly. But in the end a convention as
to what is just is the only thing which stands between the
oppressor and the oppressed.

Life is not so simple to this townsman as it seemed to the
herdsman of Tekoa. It needs disciplining, governing, guiding,
regulating. It needs law and justice, expressed in plain human
statutes and embodied in a strong governor who can enforce
these things and who will not hesitate to do so. Isaiah sees
something of the long process of time, by which these things,
the frail shelter which men have built up against the icy blast
from the outer wilderness, against the greed of their neighbours, aye and ultimately against the fierce lusts of their own
hearts, have come into existence. He sees God's hand in these
things, blundering though they often are. They may be poor
substitutes for the eternal justice which Amos desired to see
flow down like a river. But the eternal justice in all its austere

beauty is apt to be rather remote from the constant needs of time, unless it becomes incarnate in human flesh. Hence Isaiah comes nearer Hosea who had believed that Israel's institutions, kingdom and priesthood, lawcourt and lawbook, were gifts to Israel from Yahweh, who could write His Torah in a thousand statutes and set up men to teach its truth.

The king and the judge, the ordered life for which these figures stand, the mutual dependence of men on one another to which their very existence witnesses, are apt to seem remote to the dweller among the steppes or among the foothills. Often he only realizes their power when they turn to rottenness and exert a mischievous influence on his personal life. He resents them, when they are bad; he fails to be conscious of their significance for him, so long as they are good. He does not realize that men need them continually for a decent orderly existence, since he himself lives greatly without them, measuring himself against the stark processes of nature with which his daily struggle is carried on.

So Isaiah's thought of God is naturally the thought of One who is king, the lawgiver, the source of all seemly regulation and sweet order. So too his conception of the future is deeply influenced by his recognition of the need of the present which is the necessity for all time. And when the consummation arrives, when Yahweh has intervened to remake what is unworthy and to institute what is perennial, of the increase of Messiah's government there shall be no end. It is Isaiah who originates the conception of Messiah as ruler, who receives from Yahweh the sevenfold endowment of the spirit for his rule. In the end the world shall be governed because the world needs government, cannot indeed continue without it. Without government it is not a world. What is loudly calling for Yahweh's intervention at present is the utter want of discipline which is patent everywhere. I will restore, he says, thy judges as at the first and thy counsellors as at the beginning : afterwards, when this is done, thou shalt deserve thy name, the city of righteousness, the faithful city, 1 : 26. Life is an ordered thing to Isaiah, or else it hardly deserves the name, at least it is not all that God meant it to be for man. And order means law and a people which is willing to observe the law : it means a worthy ruler to enforce the law and a heart in the governed to recognize its purpose and to welcome its restraint. The shoot which springs up out of the stem of Jesse shall be of quick understanding in the fear of the Lord. He shall not judge after mere superficial appearances, nor shall he reprove after a mere casual hearing : but with righteousness shall he judge and with equity shall he reprove, 11 : 1 ff. Isaiah had the sense of the organized life of a nation where men live together in mutual society. And the organic life does not come by accident, it grows out of the ideals and the disciplined obediences of the generations. In turn it profoundly influences and deeply modifies these ideals in all the succeeding generations.

It is often taken for granted that the prophet belonged to the governing caste in Judah or even that he was in some more or less direct way connected with the royal house. To me the matter remains wholly incapable of proof one way or another, so much so that I shall not waste your time in this rapid sketch by entering into discussion of it, especially since the question does not deeply concern us. All that I should wish to say is that there is no real ground for the resulting suggestion that Ahaz was unable to brush aside the interference of one who, like Isaiah, occupied a leading position in the society of the capital, in the casual way in which Amaziah brushed aside the peasant prophet from Tekoa. For in reality I can see no evidence that Ahaz did show any special consideration to Isaiah. Amaziah, as we say, warned Jeroboam of the appearance of Amos, because he thought it possible that the prophet was the mouthpiece of popular discontent and might become the means of fanning that discontent into a flame. In a period of popular excitement any official in a modern state might find it neessary to warn his government of the appearance of some popular demagogue. In the same way Ahaz seems to have acted towards Isaiah. When the prophet appears in connection with the troubles about the coalition, Ahaz shows him the half-annoyed, half-timid deference of a government in face of a movement which it does not welcome, but cannot quite measure. " This man is quite ignorant and very troublesome. He cannot possibly estimate the difficulty of our situation between the coalition on the one side and Assyria on the other. But he comes here speaking in the name of religion and he may have behind him for all one knows a body of fanatical opposition which is capable of being very troublesome. It is as well to deal cautiously with him and not commit oneself too far ".

But afterwards, when the government with its league with Assyria was sure of itself and felt that the northern coalition had spent its force, the attitude of the court stiffened at once. And in Chapter 28 we find the leaders mocking at the prophet. " We have made a covenant with death and with hell we are in agreement ". That is to say, " our position is so secure that neither death nor hell can do us any harm. As for this babbling prophet with his talk about moral considerations and his kind of dame's school teaching about right and wrong, he does not count any more in state counsels."

ISAIAH'S CALL

We are singularly fortunate in having, in connection with Isaiah, so full an account of his call. For, in his call, in what he conceived to be the nature of Him who called him, and in what he believed to be the task to which he was called, we have his fundamental thoughts about God and about God's relation to Israel.

Notice, then, first how he fills the conception of the divine holiness with ethical content. It is not possible here to deal fully with this subject, but you should notice that *qadhosh* (or " holy ") at the time when Isaiah rose, did not carry in Israel the content which we naturally put into it. God to the Semite was holy, so far as He was God; that is, so far as He was separate from man. But He might be separate from man, because He was eternal while man was transient, because He was omnipotent while man was creaturely. Holiness marked that by which and in which God was different from man. Hence it was a purely negative term. It was that through which the divine was not human. As such, God, being separate from man, reacted against anyone who came carelessly into His presence. He could not bear the presence of this inferior creature. But He might react against man's weakness, against man's transient character.

Isaiah thinks of God as holy, separate from man. But he shows what to him constitutes this holiness, when he says what it is in him against which God reacted. The reaction of Yahweh's holiness was against that which was ethically unclean, not against that which was creaturely and weak. " I am a man of unclean lips ". Isaiah has filled the negative thought of holiness with ethical content.

In the same way, it is unnecessary to dwell on, but only necessary to underline, his monotheism. The fullness of the whole earth is the *kabhodh,* the self-manifestation of Yahweh. That leaves room in the world for no other than one God. Isaiah is conscious of living in a universe which is a universe, because its fullness is divine.

Only it is well to recognize again that these two convictions about God are not accidentally combined in the prophet's mind. They appear together in the prophet's mind at the beginning of his life-work, because they belong together. What Amos had already clearly felt, Isaiah clearly expresses. The world is one in the ethical purpose of Yahweh. What gives it content and meaning is that it embodies a self-manifestation of God. There is only one will which controls all things and which gives significance to this multiform world. There is only One and there can be but one way of serving His will.

So far, you notice, Isaiah brings out more sharply what Amos had felt after, and he begins from it. It gives him his favourite thought about God, as the moral governor, the king of Israel first, and then of all things in heaven and earth. But it gives him also his valuation for everything which, however brokenly, reflects or maintains the order God has set in His universe. All good order is of God, whose will is no mere transcendental thing. It makes the meaning of the universe. But, in particular, it has intervened to guide Israel's history, and it is about to intervene again. Only, before it manifests itself, Yahweh has come to make known to a prophet what He is about to do. He even calls a man, who is conscious of his unfitness for the task, to be this prophet. The will of Yahweh is not merely that which fills the whole earth with the splendour of His purpose : it has manifested itself in Jerusalem and in the temple, which are Judah's capital and Judah's place of worship. It now manifests itself there to such

7*

a man as Isaiah knows himself to be. So far again there is
no great difference between Isaiah and Amos. Amos also
had believed in a special revelation to Israel, for Yahweh
raised up prophets there. Amos too had told Amaziah how
hopeless it was to stifle prophecy, since God revealed His
mind to a herdsman.

Yet one cannot ignore that Isaiah saw God in the temple.
We need not, must not, press the matter too far, as though
it meant that he took a less severe view of the cult of his time
than his predecessor, for he did not. In his definition of the
divine holiness he was controverting the ideas in his people's
law. As little, however, ought we to ignore it. Amos comes
from the open hill : Isaiah from the historic emblems and the
historic places of his people's worship. It would be a mistake
to conclude that he counts these things necessary; but it is
legitimate to believe that he regarded them as valuable and
capable, if rightly used, of being helpful. He himself found
God through them and even counted it worth while to say
that he found God through them. These outward forms, in
which men had tried to express their thought about God,
are not merely dear to him through old association : they
have been helpful to him in his personal life. So helpful have
they been, that he finds it possible, and even natural, to
clothe his new commission and his new thoughts in these old
formulæ. They have served a great purpose and something
like them *may* be needed to serve the purpose for which
the prophet knows himself to be summoned. This seems the
thought which lies behind the fact that Isaiah valued the
temple and Jerusalem as other prophets did not.

What that purpose is is to declare the end of the self-
revelation of Yahweh who is about to appear in the world
and in Israel's history. Now, Amos, as we saw, had been
content to insist that this self-revelation must imply chastisement. And, while his thought inevitably implied more than
chastisement, the larger end never emerged into the foreground of his teaching. Isaiah could not keep in the background the ultimate end for which chastisement is only the
preparation, for the simple reason that he himself had received so much more. Isaiah cannot declare that the end of
the divine self-revelation is chastisement, because it has not

been so to him. A prophet declares what he has found in God, in his singularly intimate communion and his personal relation. Now Isaiah found that Yahweh redeemed him. And, as he knew himself to be no better than other men—" I am a man of unclean lips and I dwell among a people of unclean lips "—he knew that the end of the divine self-revelation to his people must be the same as its end to himself : it must be to redeem them.

In connection with Isaiah's emphasis on the uncleanness of his own and his people's lips it is necessary to remember that " in Hebrew idiom a man's words include his purpose on the one hand, his actions on the other, and thus impurity of lips means inconsistency of purpose and action with the standard of the divine holiness ". Thus Jerusalem is said to be ruined and Judah to be fallen, because their tongue and their doings are against the Lord to provoke the eyes of His glory. (3 : 8). The idea is that they have set themselves, alike in the outward and inward drift of their lives, against the divine will which upholds all things. But further Isaiah shows what he means by uncleanness in 1 : 16 ff. " Wash you, make you clean, put away the evil of your doings from before Mine eyes, cease to do evil, learn to do well, seek judgment, relieve the oppressed, judge the fatherless, plead for the widow." When therefore the prophet, knowing himself to be in the presence of God, declares himself and his nation to be of unclean lips, he means that God's presence reacts against such impurity. It does not react to him in the way in which it reacted against Uzzah's deed in touching the ark. When God in His holiness draws near to man in order to make His will known, the one quality which is needed in those who are to endure His presence is purity. He expects and demands it because of what He is in Himself. The title holy was of very wide connotation and above all it was purely negative. That left it open for each prophet to attach to the divine nature what seemed to him most important.

No sooner had Isaiah uttered his confession of sin and need than Yahweh removes the sin and fulfils the need. At a touch, on the divine command, he is renewed. Someone has said that Isaiah has made the action and the means of the divine forgiveness very easy. And what he intends to suggest is that

the prophet makes it too easy, easier than we, with our knowledge of what is implied in it, can readily conceive. I should
not refer to this at all, were it not that it gives one the opportunity of saying that Isaiah finds redemption easy, because of
what was behind it. Behind it was all the purpose of Almighty
God, everything which prompted Him to intervene at all in
this world of men. He came to chastise the old. Yes! But He
came ultimately to recreate. When He came first, it was to
create a world, the fullness of which was His self-revelation.
When He comes again, it is to recreate a broken world.

Note that there is nothing corresponding to this in the attitude of any preceding prophet. Elijah counted it the melan-
choly feature of his situation that he alone in all Israel was
found faithful in his testimony for Yahweh. To this must be
added the fact that, when the divine revelation came to him
at Horeb, it was to tell him that he was mistaken about other
people, not that he was mistaken in his opinion of himself.
What he learned was that there were still seven thousand in
Israel who had remained faithful, not that he had at all failed
in faithfulness. That is to say, in his intimate intercourse with
God, Elijah was not made conscious of his failure or his
sin.

"Go, prophesy against My people Israel", is the divine
commission to Amos. He was conscious accordingly that he
stood alone with and for Yahweh opposed to a disobedient
nation. Even in Hosea the means through which he came to
learn God's compassion was to recognize that he must remain
faithful to his first affection and to his first vow, though his
wife had outraged both. His commission also separated him
from other men. He became a preacher of the divine mercy,
not because he had come to realize how much he needed it,
but because he saw that he could not refuse mercy to someone
else.

But Isaiah had begun by identifying himself with his
people. He, equally with them, was unfit to bear the near
presence of their common God. Only when he acknowledged
himself a sharer in their guilt had he received reconciliation.
But no sooner had he acknowledged this guilt than he was
restored to fellowship with God and was even commissioned
to become the messenger of the divine purpose to the guilty

people. His right to speak of what Yahweh's purpose was rested on the fact that God had redeemed him. He knew himself restored to a right relation with the great will which controlled all things and Yahweh sent him, endowed with this knowledge and having passed through this experience, to speak to other men about His will. Obviously, then, the prophet could not denounce on a guilty people a chastisement from Yahweh which held no hope, since what was fundamental to his personal conviction about his relation to Yahweh was that, in spite of his guilt, God had not only restored him, but had also commanded him to become His prophet.

What has made it difficult to hold this, however, is the interpretation given to the message which he received immediately after his call. As it stands in the M.T. and as it appears in our E.V., the message ends in v.13 on a note of hope. Before that, however, it speaks of chastisement in very strong terms. It states that one result of the prophet's work must be simply to rouse envenomed opposition and so serve to make men worse. When Isaiah said that the effect of his mission in certain quarters would be to make men more deaf and blind to the divine purposes with them than before, he said in vivid phrase what our Lord meant when He said that one effect of His coming would be that men would have no cloak for their sin. Men who positively reject a divine warning or a divine appeal are in worse moral estate than if they had gone on in evil unthinkingly. There is even a judicial hardening of the heart produced by God's setting the clear issues before men, so that the refusal to listen may be ascribed to the action of the Almighty. The prophet was there sadly recognizing one fact in human history and human experience which is summed up in our homely proverb : There are none so blind as those who *will* not see.

Then, further, Isaiah emphasizes that the effect of the divine coming which it is his to announce must be, in New Testament phrase, a fearful looking for of judgment. He says that only a tenth shall be left in the nation. There he was following Amos, who had said that the town which went out a thousand should have only a hundred left, that the town which went out a hundred should have only ten left. Both prophets declared that the first effect of the judgment should be the destruction of all but a tenth of the people. Then Isaiah continues that even this tenth should be made subject to a further testing, so thorough should be the work of God in the world. But when all this was past, when the first remnant from the trial of God should be tried to the uttermost, the case would be like that of a tree which men cut down to the very roots. Even though its trunk is gone, the root and stump are left and the new shoots spring to life. So the holy seed, that is, the remnant which partakes of the character of Him who has brought this trial and which accepts the standards of the divine judgment should spring from the stump of ruined and broken Israel.

What led men, however, to question this connection of thought was that they hesitated to accept the last clause of the whole. It was believed that this sentence " the holy seed shall be the stock thereof " was absent from the LXX, and it was said that this was an addition, made by a later editor, who desired to soften Isaiah's harsh judgment by adding here some reference to his peculiar doctrine of the remnant. And Marti was able to appeal to this, which he held an addition, and to say that originally Isaiah, like all the early prophets, was merely a prophet of doom and held out no promise of restoration.

I should like to add that at one time I agreed with these expositors and in my early volume on the *Religion of Israel under the Kingdom* took the same attitude, but made an effort to escape from its consequences. But later I worked over the material of Isaiah again and came to the conclusion that the idea of the LXX having omitted the clause is a mistake. I had accepted too readily the judgment of my predecessors and had not sufficiently examined the facts for myself. It is another illustration of the truth of the old saying that you should always verify your references. In my judgment it is impossible to agree with the verdict that the clause is omitted by the LXX. As the LXX reading stands, it rather witnesses to the presence of the closing clause in the passage and indeed serves to improve its reading.

Now the view expressed here helps to resolve the difficulty which Skinner expresses in the second edition of his Com-

mentary on Isaiah.[1] He says : " It must have been soon after
the inaugural vision that a son was born to Isaiah whom he
named Shear-jashub, that is, a remnant shall return, thus
giving expression to a distinctive element of his teaching, *viz.*
the conviction that there was in Israel an indestructible spiritual kernel which should survive the impending judgment and
form the nucleus of the new people of God ". That is to say,
from the earliest period of his public appearance as a prophet
he came, not only with the announcement of the judgment,
but with the conviction that the judgment looked beyond destruction to an issue which was mercy. The boy, he states was
already old enough to walk when his father brought him
with him to meet Ahaz. Skinner's difficulty is to reconcile the
conviction expressed in the boy's name with the closing verse
of Isaiah's commission which Skinner also takes to mean
judgment without a hint of mercy.[2] The name of the boy is
really the expression of the same conviction as that which
came to the prophet at the time when he received his commission. And his commission in turn is integrally related to
his experience at his call. He himself in spite of his sin had
been redeemed by God and sent to declare His mind to
Israel. God's mind is thus essentially related to a purpose of
redemption for His people. Hence the prophet, when he is
told to denounce woe on Israel, instinctively asks, " Lord,
how long?" As natural is it for Yahweh to respond to this
question " how long?" with an answer which marks the *ter-
minus ad quem* of the judgment. The judgment itself may
be long : it must be appallingly severe, but it must issue
in something larger and richer than mere destruction.

Then further this recognition of the form in which this
conviction came to the prophet makes another point clearer.
He has spoken about the holy seed being the shoot from the
stock left after the judgment. And so afterwards he speaks
about Messiah the head as the scion from the stem of Jesse.
The whole thought of the prophet is seen to be closely related
and consistent throughout.

The man then has learned that he, in spite of his unworthiness, has been forgiven by God and has even been counted

[1] *The Book of the Prophet Isaiah, Chapters I-XXXIX.* Revised
Edition, p. xxvi.
[2] Not quite accurate. [Ed.].

worthy to be the divine messenger to his nation. Since this reality of his forgiveness is fundamental to his thought of God in His relation to himself, it must also be fundamental in the divine relation to the nation. But this large and generous conception of the divine grace, because of its very largeness, is not one which can be assimilated all at once. It needs to be pondered, and brought into relation to all the other thoughts of the young prophet.

Moreover, the divine forgiveness has only come to him, because he has acknowledged his unworthiness, and, by acknowledging it, has expressed his desire to be purged from it. His experience of grace has been conditional on humility and repentance. If the nation is to enter with any reality into that which he has to teach, it must appropriate the mercy of God by the same way of repentance and confession. Hence it is not surprising to find that the earliest oracles of Isaiah turn upon doom. And here he follows very closely in the footsteps of his predecessor Amos, using largely his conceptions. There are not many of these early utterances. This is natural, partly because men did not preserve the words of the new prophet until he had made himself and proved himself a force in the community by his meeting with Ahaz. After that no one could well ignore him or his message. We can however distinguish a few such utterances and group them together.

Thus we notice that he too, Judean though he is and native of Jerusalem as he must always remain, feels himself called to speak to the house of Jacob (2 : 6-22). To him the house of Israel also is the vineyard of Yahweh Zᵉbhaoth, the men of Judah are His pleasant plant (5 : 7). In the same way Amos had addressed himself to the whole family which Yahweh had led up out of Egypt. To both prophets the two branches of the nation are still one, as having equally received the mercy, as being equally exposed to the judgment, of God. Both are under the charge of the prophet whether he comes from Israel or from Judah.

Again Isaiah even copies his predecessor in his view of Northern Israel as the place to which the primary activity of Yahweh is directed. Amos knew himself to be sent to the whole family which Yahweh had brought up out of Egypt,

but he had turned his chief attention to Northern Israel,
whether because it was the more important section or because
he knew its life better than that of Judah. Isaiah says:
"Yahweh sent a word against Jacob and it hath lighted in
Israel" (9 : 7). We must put this early, because, as soon as
Israel allied itself with Damascus, the prophet took a wholly
different attitude to it while earlier, even to this Judean
and man of Jerusalem, Northern Israel came first. The man
is still something of a copyist of the manner of his forerunner.

Again in Chapter 2 Isaiah gives his early views of the day
of the Lord. It is wholly for judgment and it includes the
whole world, and when I say the whole world, I do not mean
merely the world of man, but the world of nature also. Thus
it is to involve the bringing down of everything which is
high and lifted up; and among the things high and lifted up
which shall be levelled in the day of the divine revelation are
included the oaks of Bashan, the cedars of Lebanon and all
lofty mountains. One might explain the inclusion of the oaks
of Bashan and the cedars of Lebanon in the terms of the
divine judgment with the sense that these things are swept
away because they have been used to minister to Judah's pride
and Jerusalem's vainglory. They have served to build the
ships of Tarshish which are also mentioned and the lordly
houses of the capital. To denounce these oaks and cedars
might then be no more than a poetical method of denouncing
all forms of national vainglory. But one cannot so explain
the lofty mountains, and the inclusion of these as brought
down in the day of the Lord is enough to prove that the oaks
and cedars also are there for themselves. The day of the
Lord means a world catastrophe, which includes within its
scope inanimate as well as animate things.

Duhm in his *Theologie der Propheten* has confessed himself puzzled by this unethical trait connected with the judgment, which appears very surprising to him in a prophet so
penetrated by ethical considerations as Isaiah. One must
connect it with the saying which appears in his call—the
fullness of the whole earth is the self-manifestation of Yahweh.
One must also connect it with the later saying that in the
consummation not only shall the sin of man disappear, but

the very nature of the brute creation must be changed. But principally one must note how, like Amos, Isaiah begins with the thought of a world revolution, not merely of a judgment on Israel.

Thinking along these lines, seeing Yahweh rise up to judge His world and to renew it, the prophet at first says as little about the instrument of judgment as Amos had done. Not only does Assyria fail to appear in these early oracles; but there is a reason why it should not appear. The catastrophe with all that it includes is on such a scale that no earthly power, Assyria or another, could ever be expected to carry it into effect. In connection with this early oracle, 2 : 6-22, Cheyne notes that Isaiah " rises completely above local and national circumstances and idealises the national almost into a universal judgment : not Yahweh and Israel, but God and man, fill up the painter's canvas ". This is well said, except that I should omit the " almost ", and should not say " idealises ". For the use of such a phrase as " idealises " implies that one starts from Yahweh and Israel. Now the impression left on me by the oracle is that Isaiah starts from God and man, and, like Amos in his vision of the nations, is thinking first of these two. From them he comes to Yahweh and Israel.

Again the scope of the judgment is as wide as the world, and as, agreeing with this, the instrument of the judgment does not come into view at all, so is its issue confined to condemnation. In 17 : 6 Isaiah says that, when Yahweh has finished with Israel, there shall be left therein only gleanings. The translation of our R.V., " yet there shall be left gleanings " transforms the whole slightly in words, but significantly in sense. What this translation implies is that, in spite of the judgment or after the judgment is done, the tree will not be left quite stripped. There will be something left. This translation sets a limit to the judgment. The true sense —there shall nothing be left but gleanings—suggests the searching character of the judgment. And the gleanings are not the gleanings of the harvest field, which the women gather as Ruth did—full ears and profitable for food or for seed-corn. They are the gleanings of the olive tree, the sapless, half-filled, ill-ripened berries which the harvesters leave hang-

ing on the ends of the branches, because they do not repay
the trouble of climbing for them.

The translators, it will be noted, have unconsciously been
influenced by the recognition that Isaiah's leading thought
about judgment is that it does leave a remnant which, with
all its poverty, is yet sufficient in the divine mercy to become
the basis for a new creation and the means for a new world.
The fact that they felt the phrase to contradict this later idea
so characteristic of Isaiah and so pregnant in suggestion, emphasizes how here also he is dependent on his forerunner and
is reproducing his thought. The leavings on the olive branches
are just the shin-bone and the ear-tip which are not worth
gathering after the lion has finished its meal.

In all this Isaiah has not yet come to himself. He is uttering the common message of all prophecy, the sure intervention of Yahweh to punish a guilty world. He can therefore
use language very similar to his predecessor. He has not yet
correlated this truth to his own experience of Yahweh's ultimate purpose with him and therefore with the nation and
with the world. What he has learned in one great hour of
experience has still to be made his own and to be reinter-
preted for the life of the people to which he has been sent.

ISAIAH IN THE CRISIS OF SYRO-EPHRAIMITIC WAR

The occasion on which his own view came to the front was
the threat of combined Syria and Northern Israel to which
I have already referred. In this day of testing as to what
Judah stands for Isaiah comes forward with his own peculiar
message.

And two things mark it at the very beginning. One, the
meaning of which we are left to discover, is that, from this
time forward, Isaiah has no more to say to, and little to say
about, Northern Israel. He had already denounced woe on
Samaria in 5: 1ff.: he now adds vv. 27-30 to his original
oracle and from that time dismisses Northern Israel. One
might be tempted to say that the prompting motive was patriotism. Pekah has leagued himself against Judah and against
the holy city, and a patriotic Judean might well be excused

for ceasing to have patience with a people which took this
position against its brother nation, sharer in a common life-
task. But, even when Assyria was ranged against Judah,
Isaiah was able to speak of it as a rod in the hands of
Yahweh for the chastisement of his own people. Evidently
then there is something more in his contemptuous dismissal
of Northern Israel. One can only, I think, find it in the
recognition that Samaria has leagued itself with heathenism.
It has sought protection from a combination with Damascus:
as Hosea put it, it has mixed itself with the nations. It
should share the fate, mutable and uncertain, of the heathenism with which it has allied itself. Unconscious of its dis-
tinguishing element, of that which made it and Judah different from all the surrounding world, it has been content to
find its support in the force on which the other nations rely
for their strength: it is lost in the heathenism to which it
has turned.

The other element, the meaning of which we do not need
to conjecture, since it stares us in the face, is that Isaiah
goes to his own people with a definite message, and that one
of hope. He goes to meet Ahaz, leading his little son by the
hand. The boy is the future: and the boy's name contains
the assurance of the future, Shear-jashub, a remnant shall
return. The reconciliation which God has made possible and
real in the prophet's own life and through which he has been
made fit to be a prophet, is fundamental to all his outlook.
What is true for him is true for the nation of which he forms
a part not merely by the ties of nationality but by the tie of
a common need for salvation. If he was able to return, if God
intervened to make it possible that he should return, so may
Judah.

He comes to Ahaz then, not primarily to announce a catastrophe as the result of the sure emergence of the day of the
Lord; he comes to plead that Judah may set itself right with
the God who is about to intervene. He has a right to plead,
because he knows how blessed and how possible it is to welcome God in His coming. He himself through that surrender
has found his whole life re-created in its outlook and its issues.
If his people can surrender to that direction, they shall find
it, not their ruin, but their salvation. He must speak of

Yahweh's intervention, however sharp and sore its first effects may be, as having its ultimate result in redemption, because it has redeemed him. Therefore he came to meet Ahaz, leading by the hand the boy whose name expressed this faith and the hope which sprang from it.

Isaiah found the minds of Ahaz, his court and indeed the minds of all men in Jerusalem gravely preoccupied. Their heart was moved as the trees of the forest are moved with the wind (7 : 2). Their agitation and preoccupation were natural, for on the issue of these few days hung the fate of their country. Ahaz had resolved to submit to Assyria and had probably already sent away his embassy, offering tribute and asking protection. Meantime he was looking to the defences of Jerusalem, in the hope that, if the League attacked, he might be able to make good his stand until Assyria advanced on Damascus. There is nothing very contemptible or very wicked in all this : one may even venture to think that this was what the civil ruler of Jerusalem and Judah was set over the people to do—take the wisest course possible in any given circumstances for the safety of his state.

Isaiah's thought is moving along an entirely different plane, and he is engrossed with entirely different questions. I think one has to recognize this fact, if one wishes to do justice to one or other of the two men and to realize their attitude to one another. The prophet believes that Yahweh is about to intervene in a great act of judgment which shall include the whole world. This cataclysm may arrive at any hour : all that is certain about it is that it cannot be long delayed. Naturally the one thing which matters to Isaiah is how Judah can meet this day of judgment, how it can meet the God who summons it to judgment.

Any man whose mind is engrossed by such a vision can only regard the danger from Syria and Northern Israel as trivial and insignificant. What can Damascus and Israel do, these two stumps of smoking firebrands, 7 : 4? They themselves are doomed in the day of the Lord, doubly doomed since they had proved by their attack how little they cared for, or were interested in, the greater kingdom already on its way. Let men in Judah lift up their hearts to the anticipation of the greater thing which is coming, let them commit themselves to the Lord who is already on His way, and they shall be secure with a security which goes beyond fear of temporary changes such as Pekah and Rezon plan, a security which is based on eternal things. But if ye do not believe, if ye do not base on these eternal verities, ye shall never stand fast, 7 : 9 :

So a man might speak to-day who, in the multifarious schemes for patching up a temporary shelter in the fluctuating social and political conditions of our time, tried to make men envisage the bigger future. So a man might urge men to look beyond the distracting anxieties of a writhing world to the few sure lines on which alone human society can base itself and can hope to last in the future. And so, it may be added, such a man might be unjust to the men of his own time who refused to be distracted from the instant present by such distant views and who said that meantime women and children need to be fed and housed in the cities of Europe. So Ahaz might well retort to Isaiah that meantime "the walls and the water supply of Jerusalem need to be looked to, because Pekah is twenty miles away up the Shecham road. It may be quite true that Samaria and Damascus have no place in the eternal scheme of things and are but empty shells with no reality. But they are uncommonly inconvenient factors in this uneasy present in which I, Ahaz, am made responsible for this city, Jerusalem, which is the capital of the kingdom of Judah and incidentally your home".

See the situation after this fashion and you see at once that these two men stand there, not merely as the representatives of two conflicting policies in an obscure period of the life of the little state in the Middle East during the year 735 or thereby. They stand as representatives of two conflicting factors in human life everywhere and at all times, so long as men are seeking to prepare a Jerusalem which hath foundations and yet are required to live in a Jerusalem which has very shaky walls and an extremely poor water supply. The horizons widen out round us.

Isaiah then returns to the charge and ventures to deliver a remarkable challenge. He believes, let it be remembered, in the certainty of the divine intervention for judgment and in its coming soon. Believing that, he bids Ahaz ask a sign from

Yahweh, as to whether the prophet's message is not true. Ask a sign which may convince even your dull heart that God has His purpose to serve here. And Ahaz refused.

Again, let us try to be just to the king. In our ignorance of many factors in the situation, it is easy to call him weakly and shortsighted. But here is an unhappy man, responsible for his kingdom, seeing apparently irresistible danger at its door, distracted about questions of food supply and water supply and munitions, looking anxiously as to how he may not only prop his tottering throne, but thereby guarantee decent living conditions to his nation. His counsellors and he have resolved that the best thing to do is to bow to the inevitable and ask help from the eastern colossus, though that must to some extent imperil their independence. He knows or suspects that certain elements in his kingdom may not, probably will not, welcome such a novelty in their foreign policy. Especially those intransigent elements, which find their support in the fanatical religion which sways large bodies of men, may set themselves against such a policy.

Such a man cannot be expected to take account of the great eternal principles which lie in Isaiah's demand. He has no time to turn over what these may imply and he has no great inclination to try to realize what the prophet means. With his limited interests and narrow outlook all he can see about Isaiah is what Amaziah saw in Amos, a voice which may arouse the masses. This man with his weird talk about the coming of Yahweh may yet be able and be desirous to rouse those sleeping depths in his people which he himself does not understand or share, but which he fears the more because he has no share in them which might enable him to understand them. So he covers his refusal by the excuse that it is not for a man like him to tempt Yahweh. It was a clever, because on the surface a reverent, method of escape from the question. He does not break with the religious party : he merely bows them out quietly from interference.

Isaiah replies that the fact of men having for any reason refused to recognize the intervention of God cannot prevent Yahweh from intervening. The fact remains, whether men welcome it or not, that Yahweh Himself will give a sign. Only, of course, the character of the sign, or rather the effects of that which it signifies, must change according to the attitude of those to whom it is sent. The prophet's whole interest was gathered up in the commanding desire to convince his nation that, since they were in God's hands, their attitude to Him was their prime concern. The terrifying conditions in which they were placed had for their purpose, as they must have for their result, to bring clearly out how they faced this ultimate concern.

Samaria had so been tested and had answered the test by allying herself with the heathen, ignoring the ultimate things and thinking only of the immediate present. Samaria and its ally shall pass away with all the world of the immediate present which is already doomed, 7 : 5ff. Ahaz and his court have answered the test by allying themselves with the heathen power. The power in which they trusted shall sweep them away (7 : 17ff.). They were doomed by the very means on which they rested for deliverance.

The indifference of men could not turn Yahweh back from doing that which He was about to do : it could only result in making the effect of this upon themselves different. Yahweh was unalterable and would do as he had resolved to do. Ahaz and his court had, through a prophet who showed them the counsel of the Most High, been given the opportunity of setting themselves right with the greater purpose about to realize itself in the world. They had been called upon to recognize it, and so to welcome and serve it. But they had buried themselves in the immediate present with its pressing cares and its immediate remedies. They had remained part of the world which was already judged and condemned by Yahweh and which was ready to vanish away. They would vanish with it. Yahweh, when He came to fulfil His counsel, would need to overturn them and their counsel. Immanuel, God with us, God's presence among us, says Isaiah in Chapter 7, meant first God in judgment on Ahaz and his court.

I do not here enter into the debatable question as to the meaning of Immanuel, partly because it would take too long in this sketch of Isaiah's work, still more because it must deal with niceties of interpretation which would be out of place here. It must suffice to say that I accept the old interpretation of Immanuel as essentially Messianic. Only I must ask you to recognize that it is Messianic in the sense which we to-day have come to attach to the word Messianic. It is not, that is to say, a direct prophecy of Jesus Christ, which could only be understood after the coming of the Lord and which remained a profound secret to the men who actually heard it. It is a Messianic prophecy with only the content which Messianic prophecy then had, and so was the better fitted to fulfil the purpose for which it was uttered, i.e., to impress the men to whom, and influence the time in which, it was spoken.

And what I ask you to notice chiefly is that the word Immanuel Isaiah chooses, and I believe deliberately chooses, is a name which is ambiguous, which is double-edged. For God to be with men may mean blessing or curse, but it always means testing. God comes to prove men, and, according as they bear the test of His appearing among them, so shall His being with them result in their judgment to condemnation or their judgment to benediction. Isaiah learned this in his first communion with Yahweh. He now applies it to his nation.

But Immanuel is the agent of Yahweh and fulfils the purpose of Yahweh—a purpose the content of which the prophet has learned and which he is commissioned to declare. Because Immanuel is this, and because the self-manifestation of Yahweh brings more than the destruction of whatever is opposed to him, the coming of Immanuel implies more than ruin. His advent has a positive content, because He serves One whose purpose is primarily for redemption.

This side of the meaning of Immanuel is presented in Chapter 8. The prophet came with his second son " Spoil speedeth, prey hasteth " but this time, be it noted, he came, not to Ahaz and the royal court, but to the people. Again he insists that what alone is of significance is the action of Yahweh Himself and the attitude Judah took to its God. But that is so, because this great hour of history has brought that clearly forward, it has brought to light the underlying thoughts of men's hearts and the things on which they ultimately put their trust. Syria and Ephraim, then, are doomed and have no more significance in the world (8 : 4). " This people " through its rulers has, in its terror before[1] Rezon and Remaliah's son, turned its back on the peace of the divine protection (v. 6). Their terror before an immediate and passing danger has shown how they are ready to grasp at any succour, and for the sake of immediate deliverance ignore the future and the enduring things. They can but pass away through the very means at which they have clutched to rescue them (v.7), these men who mortgage the future for an instant success and who betray the dearest interests of their world in order to stop a gap in a crumbling dyke. But though the flood sweeps over them and all their works, drowning them from men's sight : Immanuel : God is with us. The land over which the waters burst is Immanuel's. And so, though all the nations should enter into league, they cannot do more than is permitted to them by Him who has said that He is with us (vv. 9 ff.).

Already Isaiah has asked Ahaz to believe that it was not Rezon nor Remaliah's son nor even Tiglath-pileser who governed history, and had urged him to realise the mightier will behind them all. Now he said that these powers of a little day were but instruments in God's hand, broken and cast away when they sought to advance a step beyond their allotted sphere. To lift up the heart to Him who held the world in the hollow of His hand was to be of quiet heart (vv. 13 ff). To such men Yahweh was a sufficient sanctuary.

The world was in the hands of God who was about to reveal Himself in a new way in it. The result of this self-manifestation must be that all who refused to look beyond the immediate present and had no hold on the divine future should be swept away. But the men who were sure that all things, themselves included, were in God's hands, could wait with patience through a dark time, confident of a future which Yahweh Himself should secure to them. The world was delivered over to confusion. " Spoil speedeth, prey hasteth " : but God is with us.

You will have noticed that my discussion of Isaiah's attitude to Ahaz rests wholly on the assumption that the prophet's thought moved on an entirely different plane from that of the king; that he was the bearer of a definitely religious

[1]Emended text.

message, not the adviser of a particular policy. Again, you should make clear to yourselves whether you construe Isaiah as a species of super-statesman, whose eyes had been cleared by his including religion and moral issues in his programme. If so, what was the political line which he wished the king of Judah to take? Presumably it was the line of neither joining the coalition nor of relying on Assyria, but of relying on Yahweh. And this reliance on Yahweh was to bring it about that Yahweh should, through some act of intervention, protect the capital and the temple, not only from the present threat by the coalition, but from any future danger through the advent of Assyria. Somehow or other, in a way which is never specified and which is very hard to specify, Yahweh was to intervene for the defence of His beloved city.

Now, if we take this line of interpretation, we must take its consequences; and its consequences are that at a later period Yahweh did not intervene for the protection of Jerusalem or the vindication of Judah. He allowed them both to go, overwhelmed in the storm of Babylon's war. And Jeremiah had to face the question of how religion could continue in spite of this, how men could continue to believe in God, though God had not done for Judah what a prophet like Isaiah, speaking in the name of Yahweh, had led them to expect that He would do. And what Jeremiah said to his fellow-citizens was that the ruin of city and temple was the will of Yahweh. That is to say, what he taught was that it was in the interest of religion that both temple and city should be brought to an end.

This, of course, is a perfectly legitimate line to take. The fact that a later prophet did not agree with Isaiah does not prove that this may not have been what the earlier man believed. But it means that Isaiah was plainly wrong, not on a mere matter of fact, but on a religious principle. It means that he believed temple and city to be so necessary for the right worship of the nation that Yahweh would interfere in order to prevent them from being swept away, while Jeremiah could teach that the religion of Israel would be all the better if both temple and city disappeared. In that case Isaiah then was on a lower plane than his successor, and on a lower religious plane. That, of course, is also a perfectly legitimate line to take. But we ought to recognize it to be the inevitable consequence of one particular method of interpreting the prophet's attitude. But, before committing yourselves to it, you ought to hesitate and to test very carefully the assumptions which lead to it.

Now the main assumption which has brought men to take it is that Isaiah was a superior type of statesman, with a wider view than his fellows, whose business it was to recommend in the name of Yahweh the political line which Israel ought to follow at this period. If he was not that, but was urging a purely religious message, then we should be free to seek some other explanation of his conduct and his words. And certainly we have seen that both his predecessors were emphatically religious men who were eager to utter a religious message. And neither of them was particularly interested in the continuance of the outward forms of the national existence— temple or capital. Indeed both of them announced that Yahweh was bringing the nation to an end. Yet we are to believe that the continuance of these things appeared so valuable to Isaiah that he was prepared to declare that Yahweh would intervene in the world's history in order to preserve them from destruction. Isaiah, on this interpretation of his action, must have deliberately departed from the attitude of his predecessor. He was not, of course, bound to say exactly what Hosea and Amos had said. Still, if Hosea was able to believe that Israel was to disappear from history as a nation, but that the religion of Israel in its essential features would still continue in the world, and if Isaiah, on the other hand, could not conceive of Israel's religion continuing without the temple and the city Jerusalem, and if he staked the future of his people's religion on Yahweh's being so convinced of this that He would intervene to guarantee the continuance of these things, Isaiah not only differed from his predecessor, but was at a lower stage of religious thinking.

I repeat that we ought to hesitate before we accept a situation which brings us to this conclusion.

Again, about this period falls the prophecy of Micah, at least the part which consists of the first three chapters. We cannot be absolutely certain of the date when Micah's oracles were uttered, but from 1 : 3 ff. we may conclude that they

were spoken before the fall of Samaria. Micah lived at Mar-
esha or Moresheth Gath near the modern Beit Gibrin on the
Philistine border. I recommend you to read the chapters, but
I have not included a study of Micah here, because they do
not *add* anything to what we have learned from Amos. The
teaching of Micah runs much along the line of Amos and
shows singularly little affinity with the greater thoughts of
Hosea. Possibly that is due to the fact that, living as he did
on the Judean side of the Philistine territory, he came into
less close contact with the specifically north country prophet.
Possibly, however, it may point to his not having been capable
of appreciating the more spiritual tone of Hosea. I say that
the more readily, because he does not seem to have penetrated
very deeply even in the thoughts of Amos. He is a rather
superficial man, a man who denounces in pure rage, a man
who makes individuals and classes responsible for sins and
sorrows for which the whole nation was really responsible.
This means that he is able to see, and does see, the root-
cause of the sins and sorrows in a superficial way. He is able
to believe that, if you can put this thing right or that thing
right, you will have reformed the condition of society. The
result is that he has no great fundamental reconstructive
quality in him. Micah is rather a man with a programme
than a man with a gospel.

He deserves notice, less as a voice which can proclaim
the remedy for the wounds in his nation's life, than as a
voice bearing eloquent witness to the mischief which is there.
He gives utterance to the burning, bitter anger of great classes
of society against injustice and wrong. In so witnessing, he
makes clear the truth of the pictures of Isaiah's and Judah's
condition given us by the other prophets.

Yet this man was able to say and did say : " Zion shall be
ploughed as a field, and Jerusalem shall become heaps. The
mountain of the house shall be like the high places of the
forest " (3 : 12). The saying clung to men's minds. We find
Jeremiah in his 26th chapter declaring much the same thing,
declaring that Yahweh was about to abolish the capital and
destroy the temple. The officials were shocked by the utterance and hoped to silence Jeremiah on the charge that he was
uttering blasphemy and that he was wanting in true patriotic

feeling. The common people however interfered and secured the prophet's acquittal by appealing to the fact that Micah had said what was quite as bad and had not been punished for it. That is to say, they bear witness to the fact that Micah stood for a religion which was spiritual enough to be able to be independent of such holy places as Zion and Jerusalem. He could not only speak in the name of a God who could continue His work without these accessories to his worship : but he could in the Jerusalem and Judah of that period find sufficient support and understanding of such an attitude to escape persecution. When one realizes that a prophet who is not of the highest order was able to conceive a worship independent of place, and realizes that the prophet was not too profane for ordinary men in Jerusalem, one has greater hesitation than ever in believing that Isaiah thirled the true religion to city and temple and made it an essential of faith that Yahweh should intervene on their behalf.

ISAIAH AND THE IDEA OF THE CHURCH

Now the situation in Judah and the teaching of Isaiah, as I am compelled to interpret it, only force upon us afresh and with much greater weight the difficulty which we have already met in connection with Hosea. Was the course of action which both prophets demanded such a course as could be demanded from, or expected from, a nation, situated as Judah then was and constituted of the elements which make up all nations? Only the matter comes before us more clearly and with much greater force in the period of Isaiah than in that of Hosea. We do not know where or to whom or in what circumstances Hosea uttered his prophecies. He may have uttered them, like Amos, at one of the shrines of Northern Israel; and there are many things which make such an idea possible. His use of the legends about Jacob's life, his quotation of a sanctuary hymn used at one of the festivals, united with the fact that at one of the shrines he was likely to find an audience, and an audience already interested in religious questions, make such a supposition very probable.

In the case of Isaiah we are not left to probabilities. We know. He spoke these early oracles in the presence of King

Ahaz and the courtiers. He uttered them, too, when the men were busy with questions of the defence of the capital and engrossed with anxiety as to the present danger in which the city stood. Could you expect a body of men, already busied with such grave concerns, to postpone the whole question of the present need of their nation to the fundamental matters of spiritual religion to which the prophet asked their attention? And, if we are right in supposing that the basis of the prophet's thought and its entire presupposition was the expectation of the near day of the Lord, could it have force with men, some of whom no doubt did not believe in that which was the very foundation of Isaiah's attitude?

As soon as you grasp the situation in this way, you see that all the great prophets with whom we have been dealing were hampered by their situation over against a national religion. The religion with which they were actually in contact was a national religion; and they were trying to make it fulfil functions for which it was hopelessly unfit. The only result must be that this prophetic religion, which was really a universal religion, must burst the limits of nationality sooner or later.

Amos, for example, sees in Yahweh, the God of Israel, not the incarnation, or the embodiment, but, let us say, the representative of the conscience of humanity. He judges all the world on the basis of a law, which is not Israel's historical law, but which is revealed to humanity in varying degrees of clearness, which is therefore international. " *Ce peuple rêve toujours quelque chose de l'international* " (Renan). The institution, then, which in turn incorporates the law, which maintains and represents its sovereign sanctions, must be the embodied conscience of mankind. It cannot be a little nation like Israel with its historical past and its limited and temporary legislation : it must be the Catholic Church of all the men of good will.

Hosea, again, sees in Yahweh the One on whom all depend and to whom they surrender themselves in a great act of supreme recognition and humility. But men can do this and find their joy and peace in the deed without regard to physical limitations like those of Israel. And many men who are formal adherents of the historical religion of Israel have never

dreamed of the need for such a faith. Again, the bond of
union is too subtle and too spiritual to find its embodiment
in a national religion or to be satisfied with a national expression. Such a bond of union can only exist in the Catholic
Church of the men who have made the great surrender and
who are consequently united by a common spirit.

Isaiah sees the eternal world looming up clearly beyond the
mists and shows of time, never blotted out by the drifting
phantoms of kingdoms and empires which rise for a time
and vanish. He asks men to commit themselves to these few
things which are sure. He bids men set their feet on these
sure foundations and let the temporary things go, as Yahweh
orders them. But a little kingdom like Judah, which came into
existence with time, and which is constantly conditioned by
the things of time, a kingdom which has its physical place
in this world, and must reckon continually with this world,
cannot exercise such a faith and yet expect to continue as
other kingdoms have continued. But the prophet too is out
beyond the limits of national religion : he is looking for a city
whose builder and maker is God. The men who are capable
of doing what he asks are the eternal and Catholic Church,
not born into these interests by flesh and blood, but
new born into them by accepting for themselves the new
standards of a world, which, because it is always coming, is
the eternal world, which, because it is never here, never van-
ishes and never disappoints. They are the men who are born
from above. Hence Isaiah's demand for faith.

Fundamentally through no accident of its history, but
through the necessity of its principles, this religion which is
represented by the great prophets; was not Judaism in its
narrow, national sense : it was a universal religion. Its implications did not appear all at once to the men who held it.
The fact even of its incompatibility with the national religion
which was held by the priests and people was not apparent
to the prophets. If Isaiah had seen it, he would probably
never have gone to make the demands he did on Ahaz. But,
since he comes third in the great succession, some of its
implications are already becoming visible to him; and he
begins to utter them. In particular, he has found that Ahaz
refuses to listen to him, and he has also found that the people

as a whole cannot even understand what he urges on their notice. From this time he turns to those who share his convictions. " Bind thou up the testimony, seal the law among my disciples, and I will wait for Yahweh that hideth his face from the house of Jacob ", 8 : 16 ff. The hope of the future is to be found among the like-minded, in the communion of those who are held together by a common conviction. These are Isaiah's remnant, the men who hold the future for religion in Judah.

You see, I hope, how fundamentally related the position is to the two great lines of Isaiah's teaching. On the one hand, the existence of a remnant, which, because it is committed to Yahweh's will, is indestructible, represents the prophet's fundamental thought that Yahweh's coming cannot be confined to doom. It looks beyond doom to salvation.

On the other hand, the bond which holds these men together is the bond which unites them to God. And, since it is divine in its character, and since it is spiritual in its nature, it has little or nothing to do with the physical bonds of nationhood. It represents the prophetic side of the prophetic religion.

One sees again both Isaiah's certainty of judgment and his conviction as to God's purpose going beyond judgment in Chapter 28, a chapter which belongs to the period after the scare over the Syro-Ephraimitic invasion had died down. Ahaz and the court were feeling secure through the treaty with Assyria and congratulating themselves on having so shrewdly baffled their enemies. Perhaps the fact that there had been no sign of Yahweh's intervening in any way had further discredited Isaiah in their eyes. So long as the treaty was still indeterminate and so long as there seemed to be a possibility that a prophet appealing to the fanatical multitude might upset all their plans, they had temporized. But now they feel themselves secure, and at once let drop the mask. The prophet is received with a burst of ridicule. " We have made a covenant with death and with Sheol we are in agreement " (v. 15). Evidently the phrase is a provincial one for any condition which makes a man feel utterly secure. " We are guaranteed against failure and defeat, since we have Assyria on our side. Neither death nor hades can hurt us now. And

8

as for the prophet with his effort to teach grown-up men and statesmen by reiterating the commonplaces of morality and religion, he may go hang. We have left school and have no more to do with his "tsaw latsaw qaw laqaw" (v. 10). No translation can reproduce the meaning of this clause : in fact any translation prevents its sense. The words are mono-syllables, not selected because of their sense, but because they are monosyllables, the kind of words which were used to teach a dame's school. "We are done with all the A.B.C. about faith and duty. It is good enough for children : but we are grown men whose business is to rule a state."

The men are drunk with success and drunk with wine (vv. 8 ff.). And, as men often do in such circumstances, they betray more than they know; they betray the secret purposes which control their conduct. Above all, they betray just that fatal idea which is the curse of all politics, that, when you are dealing with great questions of humanity in the mass, you need no more than cleverness and quick wits, and can afford to ignore the elemental things like justice and honour and truth and brotherhood.

"You are set free from the childish teaching of the elemen-tal truths of religion," says the prophet. Set free for what? "Set free to enter a new school, where you shall learn your lesson from men of a strange tongue and by a fearful disci-pline. You would not hear when I taught you as though you were children. The Assyrians to whom you preferred to go to school will teach you, men with no childlike monosyllables, but men of an uncouth tongue. The foreigner in whom you trusted shall become your master (v. 13), and you yourselves shall be merged in, and share the fate of, the heathenism you have chosen."

For the peril they have to meet is not a casual thing but an eternal. It does not come from Syria or from Samaria, or from these two in league. It comes from Yahweh. " It was Yahweh I called you to prepare to meet first : and it is Yahweh whom you have to meet still. A league with Assyria can meet the league of Damascus and Samaria, but it cannot meet this situation." " The bed is shorter than that a man should stretch himself in it, the covering is narrower than that he can wrap himself in it." Why? "Because Yahweh will rise up " (vv. 20 f.). If the men had only had to do with Ephraim and Samaria, their clever little arrangement might have met the situation. But they have ultimately to do with Him who orders both Syria and Ephraim and who is behind them both. What have they in the day when He rises up?

So far, you see, Isaiah says not much more than we have heard already. But at once the prophet continues, because Yahweh's rising up implies to him more than destruction, God's coming is far more than a mere negative, the sweeping away of the refuge of lies. It has also positive content: and its destruction of false security is meant to lay bare the one abiding security. In Zion Yahweh is laying a foundation (v. 16).

What does he mean? If Isaiah meant simply that God was not going to allow Jerusalem and the temple to be swept away in spite of the folly and faithlessness of Ahaz and the court, then I acknowledge the German scholar Marti is perfectly right. His promise does break the point of all his previous threats, and, in particular, makes his denunciation of these men peculiarly silly. It amounts to saying that, let them do what they like, God will stand by the Jewish state and guarantee it. But Isaiah says the foundation is laid at the very time when the empirical state was proving itself most unwilling and most unfit to become a foundation for anything at all. Instead of what has proved itself thus unfit, Yahweh has brought in a new thing. Its novelty made it certain that the old must be dissolved (vv. 17 f.). The one fact which guaranteed the permanence of the new foundation, the fact that Yahweh founded it, the fact that it was founded on nothing less than the will of God, made it sure that all who were looking for their security to other support than that will must pass away. But, as for the new thing, that it was of God's ordering and was serving His purposes in the world made its continuance sure. Its stability was as certain as the instability of the old: for both rested on the same basis, viz. on the certainty of God's purpose. " He that believes shall not be ashamed " (reading *yebhosh* in v. 16).

Now, one thing is quite clear: Isaiah has given up the idea, if he ever held it, that Judah was a possible vehicle for the accomplishment of the divine ends. Because those ends were so conditioned by, and based on, faith, that is, because they were in their essentials religious ends they could not be fulfilled by any except religious men. Hence, sometimes, Isaiah speaks about the men to whom the future is promised as those who have faith. Or, in 8 : 16, he speaks about the inheritors of the future as " my disciples." They are there described as a people apart, who preserve the testimony and the teaching, that is, who preserve the religious convictions and traditions which are his.

Two matters deserve attention there. The one is that Isaiah is out beyond Amos in his doctrine of the remnant; has indeed passed beyond his own earlier ideas on the subject. The remnant to both of them was simply the leavings after the judgment was over : in the case of Amos the shin bone and ear tip, in Isaiah's case the useless olives which were left after the crop was gathered. To both, therefore, the remnant was negligible : no fruitful future could come from it, indeed nothing could come from it at all. It had no hold on God's mind or purpose, except so far as it proved how thorough and how searching His destruction must be. But now, to Isaiah, the remnant has the sure certainty of continuance, since it has behind it the will of God. On it, therefore, so far as it expresses the divine mind, everything can be built. The remnant is the fruitful source of all future growth.

But this remnant also comes out of Israel. It has its roots in all the work of God for His people and in all His revelation of His mind for their help. It is constituted for its place in God's plans through the discipline and pain and blessing of all God's dealing with the nation. That is to say, Isaiah too is breaking with Amos's conception of the coming of the day of Yahweh as cataclysmic, since that implies a clean break with all the past. The past contributes to the future : it contributes the remnant who are to be the foundation of all the future. Yahweh can use them and He will use them for His own ends. This, of course, means some form of evolution as over against cataclysm.

It is very interesting and very significant to find both the great prophets, Hosea and Isaiah, breaking with cataclysm and feeling out after a richer and bigger idea. For, so far as I can judge, they do it quite independently of one another, and, when they do it, they do it in totally different forms, as if each of them had arrived at it from his own point of view. There does not appear in Isaiah any signs of direct influence of Hosea on his thought, as there is clear evidence of the influence of Amos. Indeed there is rather evidence to the contrary in the fact that Isaiah begins his public career with the conception of cataclysm. No one who had really assimilated the thought of Hosea could have spoken as Isaiah did in the first period of his career.

What this means is that each prophet worked in his own way to the new idea from his fundamental thought of God and of God's relations to the world. We can see now, looking back, that the idea of evolution was inevitable in Judah, since Judah believed in a self-revealing God. The world was one form of His self-manifestation—as Isaiah put it, the fullness of the whole earth was His glory. Each new stage then, in its history, since it was a fresh stage in His self-manifestation, brought with it the fullness of the past, lost nothing real out of the great past, but preserved its contribution to the greater thing which was to come.

These things, I say, are clear to us now. We have even beaten out certain ways and certain language by which we may express these ideas to ourselves. But these two men in old Israel had not even the language by which they could utter these matters. Yet, by what I can only call the unconscious logic that lies in all fruitful knowledge of God and His will, they are moving by converging routes to the same point.

I think it may help us to get clear on the very important question as to why the prophets took the view they did about the destruction of the nation in its independent kingdom, if we look for a little at the time and the occasion when the prophets began to say what they did. In Northern Israel it began as early as the time of Elijah in the reign of Ahab. Now, this was precisely the period when the kingdom first allied itself with a foreign power. Ahab's father Omri, in order to secure the nation against the threatened advance of Damascus, made a treaty with Phoenicia, by which the two kingdoms for their own safety sought to secure themselves against their formidable neighbour. He made the alliance more enduring

by marrying his son to a princess of the reigning house of
Tyre. Then Elijah intervened with the declaration that Yahweh would overthrow the kingdom of Israel.

Nothing of the sort appeared in Judah at this particular
period, because Judah was not mixed up in this alliance. But
it appeared under Ahaz. This is the first time that the kingdom proposed to ally itself with a heathen power. The power
now was Assyria, but the motive was the same, to secure
the nation against powerful neighbours who in this case were
Pekah of Israel and Rezon of Damascus. Then Isaiah intervened with the declaration that God was to hew down Judah
to a mere stump.

But you will notice that neither of these prophets believed
and said that the act of God which they both predicted would
involve the disappearance of the true religion. Elijah was told
by the angel, when he claimed to be the only faithful adherent of Yahweh who remained, that God had seven thousand
in Israel who had not bowed the knee to baal. Isaiah was to
declare that, even when there was only a stump left in Judah,
it would throw up a fresh and vigorous sprout. The mere fact
that both men said that Yahweh was about to work the ruin
they were commanded to declare is enough to prove that
they did not expect from it that religion should come to an
end.

If we would see what roused the prophets, we need only
recognize the effect produced on the nation by those two
alliances with heathenism. In Ahab's case it meant that the
heathen princess was allowed to practise her own cult in
Samaria. She introduced a temple of baal and worshipped
there. The nation began to be seduced to heathen practices.
She brought too her ideal of that which constituted a king
and a kingdom. This contradicted the fundamental principle
of Yahwism. At her instigation Ahab murdered Naboth. This
was the natural line for a Tyrian princess to take. Set force
in the form of baal on the throne of heaven and you set
force in the form of a king on the throne of earth. The king
of Israel could do whatever he chose with no respect for the
law of justice. This meant transforming the kingdom. The
prophets had not helped to set up in Israel a kingdom like
that of the nations round about them, another of those

dreary despotisms which poisoned the Semitic world. A kingdom such as this, said Elijah, Yahweh must sweep away.

In the case of Ahaz the result of his step of alliance with heathenism was even more direct. For Assyria demanded alike from its allies and in its subject provinces the national recognition of its national god. Accordingly we find that, as soon as his alliance with Assyria had been brought about, he visited his suzerain at Damascus, from which he sent the pattern of an altar which was to be set up at Jerusalem at the place where the old Yahweh altar had stood. At this altar the king was to sacrifice. The high priest should continue to sacrifice on the old altar to Yahweh. The meaning was that in the temple Yahweh remained, but took a subordinate place. He gave way to Asshur. The kingdom had thus bartered away its allegiance to its God for the sake of security.

You see what was being forced on the nation through the fact that its religion was national. That did not matter much so long as, in the days of David, the only relations the nation held to the outside world were those of conquest. But such a situation only continued through the accident that both the great empires on the Nile and the Euphrates were in David's days impotent to hold their place in Palestine. It was inevitable that, as soon as these empires recovered, the entire situation should change. It did, when Damascus attacked Samaria and Damascus and Samaria together attacked Jerusalem. The only condition on which the little kingdom could endure was by making terms. But, when it came to the question of the terms which were admissible, the two sections of the nation went different ways.

The statesman said that they must maintain the kingdom at almost any cost. " Even for the sake of our distinctive life and of our religion this must be done. For, if the kingdom goes, the religion goes with it."

The prophets on the other hand insisted that at any cost the soul of the nation, which consisted in its distinctive life and its peculiar religion, must be preserved. " If this is gone, everything is gone." As Hosea put it, when Israel loses its identity which rests on its religion, it is merely mixed among the nations, one more in the grey common mass of heathenism.

You can see at once why all the prophets say that Yahweh is going to destroy the kingdom. Amos and Hosea said that this was due to His direct action, for they never spoke of any instrument He should employ for the purpose. Isaiah said that He was going to use the Assyrians for this end. Jeremiah believed it was coming through the Babylonians. But both these held that the Assyrians and the Babylonians were mere unconscious instruments in the hands of God. Ultimately the ruin of the kingdom in Israel was due to His act. God was doing it, not as a bit of petty anger because He was not receiving His due. He was doing it in fulfilment of His purpose with Israel. He was doing it to save its religion which was its very soul. What the men were saying was that the nation did not make its religion and could not maintain its religion. Its religion had made the nation and had built its temples, its cities, its kingdom, its nationhood. These had served well during the early years. But now with the changed conditions the institutions were becoming a danger to the purity of its religion. Therefore they must go and the faith must create new forms to suit its new conditions.

POLITICAL HISTORY : HEZEKIAH'S REIGN

Shalmaneser died and was succeeded by Sargon in 722, who in the very beginning of his reign, in fact in its first year 721, had to face troubles in Elam under Humbanigash, an ally of Merodach-Baladan, king of Babylon. He was severely defeated at Dur-ilu, and the news of this defeat put the coal in the thatch among the Western Nations. Arpad, Hamath, Damascus, the Philistine city of Gaza were all in revolt, supported by Egypt, for we hear of Pir'u king of Muzri and Sib'i, his tartan, as having a hand in the plot. Samaria had already in 722 fallen to Sargon but the poor remanent Israelites did what they could to support the coalition.

Sargon was weakened, but in 720 he mustered sufficient force to march westward and subdued all the coalition with thoroughness. He even reached as far as Gaza and near that city, at Raphia, defeated the allied forces of the Egyptians and Philistines. The incident is noteworthy, since it is the first clash in history between Assyria or Babylon and Egypt: and it interests us to-day, as illustrating in the past what we have seen in the present, how Gaza is the gateway into or out of Egypt.

Judah was not directly affected by these events, for Ahaz consistently clung to the policy he had adopted in 735 and remained loyal to the vassalage which he had proffered to Assyria. By this means he and his kingdom escaped the horrors and weakening which resulted from this war. And no doubt he congratulated himself on his good sense in accepting the inevitable and felt sure that events had justified his attitude.

Let me say that I have no objection to anyone saying that this was politically the shrewd line to follow and adding that, when once he had taken his line, he was wise in remaining faithful to it. But I venture to enter a caveat against our concluding from the failure of the others that their desperate efforts to resist the colossus of Assyria were contemptible, to be sneered out of court. There are passages in Dr. G. A. Smith's Commentary on Isaiah and in his notes on this period which seem to suggest, and more than suggest, that we must necessarily despise the wild struggles for independence on the part of the little states, merely because these failed and in the circumstances were doomed to fail. In my humble judgment we should not conclude too much from outward and apparent failure. The three years' gallant resistance of Samaria, isolated, weak, hopeless as it was, appeals to me as belonging to the same order in history as Thermopylae. And it is worth remembering that history has counted the futile failure at Thermopylae as being great, greater even than Xerxes. The men who could only die in a struggle against overwhelming odds, but who died for liberty, are to be held in everlasting remembrance. And further, when everything is said about this failure, this failure is more apparent than real. The unreal thing was the power of Assyria, resting as that did on the denial of the right of the little nations to their individual life and their individual contribution to the life of the world. The men who died rather than submit kept alive the individuality of their nation, the thing which survived Assyria and which, when Assyria crashed down in its

8*

inevitable and well merited fall, rebuilt the world as it sprang up out of the ashes of its old fires.

There is much uncertainty about the year of Ahaz's death, when his son Hezekiah succeeded. But in a prophecy (14 : 28-32), dated in the last year of Ahaz's reign, Isaiah is warning the exultant Philistines that, so far is the power of Assyria from being broken, that out of the serpent's brood will be bred an adder. No event belonging to the political world of the time was so well fitted to suggest high hopes to Philistia as the defeat of Sargon at Dur-ilu; and we may, accordingly, tentatively assume 720 as the year of the death of Ahaz and set down to this year the accession of Hezekiah, an accession which meant also, if not the rise of anti-Assyrian policy in Judah, at least a stiffening of resistance against the policy which meant perpetual tribute and perpetual strain. At least there is an indication of restlessness under the Assyrian yoke in an inscription of Sargon belonging to the year 711. In it he describes[1] how the peoples of Philistia, Judah, Edom and Moab, who had to bring tribute and presents to " Asshur my lord " but who now meditated hostilities and plotted evil, sent their tokens of homage to Pharaoh, the king of Egypt, a prince who could not save them, and sought an alliance with him. Evidently Raphia had convinced the Egyptians that it was only a question of time till they must come face to face with Assyria and so they were making more desperate efforts than ever to stir up Palestine. The reference to Egypt, as a prince who could not save them, sounds to me like propaganda in the interests of Assyria among the nations of Northern Syria. " Codlin is the friend, not Short." The centre of this rising would seem to have been Ashdod in Philistia, for Sargon sent an expedition against it under his tartan or commander-in-chief (20: 1-6). The city was captured and the rising collapsed. Hezekiah may not have been very deeply committed, or may have withdrawn from the combination in time : at least Judah was left unharmed by Sargon and continued to pay merely its customary tribute.

The successor of Sargon was Sennacherib 705-681 : possibly Sargon was murdered.

[1]Luckenbill, *Ancient Records of Assyria and Babylonia,* II, 195, p. 105, Gressmann *Altorientalische Texte zum Alten Testament,* p. 351.

In Egypt the country had been brought under one government under the sway of the Ethiopian king of Napata, and
unity under a single head had given more definiteness to her
policy and more continuity to her efforts. She was now prepared to intervene more vigorously than hitherto in the condition of affairs in Palestine. How active she had become one
may see from the vivid picture Isaiah has given of the arrival
in Jerusalem of envoys from Napata (Chapter 18). In Babylon
Merodach-Baladan reappeared. Sargon had succeeded in
driving this vigorous champion of Babylon's independence
into Elam, eastward of Babylon, but he returned on the news
of Sargon's death and even took his seat on the throne of
Babylon, 702. In all probability the embassy from him recorded at some length in Chapter 29 falls about this period.
In any case, though the new king may not have been able
to send an embassy, the news of his revolt against Assyria
must have reached Palestine and excited its little kingdoms
into the hope that now at last was come the opportunity to
rebel.

For the whole of Palestine was in revolt. Egyptian envoys
were promising help. Sennacherib seemed busy for some time
in the east. The Palestinian and Phoenician states renewed
a league of resistance and this time Judah was drawn out of
her isolation into the coalition.

Sennacherib was too prudent to attack them at once. He
had to dispose of Babylon before he could venture on a campaign which would have left Assyria exposed to the danger
of invasion. But Merodach-Baladan was not an easy conquest. In the days of Sargon Babylon had put up a desperate
defence for twelve years and had been subdued only after
severe efforts. It cost Sennacherib in turn two hard-fought
campaigns before he could announce to his people that he
had accomplished Merodach-Baladan's destruction.

Then Sennacherib turned to the west. This time Judah was
not only committed to the league but held a prominent place
among the allied nations. The fact that, when the inhabitants
of Ekron rose against their king Padi, a vassal-prince nominated by Assyria, and joined the coalition, they consigned Padi
to watch and ward under Hezekiah, is enough to prove how
this time Judah was committed beyond recall. Judah could

not hope to escape now by mere restitution of its earlier vassal condition : Ammon, Moab, Edom did so escape, but Judah must look now for the full weight of the Assyrian vengeance in case of her defeat. So we find Hezekiah, according to the Old Testament, looking well to the defences of the capital and, according to Sennacherib, even admitting Arab mercenaries to strengthen his garrison.

Sennacherib recounts the events of this famous campaign in two inscriptions which have both survived. The one is the Taylor prism in the British Museum, which is translated in the *Records of the Past:* New Series, Vol. 6, pp. 80 ff. The other, somewhat more brief, is taken from the winged bulls which guard the palace at Nineveh.

The Old Testament gives its account also in two places, 2 Kings 18 : 13—19 : 37, Isaiah 36-37. I say in two places, because when one examines these parallel accounts from the Book of Kings and Isaiah, one finds that they are composed of two narratives which do not wholly agree in detail.

Let me give you the Assyrian account in full, since this is less accessible to you. Then I shall ask you to note its agreement and its disagreement with the account which is given in the Old Testament story and we shall try to see as clearly as possible what actually happened.

After this comes the question of Isaiah's attitude to these events. But, as this hangs together with the general question of Isaiah's attitude to the world power and how we interpret his general position in the political situation, it were best to leave this to itself. I shall try to gather from what we have already studied what is Isaiah's position, that of a religious teacher or that of a politician, what is his view of the heathen nations, and then try to conclude what was his attitude on this particular occasion and in connection with this particular event. All this will take some time and great care. But I venture to ask your close attention to the matter, because in my view the attitude of Isaiah was peculiarly significant, and even more significant was the view taken by the men of his own time, in my opinion a mistaken view, as to his position. It impressed itself with singular power and singular influence for good and ill on the later development of Judaism.

First then, here is Sennacherib's account which, as a mere

recital of facts, is easily put together. The great king overran
Phoenicia and set up Eshbaal in Sidon as a counterpoise to
Tyre, which town he was unable, or had no time, to capture.
He then turned southward along the coast and captured
Askelon, deposing its king Zidqa, and was about to proceed
to the siege of Ekron, when he was called to meet what he
names " a force without number " of Egyptians and Ethio-
pians that had come from Egypt to the relief of the threatened
town. The relieving army was defeated at Eltekeh and, as a
consequence, Ekron was forced to surrender to the brutality
of its conqueror. It is significant that, while the victor at
Eltekeh is celebrated in the inscriptions, with the usual fan-
fare of Assyrian trumpets, the account makes no mention of
the spoils which almost invariably accompanied any really
decisive victory on the part of the Assyrians. And this is the
more significant because the Egyptian army had the desert
behind it, which meant that, if the defeat had been a complete one, it had been natural to expect here in particular a
long account of spoils. One cannot help suspecting that, while
the Egyptians were powerless to prevent Sennacherib's further
operations in Palestine, they were still unbroken and, being
able to fall back unbroken on their own frontier, were able
also to bring Sennacherib to a temporary standstill.

Here is Sennacherib's own account of his treatment of
Judah and its king : " But Hezekiah of Judah who had not
submitted to my yoke, I besieged. Forty-six of his strong
towns, fortresses and small towns of their environs without
number, by casting down their walls, I took them. 200,150
men, young and old, male and female horses, mules, asses,
camels, oxen and sheep without number I brought out from
them : I counted them as spoil. Himself I shut up like a caged
bird in Jerusalem, his royal city : ramparts I threw up against
him; whosoever came out of the gates of the city I turned
back. His towns which I had plundered I divided from his
land and gave them to Mitinti, king of Ashdod, to Padi, king
of Ekron, and to Zilbel, king of Gaza and thus diminished
his territory. To the former tribute paid yearly I added the
tribute of all my lordship (probably a special levy) and laid
that on him. Hezekiah himself was overwhelmed by the fear
of the brightness of my lordship : the Arabians and his other

8**

faithful warriors whom as a defence for Jerusalem his royal city he had brought in, fell into fear. With 30 talents of gold, 800 talents of silver, precious stones . . . a heavy treasure and his daughters, his palace women, his young men and young women to Nineveh, the city of my lordship, I caused to be brought after me, and he sent his ambassador to give tribute and to pay homage."

Now, I cannot enter here into the analysis of the two passages in the Old Testament which deal with these events. It would take too long and I must refer you to a good, clear statement in Skinner's *Isaiah* in the " Cambridge Bible " (2nd Edit.) in his notes on the two chapters of Isaiah. The question at issue can be decided with no special knowledge of Hebrew and is easily determined by anyone who will take the trouble to examine it.

But, put broadly, we have in 2 Kings 18 : 13-16 a short summary of this campaign : in 2 Kings 18 : 17-19 : 37 or Isaiah 38 f. we have a long extract from a biography which specially relates Isaiah's connection with these events and shows how a biographer construed his attitude. This naturally refers to the historical events but always connects them with the attitude of the prophet.

If then, we compare 2 Kings 18 : 13-16 with the Assyrian account, we find them in agreement on two leading points, namely that Sennacherib overran Judah and captured its " fenced cities " and that Hezekiah submitted and was compelled to pay a heavy tribute. We find them in disagreement on one more important, and another more trivial point. Thus 2 Kings says nothing about an investment of Jerusalem, which, as we have seen, Sennacherib claims to have carried out, though it deserves notice that he never claims to have taken the city. The other point of difference, which is so trivial as perhaps to be negligible, is that 2 Kings seems to say that the tribute was paid at Lachish, while Sennacherib's account seems to suggest that Hezekiah's ambassadors followed or accompanied the great king to Nineveh. The latter point seems to me so insignificant that I only mention it for the sake of completeness. And even the former difference as to the investment of Jerusalem is explicable. The Hebrew account is exceedingly curt and naturally does not dwell on a siege which came to nothing. The Assyrian account, on the other hand, seeks to cover the ill success of the siege by insisting on the completeness of the investment and the helplessness of the captive.

But, when we turn to the longer narrative, 2 Kings 18 : 17-19 : 37 with its parallels, the situation is different. This narrative is confused in itself, because it has been put together from two accounts. Both of these relate an effort on the part of Sennacherib, while he was encamped at Lachish, to bluff Hezekiah into submission. But, while one declares that Sennacherib employed a considerable force for the purpose, the other states that the means used was a threatening letter. Again I must refer you for the details to Skinner's able analysis of the chapters.

Let me try now to put together my own view of what took place. I have hesitated a good deal as to whether it were better to discuss the questions involved in detail : but I have recognized that this would necessarily bring with it a great deal of elaborate and perhaps wearisome discussion of opposing theories. And so I have decided to give you my own views on the subject, at the same time warning you that opinions are very greatly divided on the question and, in particular, that there are many critics and historians who practically reject as mere fiction the whole of the accounts which are given us by the Old Testament historians, outside of 2 Kings 18 : 13-16. With this I cannot at all agree, though I acknowledge that there are somewhat legendary accretions which have gathered, as was natural, round the main account. But I can see no reason why resort should have been had to a wholesale invention at a time when the memory of men in Judah was still vividly concerned with this most important event in their history. And especially is this the case, when we can see, as I hope to be able to show, that the account in the Old Testament fits in with, supplements and makes clearer certain facts in Sennacherib's own account of his campaign.

We saw, then, that Sennacherib was left after Eltekeh with no decisive victory over Egypt : we know this, not merely because of the absence of details as to his spoil, but because as a matter of fact, the Egyptians were able to come again and offer some opposition. Naturally the Assyrian proceeded to secure his base and his flank. He reduced Ekron and Lachish. This latter fact, which has its importance because 2 Kings refers to this place, is not mentioned in the account of the campaign but is proved by a relief in the British Museum which represents Sennacherib on a throne receiving the submission of Lachish (*vide* Handcock, *Latest Light on Bible Lands*, p. 151). While he himself was undertaking the reduction of Lachish, important for his security since it overlooked the maritime plain, a contingent proceeded to eat up the towns of Judah in detail. When the capture of Lachish was sure, or even after it was completed, a strong force was dispatched under the Rabshakeh against Jerusalem. This corps may have encountered Hezekiah's field army, which contained not only Jews but the Arabian mercenaries to whom Sennacherib refers and who may now have deserted (cf. 22 : 3). The same chapter (vv. 8-11) describes the hurried preparations made after this blow for the defence of the capital.

The situation seemed hopeless when the Rabshakeh invested Jerusalem, as both Sennacherib's account and 2 Kings describe. Recognizing that it was hopeless, Hezekiah entered into negotiations with Sennacherib, sending envoys to the Assyrian who had remained at Lachish, busy with his preparations against Egypt. The negotiations inevitably included an undertaking on the part of Hezekiah to pay the tribute : whether it was paid now or afterwards does not seem clear, as I have already pointed out.

But Sennacherib was here in a far more critical situation than he ever acknowledges in his own account of the campaign. Egypt was still far from broken on his front, and, while Egypt had been forced back, it had been forced back on the Delta, where it could recruit both for men and stores. His own army had been weakened by its long continued fighting in Syria and especially by the indecisive pitched battle at Eltekeh. It was further weakened by the strong contingent detached under the Rabshakeh for action against Jerusalem. He was at a great distance from home : and remember that distance then, when the speed of transit for supplies was the speed of a cart over an unmetalled road, meant more than it means to-day. He had by this time eaten up the Philistine plain and was on the edge of the desert, meditating a plunge into its devastation, if he meant to strike at Egypt. Time was running out, for Jerusalem was displaying no inclination to yield. If he merely accepted Hezekiah's formal submission and tribute, he left the strong fortress on his flank, And, while the little city was now reduced to practical impotence, it could be an extremely inconvenient neighbour, if the great king were to suffer a check in the desert and his army in a condition of semi-rout were to come streaming back along the Philistine plain with an Egyptian conqueror hanging on its rear and pursuing it northward. Yet he could not afford time to prosecute the siege under the Rabshakeh to its victorious end, especially since the Rabshakeh might report to him how difficult it was to besiege Jerusalem.

My construction of the situation is that Sennacherib resolved to try a game of bluff. He accepted Hezekiah's submission but then sent an envoy to demand more, even the surrender of the city. His letter with this demand, which meant the absolute collapse of Judah's independence, steeled the last elements of resistance in the heart of Hezekiah. Probably knowing some of his opponent's difficulty, he determined to hold out to the last. Sennacherib found that his bluff had failed. And, since he dared not continue the siege, he withdrew the Rabshakeh and gave up the investment of Jerusalem.

This construction at least explains two interesting features in the accounts of the Old Testament. First, it explains why the peril is described on one occasion as coming from the Rabshakeh, on the other as coming through a letter. The one historian, perhaps knowing nothing of the letter which quickened the last effort of patriotism in the dismayed king, ascribed the whole course of events to the presence of the investing army. The other laid special emphasis on the letter, which, as a matter of fact, precipitated the actual finale of the whole and was the final threat from Sennacherib. More remarkable discrepanices can be found, I imagine, even in accounts of campaigns in the twentieth century.

The other matter which is so explained is that the Old Testament account speaks always as though the Assyrian had shown himself not only brutal but treacherous. Now, if the Rabshakeh had shown himself content with submission, and if the envoys of Hezekiah had been suffered to pass through his lines on their way to Lachish because they were offering Sennacherib tribute and submission, the very thing which the army was there to demand, it is impossible to acquit the Assyrian of treachery in accepting the tribute and then further demanding the surrender of Jerusalem. The Jewish historian may have been exactly correct in his record of a situation which was peculiarly liable to appeal to a nation in the last struggle for its independence. Here we know our enemy treacherous as well as powerful. " We cannot trust his promises : and it were as well to die as to submit to one who only sees in the acceptance of his conditions a reason for demanding more."

Then Sennacherib with his reunited army, after the failure of his effort, marched against Egypt to meet disaster, probably from an outbreak of plague in his camp, which enabled the Hebrew historian to say that an angel of the Lord smote the Assyrian in his pride, though it scarcely justified him in the interesting remark that, when they awoke in the morning, behold they were all dead corpses.

ISAIAH IN THE CRISIS OF SENNACHERIB'S INVASION

What, now, was Isaiah's attitude to all this condition of things? The first thing we have to find there, I think, is what he thought about Assyria. Assyria, according to him, had a place in the divine purpose for the world : it was a rod in the hand of Yahweh, it must subserve His ends and His purpose with the world. It had been ordained for judgment, but judgment was not God's end; it was His strange work (28 : 21). What expressed God's eternal nature and fulfilled His ultimate purpose was something for which Assyria could only be a preparation. Without its work on Israel Assyria had in itself no place in the consummation of all things or in the final revelation of God's will. Therefore, when its temporal task in Israel was finished, it should utterly pass away. It itself had no hold on the eternal values which Yahweh was to reveal and make permanent.

Isaiah had been content in his earlier oracles, chapters 7 and 8, to predict that the chastisement which was to precede the coming of the divine kingdom should come through Assyria. But, when Samaria had fallen and Assyria was only across the frontier, when its close proximity was appalling even good men, the prophet indicated to them that Assyria was also in God's hands (10 : 24-34, 5-19). The two oracles were delivered after the fall of Samaria (cf. v. 11). In the former of the two, the prophet went straight to the new feature in the situation which was troubling men in Judah, namely, the ease with which Jerusalem could be attacked, now that Damascus and Samaria were gone. And he described (vv. 28-32), as though he saw it, the swift unhindered march of the Assyrian armies through the gate of Benjamin. So vivid is the picture and especially so full are the details that for a long time it was supposed that the prophet was describing an actual invasion preceding the advance of Sennacherib. To-day it is generally recognised that, as a matter of fact, no such invasion ever took place. What Isaiah is describing is the ease with which the nation which held Samaria could, whenever it would, shake its hand against the mount of my lady Zion. Then over against the picture of the apparently irresistible strength of Assyria the prophet flung up the equal ease with which Yahweh could overwhelm the invader. "Behold the Lord, Yahweh Z^ebhaoth, shall lop the boughs with terror; and the high ones shall be hewn down and the lofty shall be brought low" vv. 33 f. For Assyria, however it might pride itself in its irresistible strength, was yet in the hands of God, an instrument for His purposes. If it sought to overpass its limits, the hand which used it would shatter it.

Again, in a later oracle, 10 : 5-15, Isaiah pointed out how irresistible the Assyrian advance had hitherto been. But he also gives the reason why no other nation has been able to stand against the conqueror. The reason is that the kingdoms which had been attacked had possessed no strength or endurance : they were destitute of any place in the ultimate purpose of the Almighty, v.6. Between them and Assyria the difference was merely one of strength and not of character. Assyria accordingly found no resistance to its onward march in Carchemish or Calno : but the moment it touched Jerusalem it touched something which rested on a different basis. In Zion Yahweh was laying a foundation for His new order (28 : 16) and so soon as Assyria came into contact with Zion, the conqueror touched what it could not overcome, a spiritual kingdom. Its work, so far as Judah was concerned, was to prepare the way by punishment for what was greater than it could supply itself : when, therefore, it had fulfilled its allotted task its power would be destroyed by Him who was using it for His own ends.

Because, however, it was thus an instrument in God's hands, only God had the power and the right to set limits to the instrument which He had summoned into His service. He alone could know when its work was finished and He alone could determine the hour when it was to be brought to an end. Since God was using Assyria, to resist it was to resist the divine will.

Only along this line can one hope to understand the way in which Isaiah steadily discouraged every effort at forming a league against the power of the conqueror. He is quite as uncompromising as Hosea in condemnation of any such alliance, but he seems to arrive at his conviction along his own line, which is not the same as that of his predecessor. Hosea thinks of Israel as the bride of Yahweh, living in His house and wholly dependent on Him. For her to become dependent on another power was to lose that uniqueness of character which was the thing which made her what she was. It was to serve another's will and so to become at once altered in outlook.

Isaiah thinks of Yahweh as king and of Israel as the glad servant content to be in such mighty hands, who waits continually on its master's orders. Hence in 17 : 12-14 he does not speak of the change which would come over Israel's temper from such an alliance. He emphasizes rather that Israel does not need to look for help from any other quarter than Yahweh. God meant to break Assyria, but at His own time and in His own way. No one else could know when Assyria's work was finished. For Israel to seek other help was to distrust Yahweh's wisdom or Yahweh's sufficient protection.

When, in the year of the death of Ahaz, ambassadors came from Philistia, seeking to draw Jesusalem into a coalition for freedom, Isaiah urged that the messengers be sent back without any hope (14 : 28-32). Now it might be possible and legitimate to interpret this attitude as meaning that the prophet insisted on the necessity of Judah keeping faith with the power which was its suzerain and to which it had sworn allegiance. But, unfortunately for this interpretation, Isaiah has not left us to guess why he objected to the alliance, for he has given his reasons. Philistia, he said, was doomed. Against it Assyria was irresistible, as it had been irresistible against Carchemish and Calno. None of these had any hold on any of the things which could guarantee them against the rod of Yahweh's anger. But Zion needed no protector, because Yahweh had laid His foundation there. So far as Jerusalem was a spiritual power, it could not be overcome by earthly weapons. " The Lord hath founded Zion and in her shall the afflicted of this people find refuge " (v.32).

Further, we find Isaiah giving another oracle with reference to the embassy which arrived from beyond the rivers of Cush (18 : 1-5). Again he says nothing about the need for loyalty to the suzerain power. What he insists on is that the Lord will choose His own time to rise up against Assyria. The prophet says absolutely nothing about the fate of the proposed coalition, as he did in connection with Philistia. What he urged was that the people must not set their hand to do something which Yahweh reserved to Himself and for which He must choose His own time. At present He was still, but when He chose, not when His people chose, He would lift up a signal for the nations. For Judah to take its fate into its own hands was to seek to force Yahweh to take action before His hour had struck.

The most significant illustration of the prophet's attitude, however, is to be found in Chapter 31. Hezekiah was being urged to join a coalition with Egypt. Now, Isaiah talks scornfully of Egypt as a feeble support for anybody, but that does not form the ground on which he insists that his nation should abstain from the alliance. The reason given is that the Egyptians were men and not God (v.3). To trust in men, whether strong Assyria or weak Egypt, was to forget Yahweh and the issue of seeking help from any other than Yahweh must be, that, when God stretched out His hand, both he that helpeth shall fall and he that is holpen shall stumble. To identify oneself with the heathen, that is to say, was to share their fate in the day when God manifested Himself. What Isaiah was contending against was not an Egyptian alliance, but any alliance at all. You see how wholly this agrees with Hosea's attitude. Only Isaiah, however, adds that Assyria is about to fall, but not by the sword of man and the sword not of man shall devour him (v.8). Yahweh was about to intervene. When He did, He should break the instrument He was temporarily using, because it was not fit to fulfil the larger purpose which He had in view when He intervened. But Yahweh was to intervene at His own time and in His own way. When He rose up, He would guarantee a place and a continuance to those who trusted in Him, and who proved their trust by the simple fact that they waited for Him to give them their place.

Isaiah was groping after something. Assyria's power in the world had a meaning. As the colossus overthrew one nation after another, it proved that each of them had no place in the eternal order. As Judah groaned under the oppressor, Judah could learn to set itself right with the eternal order, to choose the eternal values, and to welcome the coming kingdom. But, when Assyria's work was complete, it too was proved to have no place in the eternal order. For, when Yahweh ceased from His strange work and, rising up, began what was His eternal purpose, to set up the Kingdom which could not pass away, He should show the lighting down of His arm and through His voice should Assyria be broken in pieces (30 : 27-33). For endurance does not belong to Assyria, it belongs to the men who have faith.

This also was Isaiah's attitude on the occasion of Sennacherib's invasion. Only in one point did he go a little beyond the position which he had previously taken up. Convinced as he was that the retreat of the Assyrian was due to the divine will and so was the signal proof of how the world was in the hands of God, the prophet seems to have hoped that the whole city might now turn to its God and thus the remnant be found identical with the actual nation which he so greatly loved. Perhaps the different attitude taken by Hezekiah as compared with that which was taken by Ahaz may have contributed something to this hope. But in 22 : 1-14 he confessed the bitter disappointment which had come to him. For he saw how men in the hour of their danger had thought of nothing except the difficulty of their city, and in the hour of relief turned to feasting. He saw their joy at deliverance turn into a vulgar debauch instead of a humble recognition of the will of their God. And he said that their iniquity was found on their hearts while they lived.

Now again, in all this, Isaiah came down on the empirical world of his day with a teaching which really had nothing to do with the political situation in which Judah stood among the world forces of its time. Yahweh had a kingdom which He was about to establish in the world. It was a kingdom which expressed the mind of God. In the hope that Judah as a nation might find a place in this new creation, Isaiah urged Ahaz and his court to set their kingdom right with the purpose of the Almighty. He offered them a sign that Yahweh was behind the forces of the world and was controlling them for vast and righteous ends. When the court refused to have anything to do with such questions, Isaiah said that their neglect could not hinder the divine kingdom. It was coming : only now it must come in spite of them. Indeed, finding them in its way, it must sweep them aside. Assyria, in which they trusted for escape from the present perplexity, was to be the means of chastising their pride and the pride of the world. Only Assyria could not bring the Kingdom. The Kingdom of God was too vast and positive a thing to be brought about by Assyria, even as it was too sure a thing to be hindered by Ahaz's refusal. The Kingdom would cast down its temporary instrument and Assyria too should be doomed in the day of the end. Assyria itself and in itself stood, like all the heathen world, for immoral force, for the world of things which was destitute of moral order and right. Fundamentally it was unreal. Whenever the reality of things emerged, Assyria must pass like a dream of the night.

If Judah could hold back from relying on those unreal things, it was secure. It could and should pass into the new order and be guaranteed a continuance. For the one thing which could endure into the consummation was the world of men who rested themselves on God's will, the men who had faith. The new Kingdom is to be instituted along the lines of that very moral order, for which they have, however imperfectly, worked and to which they have committed themselves. In it, therefore, they will take their natural place. Exactly what it may be, it is impossible wholly to define, for the self-revelation of God, because He is God, must contain elements and involve changes such as men cannot wholly measure. But their place is sure, because it comes from Him whom they love and serve : and it, with all it involves, will be sufficient for all they can need. They must have no fear and need have none, because they are in the hands of One to whom they have committed themselves.

Now, such a construction of Isaiah's message has this to commend it, that it makes it self-consistent. What Isaiah urged on Ahaz he continued to urge on Hezekiah.

But all this message, which moved on a wholly different plane from the ordinary line of political thinking both then and now, came to be interpreted by men who were still bound in the chains of an Israel after the flesh. They saw Judah as a political entity, united round a king, constituted as a state, living in a capital with a dependent country, worshipping at a temple, maintaining a priesthood and a sacrificial ritual there. The moment such men took hold of the prophet's doctrine and tried to serve themselves heirs to his far-reaching religious principles, it is easy to see how hopelessly, in reinterpreting his ideals, they perverted them.

It is equally easy to see how fatally the actual circumstances of the time could play into the hands of their false interpretation and could confirm it. Sennacherib had been defeated beyond human expectation by a disaster which they could only call an act of God. Yahweh, the God of Israel, had intervened, as the prophet said He would intervene. He had proved Himself able and willing to defeat the invader at their very gates, and so to protect His own. He had preserved the things which they counted essential to their continuance as a nation—Jerusalem and the kingdom of David, the things too which they counted essential to their continuance as His worshippers—the temple and its sacrifices. No matter that Amos had said that Yahweh meant to remake the nation in the interests of religion. No matter that Micah had

declared that Yahweh would allow the temple mount to be
ploughed as a field. Isaiah had declared that Zion was in-
violate : and Zion was the Zion they saw and loved. The prophecy, as they interpreted it, and the events through which
they had lived fitted into each other as hand fits into glove.
Yahweh had proved Himself more powerful than all His ad-
versaries. Assyria had been proved impotent before a nation
which trusted in His almighty protection. The God of their
fathers had vindicated Himself in a great act of self-manifestation by which He had proved that He was not indifferent to
the conditions and needs and dangers of His people. Above
all He had proved Himself very jealous of the inviolability
of His capital among the hills of Judah and of the sanctuary
at its heart.

It was natural and inevitable that, from this time the
temple of Jerusalem, which had previously been regarded as
one of the sanctuaries of the land, given a certain prominence
as the royal chapel, became invested with a new dignity and
a new sanctity in the eyes of Judah, Yahweh had shown that
He counted it essential to His worship, since He had actually
intervened to save it from profanation by the feet of the
strangers. Yahweh, as Isaiah promised, had guaranteed to
those who trusted in Him the conditions necessary for their
continuance as His servants. The temple therefore became to
many devout men a necessity for rightful worship, rightful
worship consisting largely in a correct observance of its ritual
and its ordinances.

This is how the good in this strange and curious world
became the enemy of the better, and a prophet who saw the
gleaming of the new Jerusalem helped to make it possible
that to this day Jewry makes pilgrimage to weep over dead
stones.

THE MESSIANIC HOPE

So far, you will have noted, I have been tracing Isaiah's
view of the future almost entirely on its negative side. There
is continually a hint of a larger and more positive side. Thus
Assyria is to be rejected, because in itself it is only fit to be

an instrument for chastisement, and chastisement is God's strange work. When God turned to His real work, which is His work of redemption, Assyria can have no place in it. There you have the continual suggestion that the blessed future has a positive content, so rich and large that only God can bring it in.

What this is to be, Isaiah lets us see in Chapter 9: 2-7 and 11: 1-9. Now it is just to say that these two oracles are not universally acknowledged to be Isaianic. I cannot halt here to develop the reasons which have convinced me of their genuineness. You will find an excellent discussion of the question in Skinner's commentary, where you will find it discussed in a much drier light than I am likely to throw on it. Two things I wish to emphasize. The one is that everyone allows now that, so far as language and leading ideas are concerned, there is nothing to prevent the oracles from being dated in the period of our prophet. What prompts men to relegate them to a post-exilic period is not, therefore, an unbiased criticism, but a criticism biased by an *a priori* opinion as to Isaiah's general position. Men have approached the oracles with the opinion that Isaiah could not have uttered anything except oracles of judgment. They have not freed themselves from this bias. This is why I have spent so much time at the beginning of our study of the prophet in making clear what is involved in his call and commission.

The second thing I wish to emphasize is that we have no right to throw the oracles into the post-exilic period and then think we have comfortably disposed of all difficulty and of all questions in connection with them. The moment one asks how they could have sprung up in the post-exilic period, to whom they can be assigned there and what line of thought they belong to there, one discovers that it is far more difficult to account for them then than when we assign them to Isaiah. For these two oracles belong to a type of Messianic expectation: they both look for Messiah as a king and as one of the Davidic stock. I need not tell you how strong a hold this form of the expectation took on the imagination and thought of Judah. To see this we only need to read our New Testament and see how consistently the evangelists urge the royal entry of their Lord into Jerusalem, for example, and stress

His birth from the Davidic line. The men would not have urged these matters as supporting His claims to be Messiah, had they not themselves valued them and had they not known that they would appeal strongly to their Jewish contemporaries.

Very good, this being the case, we want to know when the Messianic expectation took this form, a form which impressed itself so deeply on the Jewish mind. To me it seems extremely unlikely that it should have sprung up during or after the exile. Because the prophets put their hopes for the future in terms which their fellows could understand, they were not likely to put them into this shape at a time when the kingdom of Israel had disappeared and when the old royal house of David had lost its dominating position. The very men who seek to relegate these oracles to the post-exilic period refuse to accept certain other oracles as earlier than the time of the kingdom, because, they say justly, such hopes would not take this particular shape until after Israel had won its kingdom. The argument cuts both ways. The oracles which do present the hope in the form of the kingdom would not spring up after the kingdom had come to an utter end. If the post-exile men continued to think of the future in terms of a Messianic kingdom, it was because that form of the hope was already traditional. They continued what had already begun, because they could not deny that their prophets had spoken in these terms, however difficult they may have found this form of the hope in the conditions in which their nation and their religion had come to exist.

We are driven to conclude that the form of the hope came into existence when Israel was still a kingdom : and I hope to let you see, as we go on, how it connects itself specifically with this prophet Isaiah. It is in close connection with the rest of his thought. You will, I hope, recall how it falls in with Isaiah's general attitude. As I said before, Isaiah believes, not merely in a great law of righteousness implanted in the very nature of man. He believes in a law which can govern through institutions, because he knows that human life needs governing, guiding disciplining; cf. 1 : 26 the oracle on the faithful city. Even the redeemed need disciplining. When Yahweh brings in the new Kingdom, of the increase of Messiah's government there shall be no end. And, remember, this is in the new order.

But it agrees further with his conviction of the need for a judgment, sure, irreversible and searching. As clearly as Amos or Hosea, he declares that Judah, as it is at present, must pass. The new shoot shall spring, but it shall spring from the stump of Jesse (11 : 1). The old kingdom must be hewn down to the very roots. For the old kingdom was not a religious magnitude at all : it stood for other things than those of the eternal order.

The new king, when he comes, shall stand only for the eternal order. He is (9 : 5) wonderful, counsellor, mighty God, everlasting Father, Prince of Peace. The effort used to be made to explain these titles as wholly compatible with a mere successor of David on the throne of Judah. Then weird explanations were offered of the separate titles, and everlasting Father was interpreted, for example, as father of booty. These, you may take it, have broken down hopelessly. They have broken down for instance over the impossibility of conceiving anyone who is at once a father of booty and a prince of peace, and over the recognition that the other title " mighty God ", is elsewhere applied to Yahweh Himself. Yet, on the other side, one must be careful to avoid putting too much content, especially too much divine content, into the titles. When we note that the spirit of the Lord is to rest upon the new ruler, we note also that Isaiah means that all that Messiah holds to equip Him for his new task he holds from God. Only he holds it in such degree and in such fullness that he can bear these titles. When he dwells among and governs the redeemed, when he administers the new order for them, he does it as the representative of God and as peculiarly endowed and fitted for his task by a special act of God. When he is present in authority over men of the new world, they may feel that God Himself in His representative is present. The new world is of such a nature that God can dwell in it in the person of His Messiah. And the blessedness of the new world is to consist peculiarly in this that God in His representative and man can dwell together there.

What I think Isaiah is insisting on here one can learn from two points. The first is the sharp limitation of Messiah's

functions. It is not his business to bring in the Kingdom, any
more than it was Judah's business to bring down Assyria.
Messiah does not break the nations or build up Judah. God
does both. Salvation is of the Lord. What Messiah does is
to continue what God had begun and done. He shall administer the new order which God alone can set up. But we
do not think of this as implying that the prophet has any
hesitation as to the use of force. Do not read more into or out
of these utterances than they were meant to say. Isaiah has
no hesitation at all in saying that, when Yahweh brings His
Kingdom, He shall do it by breaking down all opposition. He
shall even break Assyria which He has hitherto used as His
instrument. And, when Messiah takes up His functions to
continue in the new Kingdom the work which Yahweh has
begun, he shall govern, and government to Isaiah means
restraint. The prophet's objection to Israel or Judah using its
own strength to deliver itself is not, therefore, based on objection to the use of force. Force, according to him, can be
moralized, for Yahweh is to wield it and even to put it into
the hands of Messiah. He seems rather governed in his objection to Judah's relying on outward things by the sense that,
as we should put it, salvation is of the Lord.

The second is, that we must recognize how the Old Testament has no clear doctrine by which the Spirit of Yahweh
was distinguished from Yahweh Himself. To quote from Dr.
Davidson: " God, when influencing persons, is called the
spirit of God. The spirit of God is not something less than
God, it is God. And the spirit of God, that is, God in a person, remains distinct: He suffers no confusion or composition
with the spirit of man." God's spirit rests upon a man to equip
him for the task to which he is sent: and so long as he fulfils the task for the ends appointed him by God, what he
does is spoken of as done by God Himself. The spirit of
Yahweh, therefore, rests upon the scion out of Jesse's stock
to make him a true ruler of the people. And so long as he
does this, he acts among his nation as though Yahweh were
acting among them: and he can bear those divine titles as
though he himself were more than man.

What then the prophet is insisting upon there is that the
new Kingdom is to come through an act of God. God is to

constitute it and is to endow its ruler for his task. The Kingdom, therefore, is to represent the ends of God in His world and among His nation. It is to stand for the eternal and unchangeable things.

Nothing, however, shows more clearly that Isaiah was thinking of a Kingdom which must come by supernatural means than the oracle with which Chapter 11 begins. For there he shows himself to be expecting a change in the order of the world as the result of the intervention of Yahweh. " The wolf shall dwell with the lamb, and the leopard shall lie down with the kid; and the calf and the young lion shall graze together; and a little child shall lead them. And the cow and the bear shall be associated : and the lion shall eat straw like the ox." Now, this implies a change, not merely in the nature of man, such as might come about through human repentance and through men electing to live after the divine values. It implies a change in the constitution and order of nature, such as God and God only could bring about. The world also which brought forth thorns and thistles as man brought forth disordered passions, where the beasts preyed on one another for food, should be renewed. There was to be a new earth.

It might be possible to dismiss this as a mere touch of Eastern poetry, did the expectation stand alone. But it does not. It links up on the one side with the expectation in Amos that the world is to be judged. The Lord, you will remember, is to overthrow the high mountains. Its judgment, too, is only to be for its renewal. It links up on the other with a whole series of prophecies which foretells that in the new age, when the earth serves the purposes of its Creator and thus becomes able and willing to serve the uses of His reconciled people, it shall show a new and happy abundance. The sower shall overtake the reaper, the hillsides shall flow down with new wine. The weary toil of man for bare subsistence shall come to an end, for the new earth shall spontaneously serve the purpose of God by serving the uses of man. Sometimes this idea is developed into what may appear rather grotesque results in pictures which are uncongenial to our modern minds. But if we had the Hebrew sense of the unity of man and nature and Isaiah's sense that the earth is not merely the indifferent theatre on which man carries out his normal task, but is the expression of the divine glory, we should better appreciate the conception of a world which is to laugh out into abundance, as it finds its true place in serving the manifest needs of humanity, which is, then, to use all its gifts to serve God. Earth and man shall be in harmony, because, and only because, both earth and man are in harmony with the purposes of their common God.

I say that, in recognizing Isaiah's thought, you must recognize that it is to be set into connection with these sayings. All these men are looking for a new earth such as only God can make. But you will notice further how Isaiah regards the world as needing renewal. Everyone has recognized that the feature which he puts into the foreground of his picture, namely that all the animals shall eat a common food, is reminiscent of the picture of the creation, when the herb of the field was assigned to the animals while the cereals and fruit were given to men. Then it is said that he is looking for the return of the primitive, even the golden age. But the significance of the utterance in its Hebrew setting has not been recognized. For the golden age was the age when the world came first from the hands of God. For it to return to its beginning is to receive re-creation : there shall be a new humanity. And in it shall vanish precisely that which to Isaiah makes it, as it is, no place in which and with which its God can dwell. Cruelty shall come to an end, not only among men but among beasts. Isaiah's moral sense has recognised that the present world, as it is, seems indifferent to the moral task of humanity. And he looks for a world which shall in all its parts mirror something of the nature of God.

But, on the other hand, Isaiah believes that he who is to be set over the renewed humanity which is to dwell in this renewed earth shall be the scion of the house of David. He who is to preside over a renovated humanity is to do it on " My holy mountain ", which is undoubtedly Jerusalem, the capital of the little state of Judah. Has the prophet tumbled back from his grandiose vision of a renovated humanity living in peace in a renewed world into that of Jewish nationalism, and has he proved himself unable to break with the nation which he knows, with its historical past, its local outlook, even its city and temple? That is impossible in view of his belief that the world and not merely Israel is to be made anew.

You must take the thought in connection with his conception of those who are to constitute the remnant. The remnant, those who are able to pass through the judgment and take their place in the new order, are not defined in terms of Judah. They are the men who have faith, who live after the principles of the new order and who, having already achieved its dominion, naturally pass over into it when it arrives. Their head is both one of themselves and one sent and endowed by God for his functions. This means that Isaiah, because he believes that the ultimate purpose of God is redemption, has begun to break with cataclysm. The new order, because it is God's order, is the oldest of all. It has always been there. And when, through God's act, it emerges in its fullness, it cannot make a clean break with all the past. God has been in the past, in its discipline and in its activities, even in its failures. And He will not make a complete break, turning His back upon His past, as though it had not been. Nor can He turn His back on those in the past who have trusted in Him. They committed themselves in their day to what they saw of His will: and into the new thing which He is making they have freedom of entry. The stock of Jesse has been cut down, chastened, fearfully disciplined: but it has life in it. And all that is worthy in it shall be preserved to take its sure place in the world which does not pass away.

GENERAL INDEX

Aaron 52, 61-2.
Abiezer 97.
Abimelech 68.
Abner 81-3.
Abraham 50, 56-7, 120.
Absalom 83, 100ff.
Achish 74.
Adoram 94.
Adullam 85.
Agag 74-5.
Ahab 110, 186, 229-30.
Ahaz 75, 163, 179, 191-4, 199, 212-224 (*passim*), 230-1, 233, 247.
Ahijah 94.
Ahitophel 103.
Akiba 51.
Alliances, Foreign 160-3, 244ff.
Amalek 74, 90.
Amaziah 117f.
Ammon 73, 79, 81, 88f.
Amos 59-60, 130, 147, 221, Book of 107ff., Preacher, not author 107-8, Period 109ff., Occupations 112ff., Imagery 113f., Call 114ff., Visions 115, 128, at Bethel 117f., Unity of Nation 112ff., Breadth of outlook 113, 126, Monotheist 126f., Universal Religion 127f., 223, and Hosea 154f., 159, 171, 174, and Isaiah 196-7, 201-2, 205-6, 208-9, 228.
Aphek 68, 72, 77.
Apostasy 52, 58, 61-2, 110, 152, 160-2, 166f.
Arabia 94.
Aram *vide sub* Syria.
Ark 63, 68, 77, 86-8.
Armenia 130.
Arpad 131, 232.
Aschel 83.
Assyria 53, 91, 109-10, 130f., 158-63, 178-9, 190-5, 200, 212-3, 219, 226, 230-49 (*passim*).
Athaliah 95.

Baal 110, 167.
Babylon(ia) 48, 53, 126-7, 187, 232, 235.
Barzillai 103.
Bathsheba 99-101.
Benaiah 93.
Benjamin 68, 76, 82, 84, 88.
Bethel 86, 108, 112, 117ff.
Bethlehem 84-5.
Bethrehob 89.
Bethshan 79.
Bismarck 86.
Burns, R. 117.

Church 169-71, 222-232.
Covenant 50-1, 55-7, 60, 120-2, with Abraham 50, 56-7, with Noah 50, 56.
Cyrus 131f.
Cult 48-50, 111, 145, 172, 178ff., 183f., 202.
Catastrophe, World 209f., 213, 256, *vide sub* Day of Yahweh.

Damascus 74, 90f., 110, 125, 131, 192, 194, 212ff., 232, *vide sub.* Syria(ns).
Dan 68.
David 63, 67, 73, 76, 80ff., (*passim*), Early life of 73, Material concerning 80f., Organisation of kingdom 81, Extent of his kingdom 90, Religious disposition 88, Character 104.
Davidson, A. B. 58, 253.
Day of Yahweh 111, 209f., 213, 228f.
Decalogue 51, 58-9, 125, 168-9, 181.
Desert Period 152.
Deutero-Isaiah 50-1, 186.
Deuteronomy 67, 144f., 168.
Diaspora 47f.
Disciples, Isaiah 225, 228.
Driver, S. R. 139-141.
Duhm, B. 209.

261